Is Rome the True Church?

IS ROME THE TRUE CHURCH?

A Consideration of the Roman Catholic Claim

NORMAN L. GEISLER *and* JOSHUA M. BETANCOURT

CROSSWAY BOOKS
WHEATON, ILLINOIS

Is Rome the True Church? A Consideration of the Roman Catholic Claim
Copyright © 2008 by Norman Leo Geisler and Joshua Manuel Betancourt
Published by Crossway Books
  a publishing ministry of Good News Publishers
  1300 Crescent Street
  Wheaton, Illinois 60187

Cover design: Jon McGrath
Cover illustration: IStock
First printing 2008
Printed in the United States of America

Unless otherwise indicated, scripture quotations are from *The Holy Bible, English Standard Version*®, copyright © 2001 by Crossway Bibles, a publishing ministry of Good News Publishers. Used by permission. All rights reserved.

Scripture quotations marked AT are the author's translation.

Scripture quotations marked NASB are from *The New American Standard Bible.*®
Copyright © The Lockman Foundation 1960, 1962, 1963, 1968, 1971, 1972, 1973, 1975, 1977, 1995. Used by permission.

Scripture references marked NKJV are from *The New King James Version*. Copyright © 1982, Thomas Nelson, Inc. Used by permission.

All emphases in Scripture have been added by the authors.

Trade paperback ISBN: 978-1-4335-0231-6
PDF ISBN: 978-1-4335-0464-8
Mobipocket ISBN: 978-1-4335-0465-5

Library of Congress Cataloging-in-Publication Data
Geisler, Norman L.
     Is Rome the true church? : a consideration of the Roman Catholic claim /
Norman L. Geisler and Joshua M. Betancourt.
        p. cm.
     Includes bibliographical references and index.
     ISBN 978-1-4335-0231-6 (tpb)
        1. Popes--Primacy—History of doctrines. 2. Popes—Infallibility—History of
doctrines. 3. Authority—Religious aspects--Catholic Church—History of doctrines.
4. Catholic Church--Doctrines--History. I. Betancourt, Joshua M., 1978– II. Title.

BX1806.G45 2008
282—dc22

                                                              2008011649

VP   16   15   14   13   12   11   10   09   08
          9   8   7   6   5   4   3   2   1

CONTENTS

INTRODUCTION

While thousands of Catholics have converted to Protestant evangelicalism, strangely, a "number of evangelical intellectuals have gone the other way, deciding that 'Rome is home.'"[1] Some have even written books in an attempt to convert more evangelicals. While the trade-off numbers significantly favor evangelicalism, one still wonders why some evangelicals see greener grass on the other side of the ecclesiastical fence.

When the reasons are examined, we find some seek a more beautiful tradition in the Catholic Church.[2] Others see an older, deeper, or richer tradition. But many evangelicals have grown weary of the seemingly perennial problems of denominational schism and variant biblical interpretation. Catholicism seems to offer a more stable and uniform tradition in the Roman pontiff and the See of Rome. It has been said that for many of those who have converted to Catholicism, "the road to Rome is the path to *certainty*."[3] Thus it goes beyond merely an ecclesiastical or social issue; rather, it becomes at once an epistemological issue as well.[4] On the other hand, when one converts to Roman Catholicism, he or she must accept immediately as *de fide* dogma many doctrines—including papal infallibility—as binding (as a faithful member or convert) of the Catholic Church, even those that may run counter to conscience.

Ironically, this papal pillar of Catholicism has received some of its most serious challenges from Catholic intellectuals themselves. In the

1. Ralph E. MacKenzie, "Why Some Evangelicals Become Roman Catholic," *Christian Apologetics Journal* 4.1 (Spring 2005): 1.
2. Ibid., 5–9.
3. Jaroslav Pelikan, *The Riddle of Roman Catholicism* (New York: Abingdon, 1959), 206 (emphasis added).
4. Ibid. Pelikan cites one such testimony.

late 1970s a book entitled *Infallible? An Inquiry*, written by theologian Hans Küng, caught the attention of many within the Roman Catholic Church. Why was this so? Küng, a Catholic himself, penned a pointed critique of the doctrine of the papacy, i.e., papal infallibility, the notion that the pope cannot err when defining dogmas of faith and morals. Ironically, Küng was never excommunicated from the church but instead was temporarily castigated by his ecclesiastical authorities for instigating the question. Some thirty years have passed since Küng's critique appeared on the scene, and the doctrine of papal infallibility has not changed, nor can it change since it was declared binding and irrevocable by the Catholic Church at the First Vatican Council in 1870. While Küng's book raised many valid questions and concerns, and even prompted others within the Catholic Church to publish similar objections, Rome has remained insistent on this doctrine for the above reason that it has been crystallized as an immutable doctrine in the annals of the church's dogmas.[5]

The question remains, What difference does it make to non-Catholic Christians, or more specifically to evangelicals? Whatever the case for "crossing the Tiber," there remains significant theological tension that continues to keep all of Christendom divided, especially in the West. Since the time of the Protestant Reformation in the sixteenth century, the areas of disagreement have primarily revolved around the issues of personal salvation (soteriology) and of church authority (ecclesiology), though that to a lesser extent.

This topic is of great importance. To be sure, it has great theological, historical, and ecclesiastical implications. For if the infallibility of the pope stands, then every other branch within Christendom, i.e., Eastern and Oriental Orthodox and Protestant Christians, has become the obstinate stepchild to the Mother Church. If true, this would mean that the burden of proof remains on those who say otherwise. Perhaps an evangelical inquiry will help evangelicals who are considering converting to Roman Catholicism understand that it is not necessary to "swim up the Tiber" in order to become Catholic. In fact, after seriously considering the relevant evidence, perhaps they will choose just to remain evangelical, if they desire to be truly "catholic."

---

5. A more recent example is Jesuit writer Luis Bermejo's *Infallibility on Trial: Church, Conciliarity, and Communion* (Westminster, MD: Christian Classics, 1992).

CHAPTER 1

THE ROMAN CLAIM
TO BE THE TRUE CHURCH

The Roman Catholic Church claims to be the only true church and the only infallible interpreter of Christ's teaching. What do these unique claims mean? The answer can come only after looking at the historical development that led to the papal claims to exclusivity and infallibility.

The Historical Development of the Roman Claim to Papal Authority

As the saying goes, "Rome was not built in a day," and neither was the Roman Catholic Church. The belief in both the primacy of Rome and in its exclusivity did not come about overnight. As will be demonstrated, it developed gradually, step-by-step, over centuries of time. And like other gradual changes some doctrinal changes seemed imperceptible to the observer at any given time; but among the radical ones, e.g., papal primacy and infallibility, they became more perceptible with time, as we shall see.

These two Catholic claims—to papal authority and exclusivity—go hand in hand. Understanding the basis for Rome's claim of being the only true church begins with examining the history of the church, particularly as it relates to the development of the Roman Catholic authoritative structure headed up by an infallible bishop of Rome.

The Development of the Authoritarian Structure of the Roman Church

It took many centuries for the Catholic authoritarian episcopal (bishop dominated) form of government to emerge from the simple, self-govern-ing, independent New Testament churches[1] to the authoritarian papal hierarchical structure of the Roman Catholic Church. Along with this development came the evolution of the Roman claim to being the only true church of Christ on earth. The evolution may be attributed to the following seven factors.

First, the seeds of an episcopal form of government were found in New Testament times when John the apostle spoke of it in his third epistle and warned: "I wrote to the church, but Diotrephes, who loves to have the preeminence among them, does not receive us" (3 John 9 NKJV). Even in apostolic times, a false tradition began based on a mis-interpretation of some disciples about one of Jesus' statements, which had to be corrected by the apostle John (see John 21:22–23).

Second, if false traditions could spring up even during the time of the apostles, it is easy to see how quickly they could spread once there was no apostle to squelch them. Tradition, as such, is neither authoritative nor reliable, except insofar as it is accurately transmitted. And written transmission, such as exists in Scripture and other writings based on it, is the only reliable source we have of apostolic teaching. Indeed, even Cyprian, (d. AD 258), who later failed to heed his own wisdom, said, "Hence, it is in vain that some who are overcome by reason oppose to us custom, as if custom were greater than truth" (*Epistles*, 72.13). He added, "Custom without truth is the antiquity of error" (73.80).

Third, by the mid-second century, almost a century after most apostles had died—the very time that even apocryphal gospels were emerg-ing—the church embraced a more unorthodox authoritarian structure. Indeed, Irenaeus, writing decades after the time of the apocryphal *Gospel of Thomas* (c. AD 140), spoke of an emerging episcopal form of govern-ment. So there was plenty of time for false views to emerge, even among those who were otherwise orthodox.

Fourth, considering the attacks on Christianity at the time, there was strong motivation to develop an ecclesiology that would provide a united front against the divergent heretical groups emerging. This motivation is reflected in Irenaeus's emerging episcopal view of church government,

---

1. See Norman L. Geisler, *Systematic Theology*, vol. 4: *The Church and Last Things* (Bloomington, MN: Bethany, 2005), chap. 4.

a view that, ironically, did achieve a more mature form in Cyprian who himself warned against basing something on tradition, not truth.

Fifth, even if some second-century writers can be shown to favor the primacy of Rome as the center of Christianity, this does not support the later Roman Catholic claim that the pope is infallible. The early fathers constantly appealed to the original "apostles" (plural) as the God-established authority. Further, they did not single out Peter as superior to other apostles. They thought him to be, at best, only a co-founder of the church at Rome along with Paul. He was in fact on the same level as Paul and the other apostles to whom he repeatedly refers.

Furthermore, his stress on the primacy of Scripture as the final written authority of the Christian faith demonstrates that all ecclesiastical authority is based on Scripture, not the reverse. Even Roman Catholic authority Ludwig Ott admits, "The Fathers did not expressly speak of the Infallibility of the Pope."[2] And as shown above, this was true up to the time of the greatest Catholic theologian, Thomas Aquinas (d. 1274), who spoke of the pope's authority to promulgate a creed based on Scripture but not to have infallible authority in all official doctrinal decrees.[3]

Sixth, even if the disputed text of Irenaeus,[4] that "every Church should agree with this Church [at Rome]," is taken in an authoritative way (and not reflectively), it does not follow that Rome could not later deviate from the truth and be an unreliable source for all essential Christian truth. Indeed, this is precisely what Protestants believe, and they point to numerous Catholic teachings that are supported neither by Scripture nor by the early fathers of the church.[5] Nor does it mean that Rome is infallible in all its official doctrinal pronouncements.

Finally, the conversion of Constantine (fourth century) and his use of imperial power to influence the emergence of an imperial church structure were significant catalysts in the formation of the authoritarian episcopal form of government. This, combined with the natural penchant for power, produced the Roman Church with its claim to papal infallibility and other unbiblical teachings. This was well under way by the Fourth Lateran Council (1215) and culminated in the doctrinal deviations

2. Ott, in ibid., 288. Of course, Ott believed that Irenaeus and others did "attest the decisive teaching authority of the Roman Church and of its Pontiff." But there are good reasons (see Appendix 1) to believe that this is a misinterpretation.
3. See Thomas Aquinas, *Summa Theologica*.
4. Irenaeus, *Against Heresies* 3.3.2 in Philip Schaff, *Ante-Nicene Fathers* (Grand Rapids, MI: Eerdmans, 1885).
5. See Norman L. Geisler and Ralph MacKenzie, *Roman Catholics and Evangelicals: Agreements and Differences* (Grand Rapids, MI: Baker, 1995), part 2.

of the Council of Trent (1545–1547) and the eventual dogma of papal infallibility of Vatican I (1870), which has been reaffirmed ever since.

The Development of the Roman Claim to Exclusivity

With this background in mind, we are prepared to understand Rome's claim to being the one true church. There are several things to note about the claim. First, it is an authoritative claim. It is neither casual nor incidental but lies at the heart of the institution for which it speaks.

Second, it is an infallible claim and has been made at ecumenical councils such as the Fourth Lateran Council (1215) and Vatican I (1870) and by popes defining the nature of Christian doctrine. As such, it is nonnegotiable and irrevocable.

Third, if the claims turn out to be false, unsupported by scriptural, historical, and rational argument, then the very structure of the Roman Church, being built as it is on its own magisterium, collapses. Not only is Rome not the true church, but it is also false in at least two, if not more, of its central claims. Its claim to infallibility would be false, since its fallibility is proven in its claim to infallibility.

Additionally, since its claim to infallibility underlies other distinctive doctrines of the Roman Church, these too are left, by their own confession, without a solid basis for belief. By its own claim, it is the infallibility of its magisterium that grounds its essential teachings for the faithful. An infallible Scripture, they claim, is not enough. What is also needed, they say, is to define Scripture and its meaning. Without this, they claim, there is no real basis for our faith. If so, if infallibility can be undermined, then the Roman Church as a whole crumbles. The rest of this book sets out to prove that this is indeed the case.

The Background of Rome's Claims

Roman Catholicism, claiming unbroken lineage of apostolic succession since Peter, claims that through it alone can anyone receive the fullness of salvation. Such salvation supposedly comes about through the sacraments, through which one receives the actual body and blood of Christ, properly administered only through an ordained priest in the line of apostolic succession.

Cyprian (AD 259)

The bishop of Carthage in North Africa wrote:

> Can anyone water from the Church's fountains who is not within the Church? But . . . they know that there is no baptism without, and that no

remission of sins can be given outside the Church. For it is the Church alone which, conjoined and united with Christ, spiritually bears sons. But as the birth of Christians is in baptism, while the generation and sanctification of baptism are with the spouse of Christ alone, who is able spiritually to conceive and to bear sons to God, where and of whom and to whom is he born, who is not a son of the church, so that he should have God as his Father, before he has had the Church for his mother? But if His Church is a garden enclosed, and a fountain sealed [Cant. 4:12, 13], how can he who is not in the Church enter into the same garden, or drink from its fountain? Moreover, Peter himself, showing and vindicating the unity, has commanded and warned us that we cannot be saved, except by the one only baptism of one Church [by the ark illustration in 1 Pet. 3:20, 21].[6]

Of course, at the time Cyprian's statement had no creedal or ecumenical authority. However, it was picked up later by the more influential bishop Augustine of Hippo in North Africa, who did preside over a local council in his city (AD 410).

St. Augustine (AD 354–430)

Citing Cyprian, Augustine wrote: "'Salvation,' he says, 'is not without the Church.' Who says that it is? And therefore, whatever men have that belongs to the Church, it profits them nothing towards salvation outside the Church."[7] Indeed, Augustine said elsewhere, "The Catholic Church alone is the body of Christ, of which He is the Head and Saviour of His body. Outside this body the Holy Spirit giveth life to no one. . . . Therefore they have not the Holy Ghost who are outside the Church."[8]

Of course, Augustine does not take this absolutely, since he allows for baptism by martyrdom and by intent.[9] He wrote, "That the place of baptism is sometimes supplied by martyrdom is supported by an argument by no means trivial," namely, Jesus granting paradise to the dying thief without water baptism.[10]

"Imperial Edict" (AD 680)

This edict, following the Third Council of Constantinople, was posted in the church, warning, "No one henceforth should hold a different

---

6. Cyprian, *The Epistles of Cyprian* (72.10) in Philip Schaff, *The Ante-Nicene Fathers*, vol. 5 (Grand Rapids, MI: Eerdmans, 1957), 72:10; 72:24; 73:6; 73:7; 73:11.
7. Augustine, *On Baptism*, 4, 17 in Schaff, *Nicene and Post-Nicene Fathers*, 4:458.
8. Augustine, *The Correction of the Donatists*, 11, 50, in Philip Schaff, ed., *A Select Library of the Nicene and Post-Nicene Fathers of the Christian Church*.
9. Augustine, *On Baptism*, 4, 21–28, 459.
10. Ibid., 22–30, 460.

faith, or venture to teach one will [in Christ] and one energy [operation of the will]. In no other than the orthodox faith could men be saved."[11]

The Second Council of Nicea (AD 787)

The primacy of Peter and of apostolic succession are emphasized here: "For the blessed Peter himself, the chief of the Apostles, who first sat in the Apostolic See, let the chiefship of his Apostolate, and pastoral care, that his successors who are to sit in his most holy seat for ever."[12] It further speaks of "the holy Roman Church, which has prior rank, which is the head of all the Churches of God."[13]

Fourth Lateran Council (AD 1215)

> One indeed is the universal Church of the faithful, outside which no one at all is saved, in which the priest himself is sacrifice, Jesus Christ, whose body and blood are truly contained in the sacrament of the altar under the species of bread and wine; the bread changed into His body by the divine power of transubstantiation, and the wine into the blood. . . . And surely no one can accomplish this sacrament except a priest who has been rightly ordained according to the keys of the Church, which Jesus Christ Himself conceded to the Apostles and to their successors. (Fourth Lateran Council, 1215)[14]

This culminates the long tradition beginning with Cyprian (d. 258) and Augustine (d. 430) and gives the official authority of the Roman Catholic Church to Cyprian's statement that there is only one true church, outside of which there is no salvation. It was later confirmed by the Council of Trent, as well as by Vatican I and Vatican II.

Thomas Aquinas (AD 1224–1274)

The angelic doctor held that "those who lack baptism in this fashion [by rejecting it] cannot attain salvation because they are neither sacramentally nor intentionally incorporated into Christ through whom alone salvation is possible."[15] And since baptism is a sacrament of the church, this would mean that salvation is not possible apart from what is ordained by the church.

11. Philip Schaff, ed., "Seven Ecumenical Councils," in *A Select Library*, vol. 14, 353.
12. Ibid., 547.
13. Ibid.
14. Cited in Henry Denzinger, *The Sources of Catholic Dogma* (St. Louis, MO: Herfer, 1957) no. 430, 169–70.
15. Thomas Aquinas, *Summa Theologica* 3a 68, 2 (Blackfriars with McGraw-Hill, 1975).

However, Aquinas allowed for baptism by intention, as is indicated by the above phrase "intentionally incorporated into Christ." Salvation is also possible by fire (i.e., by martyrdom) without water baptism. Aquinas also affirmed, "No one achieves eternal life if he is not free from all sin and debt of punishment. Such complete absolution takes place in the reception of baptism and in martyrdom."[16]

Pope Boniface VIII (AD 1234–1303)

In 1302 the Roman pontiff Boniface VIII made a similar pronouncement on the unique claim of the Roman Church: "We declare, say, define, and pronounce that it is absolutely necessary for the salvation of every human creature to be subject to the Roman Pontiff."

The Council of Trent (AD 1565)

> I acknowledge the holy catholic and apostolic Roman Church as the mother and teacher of all churches; and to the Roman Pontiff, the successor of the blessed Peter, chief of the Apostles and vicar of Jesus Christ, I promise and swear true obedience. . . . This true Catholic faith, outside of which no one can be saved, and which of my own accord I now profess and truly hold, I do promise, vow, and swear, that I will, with the help of God, most faithfully retain and profess the same to the last breath of life pure and inviolable.[17]

Vatican I Council (AD 1870)

Here Pope Pius IX (1792–1878) said, "By faith it is to be firmly held that outside the Apostolic Roman Church none can achieve salvation. [Following Cyprian's analogy, he added] This is the only ark of salvation. He who does not enter into it will perish in the flood." But Pope Pius IX offered an important exception: "Nevertheless, equally certain it is to be held that those who suffer invincible ignorance of the true religion, are not for this reason guilty in the eyes of the Lord."[18]

Vatican II (AD 1962–1965)

Despite the appearance of liberalizing the Roman Church, Vatican II held the same view as previous Catholic pronouncements. It declared: "The church is a saving institution" and "the Church is not only a communion between brother and sister, with Christ at its head, it is also an institution to which the universal mission of salvation has been entrusted.

16. Ibid.
17. Denzinger, *The Sources of Catholic Dogma*, No. 999–1000, 303–4.
18. Ibid., 312.

. . . For this reason, the Church was presented by the Second Vatican Council as a reality . . . established as 'the universal sacrament of salvation' through the action of the Holy Spirit."[19]

The Catechism of the Catholic Church (AD 1994)

Even in this most recent and highly heralded Catholic Catechism, the claim of the Catholic Church to being the one and only true church of Christ on earth remains. It speaks of "the one and only Church of Christ."[20] And in its "Decree on Ecumenism"[21] it explains:

> For it is through Christ's Catholic Church alone, which is universal help toward salvation, that the fullness of means of salvation can be obtained. It was to the apostolic college alone, of which Peter is the head, that we believe that our Lord entrusted all the blessings of the New Covenant, in order to establish on earth the one Body of Christ into which all those should be fully incorporated who belong in any way to the People of God.

It calls the Roman Catholic Church "this one and only Church of God."[22] However, like those before, Vatican II affirmed:

> Those who, through no fault of their own, do not know the Gospel of Christ or his Church, but who nevertheless seek God with a sincere heart, and moved by grace, try in their actions to do his will as they know it through the dictates of their conscience—those too may achieve eternal salvation.[23]

This is nothing more than a restatement of baptism by intention in early Catholic proclamations.[24]

What Rome's Claim to Being the True Church Does Not Mean

Now that we have examined the background to claims of papal authority and to Rome's exclusivity as the one true church, we will look more closely at particular aspects of Rome's claim to exclusivity, beginning with what it doesn't mean.

19. Austin Flannery, *Vatican Council II* (Northport, NY: Costello, 1982), vol. 2, 568–69.
20. *Catechism of the Catholic Church* (Liberia Editrice Vaticana, 1994), no. 822 (218).
21. Cited in ibid., 215.
22. Ibid., 216.
23. Flannery, *Vatican Council II*, 367.
24. According to Catholic authority Ludwig Ott, many others held that "membership of the Church is necessary for all men for salvation" (p. 112). In addition to those mentioned above, he lists The Council of Florence (AD 714), Popes Innocent III, Clement VI, Benedict XIV, Pius IX, Leo XIII, and Pius XII (Denzinger, *The Sources of Catholic Dogma*, p. 312).

Rome's Claim Does Not Mean That All Non-Catholics Go to Hell

Roman Catholic teaching allows for salvation without baptism or communion within the Catholic Church on the grounds of invincible ignorance. The exception is made for some people, including those who desired baptism but were not able to get it (called the baptism of intent) or those who die as unbaptized martyrs (called the baptism of blood). "Those who, through no fault of their own, do not know the Gospel of Christ . . . may achieve eternal salvation."[25] Though they are called "separated brethren"[26] from "separated churches,"[27] they are still "brethren." According to *The Catechism of the Catholic Church*, "All who have been justified by faith in baptism are incorporated into Christ; they therefore have a right to be called Christians, and with good reason are accepted as brothers in the Lord by the children of the Catholic Church."[28]

In fact, they hold to the belief that not only are there true believers among non-Christians, but also that there is both truth and goodness in non-Christian religions. The Catechism declares: "Thus, the Church considers all goodness and truth found in these religions as 'a preparation for the Gospel and given by him who enlightens all men that they may at length have life.'"[29]

Rome's Claim Does Not Mean One Cannot Grow in the Faith Outside the Catholic Church

The Catholic Catechism declares that "'many elements of sanctification and of truth' are found outside the visible confines of the Catholic Church: the written Word of God; the life of grace; faith, hope, and charity, with the other interior gifts of the Holy Spirit, as well as visible elements."[30] It goes on to say that "Christ uses these Churches and ecclesial communities as mean of salvation."[31]

Rome's Claim Does Not Mean That Non-Roman Catholic Baptism Is Not Valid

Both Augustine and Aquinas allowed for baptism by non-Catholics, including by heretics, as long as it was done by water in the name of the Trinity. Even laypersons can administer the sacrament of baptism.

25. Flannery, *Vatican Council II*, 367.
26. Ibid., 162.
27. Ibid., 449.
28. *Catechism of the Catholic Church*, 216.
29. Ibid., 223.
30. Ibid., 216.
31. Ibid.

The Catechism of the Catholic Faith declares, "When the necessity of the Church warrants it and when ministers are lacking, lay persons . . . can also supply for . . . Baptism, and to distribute Holy Communion in accord with the prescriptions of law."[32]

Rome's Claim Does Not Mean That Baptism Is Absolutely Necessary for Salvation

The above exceptions show that neither baptism nor membership in a Roman Catholic Church is absolutely necessary for salvation but only normatively necessary. That is, it is the norm (rule) for all, but there are some exceptions such as baptism by intent or by blood (martyrdom). Flannery said, "In view of the stress laid upon the necessity of membership of the Church for salvation it is understandable that the possibility of salvation for those outside the Church is mentioned only hesitantly."[33]

That was so only before Vatican II, which took it out of the footnotes, as it were, and put it in the main text in bold print. There was no change in doctrine, however; only in emphasis. As noted earlier, it stated that "those who, through no fault of their own, do not know the Gospel of Christ or his Church, but who nevertheless seek God with a sincere heart, and moved by grace, try in their actions to do his will as they know it through the dictates of their conscience—those too may achieve eternal salvation."[34] This includes Jews, Muslims, and even sincere atheists. So, what was previously whispered before was said here in a clear voice.

What the Claim to Being the True Church Does Mean

Clearly, there has been a continual claim of some in the church, at least from the time of Cyprian and later by Augustine that "there is no salvation outside the Church." This claim was later made dogma by ecumenical councils beginning with the Fourth Lateran Council on through Vatican II.

In addition, their claim to being the only true church was granted by divine right, given to Peter by Christ and passed on by apostolic succession to the present pope. So it should come as no surprise that the reigning pope declares, "This Church, constituted and organized in this world as a society, subsists in the Catholic Church, governed by the successor of Peter and the Bishops in communion with him." The rest of professing Christianity is, at best, not a true church in "the proper sense." There are many "ecclesial communities"[35] but not true churches. Such communities are in fact gravely "defective" churches since they cannot trace their lineage to Saint Peter, the first pope. So says Pope Benedict XVI, the former Cardinal Joseph Ratzinger.

Benedict's claims are not new. The Fourth Lateran Council accepted these claims as ecumenical, as did Trent and Vatican I and II. Also, in 1302 Pope Boniface VIII made a similar pronouncement: "We declare, say, define, and pronounce that it is absolutely necessary for the salvation of every human creature to be subject to the Roman Pontiff."

Rome's Claim Means That in the Roman Church Alone, Christian Truth Abides in Its Full and Proper Expression

While Rome admits that some truth can be found outside the Roman Church,[36] the fullness of truth is only found within it and by "full communion" with it.[37] According to Roman Catholicism, "The fullness of grace and truth . . . Christ has entrusted to the Catholic Church."[38]

Rome's Claim Means the Roman Catholic Church Alone Contains the Fullness of Salvation

The claim that salvation is found only in the Roman Catholic Church means that "where there is Christ Jesus, there is the Catholic Church. In her subsists the fullness of Christ's body united with its head; this implies that she receives from him 'the fullness of the means of salvation.'"[39] Again, "the church is catholic: she proclaims the fullness of the faith. She bears in herself and administers the totality of the means of salvation."[40] Since salvation is mediated through the sacraments, it means that only the Roman Catholic Church is the repository for all the sacraments handed down by Christ to Peter and on to the present pope by apostolic succession.

Rome's Claim Means Non-Catholic Churches Are Not True Churches

With the exception of Eastern Orthodox churches, both Vatican II and the recent Catechism reserve the word *church* for the true church

---

35. *Catechism of the Catholic Church*, 216.
36. Ibid.
37. Ibid.
38. Ibid.
39. Ibid., 220.
40. Ibid., 230.

whose visible head is in Rome. The other Christian groups are called "separated churches"[41] and "ecclesial communities."[42] Indeed, it is the church at Rome alone to which Christ referred when he said "the gates of hell shall not prevail against it" (Matt. 16:18 ESV). *The Catechism of the Catholic Church* says clearly that "all Christian churches everywhere have held and hold the great Church that is here [at Rome] to be their only basis and foundation since, according to the Savior's promise, the gates of hell have never prevailed against her."[43] Thus, all non-Catholic Christians who have been properly baptized by water in the name of the Trinity, "although imperfect, [are in] communion with the Catholic Church." But "with the Orthodox Churches, this communion is so profound 'that it lacks little to attain the fullness that would permit a common celebration of the Lord's Eucharist.'"[44]

Rome's Claim Means That Only the Roman Church Has the Infallible Truth of Christ

As was indicated above, there were implications of the claim to infallibility of the Roman Catholic magisterium before the nineteenth century, but Vatican I was the first council to officially pronounce papal infallibility. Pope Pius IX decreed that the pope, "using the counsel and seeking for help of the universal Church," cannot err. Instead it ruled that the pope's definitions are "irreformable of themselves, and not from the consent of the Church" when speaking *ex cathedra*, that is, as pastor and doctor of all Christians.

Rome has not been shy about this claim since that time. It was repeated in Vatican II and in the recent Catholic Catechism. Vatican II declared "the primacy of the Roman Pontiff and his infallible teaching office":[45]

> This infallibility, however, with which the divine redeemer wished to endow his Church in defining doctrine pertaining to faith and morals, is co-extensive with the deposit of revelation, which must be religiously guarded and loyally and courageously expounded. The Roman Pontiff, head of the college of bishops, enjoys this infallibility in virtue of his office, when, as supreme pastor and teacher of all the faithful—he confirms his brethren in the faith . . . he proclaims in an absolute decision a doctrine pertaining to faith or morals.[46]

41. Flannery, *Vatican Council II*, 449.
42. *Catechism of the Catholic Church*, 216.
43. Ibid., 221.
44. Ibid., 222.
45. Flannery, *Vatican Council II*, 370.
46. Ibid., 389.

Likewise, *The Catechism of the Catholic Church* affirms, "in order to preserve the Church in the purity of the faith handed down by the apostles, Christ who is the Truth willed to confer on her a share in his own infallibility. By a 'supernatural sense of faith' the People of God, under guidance of the Church's living Magisterium," unfailingly adheres to this faith.[47] Of course, it is only infallibility in matters of faith and morals.[48] "The Roman Pontiff, head of the college of Bishops, enjoys this infallibility in virtue of his office. . . . The infallibility promised to the Church is also present in the body of bishops when, together with Peter's successor, they exercise the supreme Magisterium, above all in an Ecumenical Council."[49] In brief, on official doctrine for the Church, the pope cannot be wrong, nor can the bishops with him be in error in an ecumenical council.

Rome's Claim Means Anyone Who Dies Knowingly Rejecting This Doctrine Will Go to Hell

According to the Roman Catholic Church, it is a mortal sin to reject one of its infallible teachings. Unrepented moral sins lead to eternal condemnation (hell). The Council of Trent often indicated this by attaching anathema to its decrees, saying something like, "If anyone, however, should not accept the stated dogma knowingly and deliberately, let him be anathema."[50] But the claims that the Roman Church is the only true church of Christ on earth and that its pope is the infallible interpreter of Christian truth are Roman dogma, since they were proclaimed at ecumenical councils such as the Fourth Lateran Council and Vatican I.

This means that, according to Rome, anyone who knows and rejects this, as most knowledgeable Protestants do (including the authors of this book), will go to hell.

Conclusion

Our concern in this chapter has been to understand the Roman claim to being the true church on earth. Before we could evaluate this claim, we examined, first, what it does not mean and, second, what it does mean. In order to understand its meaning we studied the historical development that led to the authoritarian papal claim to have and to

---

47. *Catechism of the Catholic Church*, 235.
48. Ibid.
49. Ibid.
50. See Denzinger, *The Sources of Catholic Dogma*, 245.

interpret Christian truth. With this background, we conclude that while the claim is not absolute, allowing for some exceptions, nonetheless it is sweeping.

It means that Christian truth in its fullness and proper expression resides only in the Roman Catholic Church. It also means the Roman Catholic Church alone contains the fullness of salvation. Any other form is incomplete and diminished. It also means that non-Catholic churches are not true churches. And, finally, it means anyone who dies knowingly rejecting this and other Catholic dogma will suffer eternal punishment! So much for the ecumenical spirit. What remains before us now is to determine the truth or falseness of this unique Roman claim to being the one true church and its conviction that those who knowingly reject its claim will be punished forever in hell. We begin with an examination of the development of the authoritarian episcopal form of government.

CHAPTER 2

THE HISTORICAL DEVELOPMENT OF THE ROMAN PRIMACY STRUCTURE

f there was no apostolic New Testament basis for an episcopal form of government, particularly an authoritarian and universal one, then there is no biblical basis for primacy for anyone, Peter included. In the next chapter (chapter 3) we will discuss Peter's role in the New Testament church and among the apostles, but here we will discuss just how and when this form of government developed, and whether it has a basis in the teachings of the apostles in the New Testament.[1]

Rome was not built in a day, and we will see here that Roman Catholicism was not built in a day either. There is a radical difference and discontinuity between the hierarchical authority of the present Roman Church and that of the churches of the New Testament and early Christian centuries. First, in contrast to the claim of a divinely authoritative and infallible governmental and doctrinal structure of current Roman Catholicism, the immediate successors of the apostles

1. There are, of course, other challenges as well, such as the lack of support for the primacy of Peter in the New Testament and the lack of support for apostolic succession. For a discussion of these see chaps. 5–6.

followed the pattern of government laid down in the New Testament, namely, independent, autonomous local churches led by a plurality of elders, also called bishops.[2]

Second, it was not until the second century that even a basic episcopal form of government emerged with one bishop over each church. And even then there was no sole authority of this local leader over a given church, to say nothing of authority over even a group of churches. Further, this short step into local church episcopalism was still a long way from the later claim of Rome to have infallible authority over all churches.

Third, it took some time before more authority was given to bishops and before there was a bishop over a whole region and ultimately a bishop over bishops, the bishop of Rome. Indeed, it was not until the late nineteenth century that the papacy made the bold claim of infallible authority for the bishop of Rome in official pronouncements on faith and practice. The course of this gradual development is a fascinating study in the creeping authority that overtook the autonomous, self-governing, Bible-based churches of the apostles and their immediate successors.

Our study begins with the New Testament. Then we will look at the apostolic fathers who were contemporary with or immediate successors of the apostolic age itself and who therefore provide the most valuable historic testimony.

Church Government in the New Testament

In the New Testament there was a plurality of both elders, or bishops, and deacons in each church. Paul wrote to "the bishops and deacons" in Philippi (Phil. 1:1 NKJV). In Acts they "appointed elders" in every church (Acts 14:23 NKJV). Titus was instructed by Paul to "appoint elders in every town" (Titus 1:5). That *elders* and *bishops* referenced one and the same office is clear from the following: (1) The term *elder* was of Jewish origin, and *bishop* was of Greek origin, but both referred to the same position. (2) Paul used these terms interchangeably, saying to Titus, "Appoint elders in every city. . . . For a bishop must be blameless . . . " (Titus 1:5–7 NKJV). (3) Acts 20 uses the terms interchangeably, declaring that Paul called for "the elders of the church" and instructed them that they were "overseers" (bishops) of the flock (Acts 20:17,

---

2. See Norman L. Geisler, *Systematic Theology*, vol. 4: *The Church and Last Things* (Bloomington, MN: Bethany, 2005).

28 NKJV). Likewise, Peter exhorted the "elders" to "feed the flock . . . taking the oversight thereof" (1 Pet. 5:1–2 KJV).

Nowhere in the New Testament is the term *bishop* used of an office distinct from an elder and superior to it. Indeed, it was a plurality of leaders, or elders, of whom the writer of Hebrews says one should "obey them that have the rule over you" (Heb. 13:17 KJV). Indeed, "the elders" were told not to be "lords over those entrusted to you" (1 Pet. 5:3 NKJV). And the people were to "submit yourselves to your elders" (plural) rather than to a single bishop (1 Pet. 5:5 NKJV).

In fact, the decision of the Jerusalem church came from the "apostles and elders." Had there been a bishop over them he surely would have been singled out on this authoritative matter, but he was not. And probably the last book to be written by the last living apostle, John, still speaks of many individual churches with their own independent leaders and no hierarchy of local, regional, or universal bishops. Indeed, the only Head of these local churches was the invisible Christ who walked in their midst (Revelation 1) and held them accountable for their deeds (Revelation 2–3). The "messenger" sent to each church from the apostle was undoubtedly an apostolic delegate. These messengers are never called "bishops" nor were they held responsible for what was going on in the churches, as a bishop would have been.

Apostolic Fathers on Church Government

The late first-century apostolic Fathers and even most of the early second-century Fathers followed the New Testament pattern of church government of a plurality of elders in independent, autonomous local churches that are united by a common apostolic authoritative doctrine expressed in the Old and New Testaments.[3]

The Epistle of Barnabas (ca. AD 70–90)

Many scholars consider *The Epistle of Barnabas* to be the earliest of all early extrabiblical sources. Lightfoot places the time of its writing between AD 70 and 132, preferring a date between AD 70 and 90.[4] In view of the Jewish temple in Jerusalem being destroyed, this epistle affirms that the church is the spiritual temple of God (16).[5] The "sons and daughters"[6] in the faith to whom he addresses the epistle are urged

3. See Norman L. Geisler, *Systematic Theology*, vol. 3: *Sin/Salvation*, 118–26.
4. See J. B. Lightfoot and J. R. Harmer, eds., *The Apostolic Fathers* (Grand Rapids, MI: Baker, 1988), 240.
5. All numbers in parentheses refer to divisions of *The Epistle of Barnabas*.
6. They are also called "children of love and peace" (21).

to avoid any "schism" (19) and to make peace between contending fac-
tions. This implies that the congregation had the authority to do this.
There are no references to any bishop over a church or over any group
of churches.

Clement of Rome (ca. AD 94–95)

Clement of Rome is one of the earliest nonbiblical writers. His epistle
is written from "the Church of God which sojourneth in Rome" to "the
Church of God which sojourneth in Corinth" (Intro). He exhorts believers to be "submitting yourselves to your rulers [plural] and rendering
to the older men among you the honour which is their due" (1). He
commends them because "every sedition and every schism is abominable
to you" (2). He speaks of the apostles Peter and Paul as "most righteous
pillars of the Church" (5). He exhorts, "Let us set before our eyes [the
example] of the good Apostles" (5).

But there is no affirmation of the primacy of Peter over the other
apostles. Indeed, Clement himself assumes no apostolic authority for
himself but writes as a fellow "sojourner" in the faith (Intro). Believers
are urged to "conform to the glorious and venerable rule which hath
been handed down to us" from the apostles (7). They were admonished
to "do that which is written" in the Scripture (13; cf. 23).

He opposed leaders' exalting themselves over others, declaring, "For
Christ is with them that are lowly of mind, not with them that exalt
themselves over the flock" (16), which speaks against an authoritarian
episcopalianism of one bishop over the whole congregation. Rather, "Let
us reverence our rulers; let us honour our elders" (21), clearly indicating
a plurality of elders in the leadership of the church.

Clement speaks of "the Apostles [who] received the Gospel for us
from the Lord Jesus Christ." When they established a church they "appointed . . . bishops and deacons" (42). He even went so far as to affirm
that the apostles foresaw "that there would be strife over the name of
the bishop's office" and thus appointed "approved men [who] should
succeed to their ministrations" (44). This belies any apostolic succession
since the apostles did not appoint apostles to succeed them in every
church (Acts 14:23). He rebuked those who got rid of their sound and
godly bishops, saying, "These men we consider to be unjustly thrust out
from their ministration" (44). This illegitimate action seems to imply
that the congregations did have a legitimate role in choosing their own
leaders, which the Corinthian church was abusing. Clement speaks of the

Corinthian church's "sedition against its presbyters [elders]" (47). They were told, rather, to "submit yourselves unto the presbyters" (57).

In summary, just as in the New Testament, no distinction is made here between an elder and a bishop. Each church has a plurality of elders or bishops. There is no sign of an episcopal form of government, even in a local church, lest it be found in the warning against those who wished to exalt themselves in authority over others. The true authority in the church is apostolic (13), and their teaching is inscribed in the Scriptures (13, 23, 42, 44, 53). Even Roman Catholic authority Ludwig Ott admits, "The letter contains neither a formal statement of the Primacy, that is, an express invocation of the pre-eminence of the Roman Church, nor juridical measures."[7]

The Epistle of St. Polycarp to the Philippians (ca. AD 69–155)[8]

The value of this epistle is that its author, Polycarp, was a disciple of John the apostle. Thus, it brings us into immediate contact with the apostolic age. It begins: "Polycarp and the presbyters [elders] that are with him . . . " (Intro).

He declares, "The presbyters also must be compassionate, merciful toward all men . . . " (6). He speaks of "Valens, who aforetime was a presbyter among you" (11). That is, he was one among many. Indeed, Polycarp places himself alongside the other "elders" in the introduction (cited above). He also makes reference to "deacons," insisting they should be "blameless" (5).

The references are to a plurality of elders (bishops) and deacons and fit with the New Testament (Phil. 1:1; Acts 14:23), as does the fact that some, like Polycarp, were leaders among these elders (cf. Philem. 1).[9] There is no evidence, however, that Polycarp held any higher office than the rest of the elders. In short, the church government reflected here is not episcopalian.

Peter is not singled out in any special way. Indeed, he is not even mentioned by name. But Polycarp speaks of Paul four times (see 3, 9, 11 [twice]). He refers to "Paul himself and the rest of the Apostles" (9). He wrote of those who "are well trained in the sacred writings" (12) which

7. Ludwig Ott, *Fundamentals of Catholic Dogma* (Rockford, IL: Tan, 1960), 283.
8. See F. L. Cross, *The Oxford Dictionary of the Christian Church* (Oxford: Oxford University Press, 1978), 1107.
9. The fact that Polycarp is called a "bishop" by Ignatius is not unusual since in the New Testament these were merely different names for the same office (cf. 1 Tim. 3:1 cf. Titus 1:5, 7; Acts 14:23 cf. Phil. 1:1).

Polycarp himself quotes numerous times in this short letter, showing his belief in their importance.

The Didache (The Teachings of the Apostles) (ca. AD 80–120)

Scholars date this work to the end of the first or the beginning of the second century. Most English and American scholars vary between 80 and 120.[10] Internal evidence for an early date includes its simplicity, undeveloped doctrinal expression, and its New Testament-like form of church government.

The *Didache* begins in a Proverbs-like way: "There are two ways, one of life and one of death, and there is a great difference between them." All believers are exhorted to follow "according to the ordinance of the Gospel" as they have it from "the apostles and prophets" (11).

The form of church government was patterned after the New Testament (see Phil. 1:1; Acts 14:23). It commands: "Appoint for yourselves therefore bishops and deacons worthy of the Lord. . . . Therefore despise them not; for they are your honourable men along with the prophets and teachers" (15). While there is no affirmation of any episcopal kind of government, there is a hint of the conditions that led to the development of the primacy of bishops. It is found in the warning against any "schism" (4), the persistent presence of which led to later development of an episcopal form of government in an attempt to unify the visible church against divisions in doctrine and practice.

The Shepherd of Hermas (ca. AD 90–100)

The "shepherd" is a divine teacher who communicates this allegory to Hermas for the instruction of the church. The "aged woman" is the church, indicating her eternal election by God before the world began. The story is geographically centered in Rome. Some claim the author was the Hermas mentioned by Paul in Romans 16:14. Others follow the Muratorian Canon (ca. 180), which says it was by the brother of Pius I (ca. 140–155), but this is inconsistent with the reference to Clement (Herm. *Vis.* 4). To meet this objection, many place it around AD 90–100.[11]

The form of church government it presents involves a plurality of elders and deacons. The author refers to "the elders that preside over the Church" (Herm. *Vis.* 2.4; cf. 3.1) and who are guided by "the book" (2.4). Another text (Herm. *Vis.* 3.5) speaks of "the apostles and bishops

10. See Alexander Roberts, et al., eds., *Ante-Nicene Fathers*, 10 vols.; rev. A. Cleveland Coxe (Grand Rapids, MI: Eerdmans, 1989), 7:375.
11. See discussion in Lightfoot, *The Apostolic Fathers*, 293–94.

and teachers and deacons." Another text speaks of "the rulers of the Church" who "occupy the chief seats" (3.9). There is no reference to a bishop in the singular being over any church or churches.

An Ancient Homily (The So-called Second Epistle of Clement) (AD 120–140)

This ancient sermon by an unknown author is dated by Lightfoot between AD 120 and 140. Even though it is listed in all three manuscripts with Clement's letter to the Corinthians and is sometimes called the "Second Epistle of St. Clement," both external and internal evidence favor another author.[12] The "Scripture" is cited repeatedly as having divine authority (2, 3, 4, 5, 6, 7, etc.). Citations are prefaced with "He [God] Himself saith" or the like (e.g., 3, 4, 5). Believers are to "give heed to the things which are written" (19). Both "the Books [of the Bible] and the Apostles" declare God's truth (14).

The form of church leadership was not episcopal but more Presbyterian in so far as it had a plurality of elders. There is no mention of a single bishop in a church or over a group of churches. Rather, he speaks of the church's being "admonished by the presbyters," that is, elders (18). Indeed, woe is pronounced on those who "obeyed not the presbyters" (17).

In brief, in this tiny but early sermon we breathe the air of the apostles. In so doing we get a very New Testament picture of orthodox teaching, including an independent local church that has no awareness of the later development of a single bishop over the local church or a group of churches but rather a plurality of elders whose leadership is to be faithfully followed.

Ignatius (d. ca. AD 107 or 117)

Assuming the date and authenticity of Ignatius's epistles, Ignatius manifests the earliest form of a minimal episcopal form of church government in which each church has a bishop in addition to elders and deacons. However, there are reasons to question these dates and the exact text.[13]

---

12. Ibid., 41.
13. Many have challenged the authenticity of these works. But Anglican scholars like Bishop Ussher and J. B. Lightfoot have strongly defended them. Nonetheless, a later date is not without reasons. First, there is no manuscript evidence forcing belief in an early date. Second, there are differing manuscript traditions, one of which is shorter, indicating changes that have been made from the original. Third, the more highly developed form of authoritarian episcopal governments fits better at a somewhat later date. Fourth, the repetitive references to a single authoritative bishop found throughout these epistles seem a bit forced and contrived. Finally, if an earlier date is assumed, it contradicts other books from this period just discussed.

But even if there are later interpolations in these books, they still reflect a relatively early form of the primacy of local bishops over their congregations.

Ignatius speaks to the Ephesians about "your bishop" (1)[14] and of their need to "[submit] yourselves to your bishop and presbytery" (2). He wrote, "Let us therefore be careful not to resist the bishop, that by our submission we may give ourselves to God" (5). He adds, "Plainly therefore we ought to regard the bishop as the Lord Himself" (6). And "Assemble yourselves together in common . . . to the end that ye may obey the bishop and the presbytery without distraction of mind" (20).

To the Magnesians he spoke of the bishop as one to whom "all reverence" should be rendered (3). Of course, this respect is to be paid ultimately to God, who is "the Bishop of all" (3). He speaks of the bishop presiding after the likeness of God and the presbyters after the likeness of the council of the apostles, with the deacons also "who are most dear to me . . . " (6); "therefore as the Lord did nothing without the Father [being united with Him], either by Himself or by the Apostles, so neither do ye anything without the bishop and the presbyters" (7).

In his letter to the Trallians, Ignatius repeats his strong episcopal emphasis, saying, "In like manner let all men respect the deacons as Jesus Christ, even as they should respect the bishop as being a type of the Father and the presbyters as the council of God and as the college of Apostles" (3). Indeed, "he that doeth aught without the bishop and presbytery and deacons, this man is not clean in his conscience" (7). He speaks of not separating from "the ordinances of the Apostles" (7). It is noteworthy that he speaks of a group of "churches" (12) as independent entities that have their own elders and bishop (pastor) and of his being a "member" of a local church (13).

Another epistle is addressed to "the Church which presides in the place of the region of the Romans" (Ign. *Rom.*, Intro).[15] Ignatius disavowed apostolic status, saying, "I do not enjoin you, as Peter and Paul did." He gave equal status to Peter and Paul,[16] though he mentioned Peter as the first apostle (as did Paul in 1 Cor. 15:5) who saw Christ after his resurrection (Ign. *Smyrn.* 3). "They were apostles, I am a convict; they were

14. Unless otherwise noted, as from A. C. Coxe in the Philip Schaff ed., the quotations here are from the Lightfoot translations.
15. The Schaff edition fits the context better than the one in Lightfoot, which says, "Her that hath the presidency in the country of the region of the Romans." Even so, the "presidency" it described a few lines later is a "presidency of love" not of domination over other churches.
16. Lightfoot, *Apostolic Fathers*, 151.

free, but I am a slave to this very hour" (Ign. *Rom.* 4). He says God is the "shepherd" of the church at Syria and "Jesus alone" is its bishop (9).

To the Philadelphians, Ignatius wrote: "Be ye careful therefore to observe one eucharist (for there is one flesh of our Lord Jesus Christ and one cup unto union in His blood; there is one altar, as there is one bishop, together with the presbytery and the deacons . . .), that whatever ye do, ye may do it after God" (4). For "I cried out, when I was among you; I spake with a loud voice, with God's own voice, Give heed to the bishop and the presbytery and deacons" (7).

The Smyrnaeans were urged to "shun divisions, as the beginning of evil. . . . Let no man do aught of things pertaining to the Church apart from the bishop wither to baptize or to hold a love-feast" (8). He spoke of the apostles as "Peter and his company" (3) who witnessed the resurrection. For "it is good to recognize God and the bishop. He that honoureth the bishop is honoured of God; he that doeth aught without the knowledge of the bishop rendereth service to the devil" (9). And "let that be held a valid eucharist which is under the bishop or one to whom he shall have committed it. Wherever the bishop shall appear, there let the people be; even as where Jesus may be, there is the universal Church" (8).

Finally, he wrote unto "Polycarp, who is bishop of the church of the Smyrnaeans or rather who hath for his bishop God the Father and Jesus Christ, abundant greeting" (Ign. *Pol.*, Intro). Also, "give ye heed to the bishop, that God also may give heed to you. I am devoted to those who are subject to the bishop, the presbyters, the deacons" (6). Thus, "It becometh thee, most blessed Polycarp, to call together a godly council and to elect some one among you who is very dear to you and zealous also, who shall be fit to bear the name of God's courier to appoint him, I say, that he may go to Syria and glorify your zealous love unto the glory of God" (7).

Several things are clear from these texts. First, they represent an incipient form of episcopal church government in which each church has one bishop, many elders, and many deacons. The bishop was not just a leader of the elders but was in a position of authority above them to which they must submit. He controlled communion and baptism and oversaw everything that occurred in his church.

Further, some bishops seemed to be over a whole region or group of churches (cf. Ign. *Rom.*, Intro). However, there is no affirmation of the primacy of the bishop of Rome over other bishops. Peter is given recognition alongside Paul[17] but not over him. Likewise, the first-century authority rested in the "apostles" (plural) who are called a "council of the Apostles" (Ign. *Magn.* 6), not in any one of them. Peter is only listed as one leader, along with Paul, among the apostles (Ign. *Rom.* 4) but not as the bishop of Rome or the vicar of Christ. What is more, several times God is called the invisible "Bishop of all" (Ign. *Trall.* 3; Ign. *Mag.* 3), the "Shepherd" (Ign. *Rom.* 9), and Christ alone as "Bishop."[18] This fits with the biblical emphasis of Christ as the invisible head of the visible churches, just as the apostle John pictured in the book of Revelation (chs. 1–3).

Nonetheless, Ignatius does represent another step in the evolution of the episcopate—one where a form of episcopal government exists in each local church, as opposed to the congregation overseen by a board of elders as found in the New Testament (Phil. 1:1; Acts 14:23). Also, Ignatius may represent the first step where a region is overseen by a bishop who is the bishop of the lead city in that area, i.e., of a regional episcopate.

Fragments of Papias (ca. AD 130–140)

Papias's famous *Exposition of Oracles of the Lord* has perished, and only fragments of his writings survive. Irenaeus preserved two fragments. Other writings, including Eusebius's, contain addition material about Papias. He is believed to be "a hearer of John and a companion of Polycarp."[19]

Papias confirms several New Testament teachings on church government. First, there is no primacy of Peter. His two lists of the apostles have Andrew first and Peter second in both cases (Fragments 3 and 7). Indeed, special attention is given to John (Fragments 1, 3, 4, 6, 9, 19, 20). While later writers call Polycarp a "bishop," Papias refers to all the apostles as "Elders" (Fragment 3), showing the terms are used interchangeably as in the New Testament. He refers to "the Elder John" (Fragments 3 and 7). There are no references to an episcopal form of government in the church or churches. This would indicate that the development of episcopalism was local, not universal, and that it was not following any New Testament apostolic mandate.

17. Ibid.
18. Ibid.
19. Ibid., 527.

Irenaeus (ca. AD 130–200)

Irenaeus is an important witness in early Christianity (see Appendix 1). He was thought to be a native of Smyrna who studied at Rome. He claimed to have heard Polycarp, the disciple of the apostle John, when he was a boy. Irenaeus is said to have later become the Bishop of Lyons, France. He was the first great father of the church in the West. His major work *Against Heresies*[20] is dated between 182 and 188.[21]

On the Apostolicity of the Church

It is evident from repeated statements that the final authority for the church rests in the apostles, not in any one apostle. Even the founding of the Church at Rome was said to be by two apostles, Paul and Peter.[22] Irenaeus repeatedly speaks of "the apostolic tradition"[23] and "the blessed apostles" (plural) who "founded and built up the Church,"[24] the doctrine of the apostles,[25] and "the tradition from the apostles."[26] He wrote: "These [apostles] are the voices of the Church from which every Church had its origin . . . these are the voices of the apostles; these are the voices of the disciples of the Lord, the truly perfect, who after the assumption of the Lord, were perfected by the Spirit."[27] For "He [God] sent forth His own apostles in the spirit of truth, and not in that of error, He did the very same also in the case of the prophets."[28]

On the Unity of the Church

Irenaeus strongly stressed the unity of the Christian church. He wrote: "the Catholic [universal] Church possesses one and the same faith throughout the whole world."[29] However, as just noted, this unity is not organizational but spiritual and doctrinal. He wrote:

> The Church, though dispersed throughout the world, even to the ends of the earth, has *received from the apostles and their disciples this faith*: She believes in one God, the Father Almighty, Maker of heaven and earth, and the sea, and all things that are in them; in one Christ Jesus, the Son

---

20. See Cross, *Oxford Dictionary*, 713.
21. Alexander Roberts and James Donaldson, eds., *Ante-Nicene Fathers* (Grand Rapids, MI: Eerdmans, 1989),1:312.
22. Irenaeus, "Against Heresies," in *Ante-Nicene Fathers*, 1.414.
23. Ibid., 1.416.
24. Ibid.
25. Ibid., 1.431.
26. Ibid., 1.417.
27. Ibid., 1.431.
28. Ibid., 1.513.
29. Ibid., 1.331–32.

of God, who became incarnate for our salvation; and in the Holy Spirit
. . . and the birth from a virgin, and passion, and resurrection from the
dead, the ascension into heaven in the flesh of the beloved Christ Jesus,
our Lord, and His future manifestation from heaven in the glory of the
Father.[30]

He adds, "This one church, although scattered throughout the whole
world, yet, as if occupying but one house, carefully preserves it."[31] There
are many independent churches, but they are doctrinally united *as if
they were one house.*[32] "*Nor will any one of the rulers (Bishops) in the
Churches, however highly gifted he may be in point of eloquence, teach
doctrines different from these (for no one is greater than the Master).*"[33] In
short, Christ is the invisible head of all the visible churches, and Christ's
teaching through the authority of his apostles is the basis for the unity
of the one true church. Irenaeus declared: "The Word of God [Christ]
is supreme, so also in things visible and corporeal *He might possess the
supremacy, and, taking to Himself the pre-eminence, as well as constituting Himself Head of the Church,* He might draw all things to Himself
at the proper time."[34] Clearly, Christ has no vicar on earth; he himself
heads his church universal. As even Peter himself said, elders are only
undershepherds who lead the local congregations to follow the "Chief
Shepherd" (1 Pet. 5:1–4).

Nonetheless, Irenaeus affirmed that God desires apostolic unity in all
the churches based on "the doctrine of the apostles" (Acts 2:42). Thus,
Irenaeus spoke repeatedly against schisms, once declaring of "a spiritual
disciple" that "he shall also judge those who give rise to schisms, who are
destitute of the love of God, and who look to their own special advantage
rather than to *the unity of the Church*; and who for trifling reasons, or
any kind of reason which occurs to them, cut in pieces and divide the
great and glorious body of Christ." He then adds, "For no reformation
of so great importance can be effected by them, as will compensate for
the mischief arising from their schism."[35]

30. Ibid., 1.330, emphasis added.
31. Ibid., 1.331.
32. Irenaeus often refers to churches in the plural. For example, he speaks of "that tradition
which originates from the apostles, and which is preserved by means of the successions of
presbyters in the Churches" (*Haer.* 3.2.2, emphasis added).
33. Ibid., emphasis added.
34. Ibid., 3.443, emphasis added.
35. Ibid., 1.508 cf. 1.22.1; 1.23; 1.24–31, emphasis added.

On the Authority of the Church

A good deal of controversy revolves around a disputed text in *Against Heresies*, Book Three. Irenaeus refers to "that tradition derived from the apostles, of the very great, the very ancient, and universally known Church founded and organized at Rome by the two most glorious apostles, Peter and Paul; as also by pointing out the faith preached to men, which comes down to our times by means of the succession of the bishops." For "it is a matter of necessity that *every Church should agree* [Lat. *convenire*] *with this Church*, on account of its preeminent authority, that is, the faithful everywhere, inasmuch as the apostolic tradition has been preserved continuously by those faithful men *who exist everywhere*."[36]

J. N. D. Kelly sets forth the dispute in these words: "If *convenire* here means "agree with" and *principalitas* refers to the Roman primacy (in whatever sense), the gist of the sentence may be taken to be that Christians of every other church are required, in view of its special position of leadership, to fall in line with the Roman church, inasmuch as the authentic apostolic tradition is always preserved by the faithful who are everywhere."[37]

However, many scholars, including Kelly, have found fault with this translation for two reasons. First, the weakness of the final clause strikes them as "intolerable."[38] Second, "the normal meaning of *convenire* is 'resort to,' 'foregather at,' and *necesse est* does not easily bear the sense of 'ought.'"[39] Indeed, the editor of the *Apostolic Fathers* volume in *The Ante-Nicene Fathers*, A. Cleveland Coxe, cites one candid Roman Catholic scholar who translates it as follows: "For to this Church, on account of more potent principality, it is necessary that every Church (that is, those who are on every side faithful) *resort*; in which Church ever, *by those who are on every side*, has been preserved that tradition which is from the apostles."[40] Coxe adds, "Here it is obvious that the faith was kept at Rome, by *those who resort there* from all quarters. She was a mirror of the Catholic World, owing her orthodoxy to them; not the Sun, dispensing her own light to others, but the glass bringing their rays into focus."[41] This is in direct contrast to the proclamation of Pope Pius IX

36. Ibid., 1.415–416, emphases added.
37. J. N. D. Kelly, *Early Christian Doctrines*, 2nd ed. (New York: Harper & Row, 1960), 193.
38. Ibid.
39. Ibid.
40. A. Cleveland Coxe, *Apostolic Fathers*, in *The Ante-Nicene Fathers*, ed. Roberts, et al., 1:415.
41. Ibid.

(see below) who "informed his Bishops, at the late Council (in 1870), that they were not called to bear their testimony, but to hear his infallible decree."[42] In short, what Irenaeus meant was that Rome is the center of orthodoxy since she, by virtue of being the capital of the empire, was the repository of all catholic tradition—"all this has been turned upside down by modern Romanism."[43]

J. N. D. Kelly concurs, observing that many scholars "have judged it more plausible to take Irenaeus's point as being that the Roman Church [of that day] supplies an ideal illustration for the reason that, in view of its being placed in the imperial city, representatives of all the different churches necessarily (i.e., inevitably) flock to it, so that there is some guarantee that the faith taught there faithfully reflects the apostolic tradition."[44] That is to say, Rome's primacy is *reflective* and not *authoritative*.

As for Irenaeus's questions: "How should it be if the apostles had not left us writings? Would it not be necessary to follow the course of the tradition which they handed down to those to whom they did commit the churches?"[45] Professor Payne's comments are to the point. "First of all, the above statements by Irenaeus are theoretical; it was not necessary to follow the course of traditions, because the apostles *had* left writings. . . . Second, the above statements have as their subject the facts which one must accept to be saved, and not the degree of authority which lies behind any given medium."[46] In short, Irenaeus is not stressing the *authority* of the medium but the *accuracy* of it in transmitting the message of the apostles who alone possessed the God-given authority.

Payne adds a third point: "The above statements assume that the truths of the tradition are in fact those recorded in the Scriptures."[47] Thus, the traditions are to be judged by the Scriptures, not the reverse. It is noteworthy that the apostles did not appoint more apostles to replace themselves after Pentecost, where they became the "foundation" of the church, Christ being the chief cornerstone (Eph. 2:20). Rather, they appointed "elders . . . in every church" (Acts 14:23). Irenaeus himself speaks of "the disciples of the apostles" as "presbyters" (elders).[48]

42. Ibid., 461.
43. Ibid.
44. Ibid., 193.
45. *Haer.* 1.417.
46. Barton Payne, "Biblical Interpretation of Irenaeus," in *Inspiration and Interpretation*, ed. John Walvoord (Grand Rapids, MI: Eerdmans, 1957), 63–64.
47. Ibid.
48. *Haer.* 5.35.2.

He wrote: "We refer them [heretics] to that tradition which originates from the apostles, and which is preserved by means of the successions of presbyters in the churches."[49]

However, Irenaeus seemed to believe that each church has a single bishop over it, for he spoke of Polycarp as "bishop of Smyrna" (cf. *Haer.* 3.3.4) and a line of bishops in Rome beginning with Linus.[50] But this is in contrast to the New Testament, which is clear that every local church had its own "overseers and deacons" (cf. Phil. 1:1).[51] And it was they whose leadership was to be followed by their congregations (Heb. 13:7, 17, 24), not one authoritative bishop in a church or one presiding over all churches from Rome. Christ, the Chief Shepherd, was the invisible head of the visible church (Eph. 1:22 cf. 1 Pet. 5:4), and he commissioned the apostles to lay the doctrinal basis that is binding on all churches everywhere. For even John, the last living apostle at the end of the first century, speaks of Christ himself walking among his "churches" and rebuking them for not recognizing his headship (cf. Revelation 1–3).[52] Nonetheless, whatever the size, Irenaeus did provide the material for another step in the direction of a Roman-centered episcopal authority, as unintentional as it may have been.

Cyprian (d. AD 258)

Cyprian added a significant step to the evolution of the monarchial episcopate (one universal bishop) by insisting "there is one God, and Christ is one, and there is one chair [episcopate] founded upon the rock by the word of the Lord."[53] Under his system, "each bishop in his place succeeded to and exercised the apostolic authority. Each bishop therefore had a right to a voice in the common concerns of the whole church." But "even the bishop of Rome—who certainly enjoyed a special dignity and a special right to leadership, as successor to St. Peter—was nevertheless, substantively, the colleague and therefore the equal of

49. Ibid., 1.415.
50. Ibid., 1.416.
51. The terms *overseer* (*bishop*) and *elder* were used interchangeably in the New Testament (cf. Titus 1:5, 7), the former being the term Greeks used of leaders and the latter which Hebrews used. Indeed, the qualifications are the same for both; the duties are the same; there was a plurality of both in even small churches (cf. Acts 14:23; Phil. 1:1). Thus Irenaeus, writing over a century after the apostles, is reflecting an emerging episcopal form of government not found in the New Testament.
52. See Geisler, *The Church and Last Things*, 4.
53. Cyprian, *Epistles* 39, 5, in *Ante-Nicene Fathers*, vol. 7, ed. Alexander Roberts and James Donaldson.

his brethren."[54] However, even Roman Catholic authority Ludwig Ott admitted that *"the Fathers did not expressly speak of the Infallibility of the Pope,* but they attest the decisive teaching authority of the Roman Church and its Pontiff."[55]

The Epistle of Diognetus (between ca. AD 150–325)

This brief epistle listed in Lightfoot's *The Apostolic Fathers* is dated by him circa AD 150. Some place it as late as Constantine (fourth century). It has no mention of church officers or church government. Hence, it provides no positive help in this discussion.

Eusebius (ca. AD 260–340)

The great church historian Eusebius records other important steps in the creeping ecclesiastical authority of the Roman Church. Eventually, bishops gained authority over their areas. Before the end of the second century (by ca. 180–190) he lists bishops over various areas including Alexandria, Antioch, Caesarea, Jerusalem, Corinth, and Ephesus.[56] There arose a contention as to when the passion and resurrection of Christ should be observed. Eusebius wrote:

> Synods and assemblies of bishops were held on this account, and all, with one consent, through mutual correspondence drew up an ecclesiastical decree. . . . But the bishops in Asia, led by Polycrates, decided to hold to the old custom handed down to them [which was different]. Thereupon Victor, who presided over the church at Rome, immediately attempted to cut off from the common unity the parishes of all Asia, with the churches that agreed with them, as heterodox; and wrote letters and declared all the brethren there wholly excommunicate.[57]

This early tendency for the church at Rome, due to its size and location at the seat of Roman political power, to exercise widespread authority is a portent of things to come.

Disputes like this, and later more serious doctrinal ones, occasioned a stronger and more monolithic organization. In fact, they called for general councils of the church to decide on the matter. The first of these was the Arian dispute over the deity of Christ, which occasioned the Council of

---

54. Walker Williston, et. al., *A History of the Christian Church,* 4th ed. (New York: Scribner's, 1985), 83.

55. Ott, *Fundamentals of Catholic Dogma,* 288, emphasis added. As we have seen, the earliest Fathers do not even hold to the authority of bishops over elders in the church.

56. Eusebius, *Church History* (Grand Rapids, MI: Baker, 1990), 5.22.

57. Ibid., 5.23–24.

Nicea (AD 325). While there is general agreement in Christendom over the first seven councils (i.e., between the Eastern and Western churches), most Protestants accept only the first four.

The reasons for this parallel the development of the increasing authority of the bishop of Rome over the next centuries, as indicated by the discussion below. Eusebius reported that the action of the emperor Constantine was to encourage a unified action of the Christian church to squelch dissent. In fact, he called the first ecumenical council (Nicea) and took an active part in it. In this way he used the heavy pressure of an imperial state to bring about a more monolithic church.[58] His motives can be seen in this citation from a "copy of an epistle in which the emperor commands another synod to be held for the purpose of removing all dissensions among the bishops."[59] It reads:

> Constantine Augustus to Chrestus, bishop of Syracuse (in Italy). When some began wickedly and perversely to disagree among themselves in regard to the holy worship and celestial power and catholic doctrine, wishing to put an end to such disputes among them, I formerly gave command that certain bishops should be sent from Gaul, and that the opposing parties . . . should be summoned from Africa; that in their presence, and in the presence of the bishop of Rome, the matter which appeared to be causing the disturbance might be examined and decided with all care.[60]

Little wonder a top-heavy and monolithic Roman Church soon emerged with a structure similar to the Roman government, with a pope corresponding to the emperor at the top. Add to this the fact that Constantine put the church on the state payroll, which bound them with strong economic cords.[61]

General Church Councils

Church councils played an important role in the development of monolithic Roman episcopalism. These are numbered as twenty-one ecumenical councils by Roman Catholics. These, allegedly, are councils involving the whole church, even though sometimes major portions of the church were only sparsely represented. Local councils were only in specific geographical areas and are not held to be binding, unless affirmed by a

58. Ibid., 10.
59. Ibid., 10.5.21.
60. Ibid.
61. Ibid., 10.6.1.

later ecumenical council. Emperors convened the first eight councils, whereas popes convened the last thirteen.

From the very first council (Nicea, AD 325) called by Emperor Constantine, there was pressure to form a more monolithic ecclesiastical structure. By the eighth council (the Fourth Council of Constantinople, AD 869), this was becoming more evident. And from the twelfth council (the Fourth Lateran Council, AD 1215) the structure of what is currently known as Roman Catholicism was taking shape. Of course, the counter-Reformation Council of Trent (AD 1545–1547) solidified Romanism, and the First Council of the Vatican (AD 1870) infallibly made permanent the imperial ecclesiastical structure known as Roman Catholicism forever. And the nineteenth and twentieth councils furthered the Roman dogmas.

1) The First Council of Nicea was called by the professing Christian emperor Constantine who desired to unite the church and solidify his empire.

The council affirmed the Trinity, the full deity of Christ as eternal and of the same nature as the Father. The council formulated the famous Nicene Creed, a condemnation of the heresy of Arianism, which denied the deity of Christ and thereby divided Christendom.

In addition, Nicea set forth numerous canons that claim to be universally binding on the whole church including those mandating that bishops be appointed only by other bishops (Canon 4), that excommunication be done by a bishop (Canon 5), and that the bishops have jurisdiction over their own geographical areas (Canon 6).[62] Likewise, it affirms, "It is before all things necessary that they [who convert] should profess in writing that they will observe and follow the dogmas of the Catholic and Apostolic Church."[63]

2) The First Council of Constantinople was convened by Emperor Theodosius I (AD 379–395) to unite the church. It reaffirmed the Nicene Creed, proclaimed the deity of the Holy Spirit, and united the Eastern church, which had been divided by the Arian controversy. The emperor

62. The claim based on this canon, that it gives primacy to the bishop of Rome over the whole church, is without justification. The context makes it clear that it speaks only about different bishops having jurisdictions in their different areas, naming three centers, Alexandria, Antioch, and Rome. The text is clear: "Let the ancient customs in Egypt, Libya and Pentapolis prevail, that the Bishop of Alexandria have jurisdiction in all these, since it is customary for the Bishop of Rome also. Likewise in Antioch and the other providences, let the Churches retain their privileges" (see Schaff, *A Select Library*, 15). As Hefele put it, "It is evident that the Council has not in view here the primacy of the bishop of Rome over the whole Church, but simply his power as a patriarch" (cited by Schaff, *A Select Library*, 16).
63. Ibid., 19.

is said to have "founded the orthodox Christian state. Arianism and other heresies became legal offenses, sacrifice [to pagan gods] was forbidden, and paganism almost outlawed."[64]

The practices of Theodosius I were later codified by Emperor Theodosian II into the "Theodocian Code" (proclaimed in AD 438). This later was superseded by the Justinian Code (AD 539), which added the "novella" that provides the classic formula for the relation of church and state in which the church would take care of religious matters and the state civil matters. This code was later expanded into the *Corpus Juris Civilis* (Body of [Roman] Civil Law). During the later Middle Ages this became the basis for canon law in the West,[65] which became binding on all churches under the administration of the Roman Church.

3) The Council of Ephesus (AD 431) condemned Nestorianism, which affirms there were two natures and two persons in Christ. Since Christ is only one person with two natures, then it is proper to conclude that Mary was truly the mother of God, i.e., the God bearer or the one who gave birth to the person (Jesus) who is God as well as man. The decision of the council reads:

> This was the sentiment of the holy Fathers; therefore they ventured to call the holy Virgin, the Mother of God, not as if the nature of the Word or his divinity had its beginning from the holy Virgin, but because of her was born that holy body with a rational soul, to which the Word being personally united is said to be born according to the flesh.[66]

4) The Council of Chalcedon (AD 451) was called by Emperor Marcian to deal with the Monophysite heresy, which merges the two natures of Christ, making a logically incoherent combination of an infinite-finite nature. Of five hundred-plus bishops present only two were from the West, plus two papal delegates. Eutyches had said, "I confess that our Lord was of two natures before the union, but after the union I confess one nature."[67] The council agreed with Archbishop [Pope] Leo to "anathematize" this as absurd, extremely foolish, extremely blasphemous, and impious.[68]

---

64. Cross, *Oxford Dictionary*, 1361. See the companion article in this journal volume by Professor Nix for the implications of this action in the development of Roman Catholicism.
65. Ibid., 771.
66. Philip Schaff and Henry Wace, eds., *Nicene and Post-Nicene Fathers of the Christian Church*, 14 vols. (2nd series repr. Grand Rapids, MI: Eerdmans, 1971), 14:198.
67. Ibid., 258.
68. Ibid., 258, from Session 1.

The council reaffirmed the decisions of all three general councils before it (Session 4) as well as "the writings of that blessed man, Leo, Archbishop of all the churches who condemned the heresy of Nestorius and Eutyches, [to] shew what the true faith is."[69] The presence of an "archbishop" or bishop over bishops, represents a new state in the long development of the Roman episcopal hierarchy, which eventually culminated in the infallible authority of the bishop of bishops, the bishop of Rome—i.e., the pope—at Vatican I (in 1870).

The council also asserted its authority in the excommunication of Bishop Dioscorus, declaring, "on account of your disregard of the divine canons, and your disobedience to his holy ecumenical synod" that he was "deposed from the episcopate and made a stranger to all ecclesiastical order."[70]

The most controversial canon (28) affirms that "Constantinople, which is New Rome . . . enjoys equal privileges with the old imperial Rome" and hence "should in ecclesiastical matters also be magnified as she is, and rank next after her."[71] This canon was rejected by "Archbishop Leo" of the old Rome. But of historic importance is the statement that gives the reason any primacy was given to Rome in the first place, namely, "For the Fathers rightly granted privileges to the throne of the old Rome, because it was the royal city."[72] This confirms the interpretation of Irenaeus's statement (above) that the primacy of Rome was reflective, not authoritative. That is, Rome was given more respect, not authority, because it was the big church in the capital of the empire and, therefore, more reflective of the whole church, since representatives from the whole empire would naturally consort there. Tillemont's comment is to the point: "This canon seems to recognize no particular authority in the Church of Rome, save what the Fathers had granted it, as the seat of the empire."[73]

5) The Second Council of Constantinople (AD 553) was convoked by Emperor Justinian. It has fourteen anathemas, the first twelve directed at Theodore of Mopsuestia. A later insert places Origen's name in the eleventh anathema, something accepted by later popes. Among the heresies condemned are Arianism, Nestorianism, Eutychianism, Monophysitism (Statements I–XI), and Adoptionism (XII). The perpetual virginity of

69. Ibid., 260.
70. Ibid., 260, from Session 3.
71. Ibid., 287.
72. Ibid., Canon 28.
73. Recorded by Schaff, ibid., 288.

Mary was affirmed, being called the "ever-virgin Mary, the Mother of God" (Statements V and XIV).

One must agree with Hefele that this "Fifth Ecumenical Council should strike the name of the reigning pope [Vigilius] from the diptychs [double-leafed tablets] as the father of heresy; and the Sixth Ecumenical Synod should anathematize another Pope as a heretic."[74]

6) The Third Council of Constantinople (AD 680) was convened by Emperor Constantine IV (Pogonatus). It affirmed the "Five holy ecumenical councils."[75] In addition, it reaffirmed that Christ had two natures united in one person and that he had two wills, one human and one divine, which had a moral unity resulting from the complete harmony between the two natures of the God-Man (as opposed to the Monothelites). The Council also referred to Mary as "our Holy Lady, the holy, immaculate, ever-virgin and glorious Mary, truly and properly the Mother of God."[76] Macarius, the Archbishop of Antioch, was condemned, along with "Honorius some time Pope of Old Rome."[77]

Catholic apologists did not agree on a way to explain this dilemma of how an allegedly infallible pope can err when teaching doctrine. One scholar, Pennacchi, thinks the Council erred and the pope was right. Another, Baronius, holds, contrary to fact, that manuscripts have been corrupted. But even most Roman Catholic scholars reject this, pointing to the manuscript and citation evidence. Indeed, Schaff lists thirteen lines of evidence that the records are accurate.[78] Thus, most Catholic scholars are left with the claim that Pope Honorius was not speaking *ex cathedra* at the time. This, however, seriously undermines the claim of infallibility, since the pope was teaching on doctrine at the time. And if his teaching was not infallible, then it leaves no meaningful distinguishable criteria as to when the pope speaks *ex cathedra*. For if a pope can be fallible when affirming doctrine sometimes, then how can we be sure he is infallible when affirming doctrine at other times? In fact, how can we be sure he was infallible when he pronounced his own infallibility at Vatican I in 1870?

---

74. Cited by Schaff, ibid., 305. Pope Vigilius subsequently recanted after the council condemned him and died on the way home but only after he approved of the action of the council which he "by the [alleged] authority of the Apostolic See" had forbidden them to do (see Schaff, ibid., 321–23).
75. Ibid., 345.
76. Ibid., 340, from Session 1.
77. Ibid., 342, Session 8.
78. Ibid., 351–52.

This council claimed to be not only "illuminated by the Holy Spirit"[79] but also "inspired by the Holy Spirit."[80] Thus, it claimed to provide "a definition, clean from all error, certain, and infallible."[81] What is of note from the church/state standpoint is that following the council the emperor posted an "imperial edict" in the church, noting the "heresy" and warning that "no one henceforth should hold a different faith, or venture to teach one will [in Christ] and one energy [operation of the will]. In no other than the orthodox faith could men be saved."[82] Punishments were listed.

7) The Second Council of Nicea (AD 787) was called by the Emperors Constantine and Irene and attended by legates of Pope Hadrian, and it dealt with the iconoclastic controversy. It ruled in favor of venerating images: "Receiving their holy and honorable reliques with all honor, I salute and venerate these with honour. . . . Likewise also the venerable images of the incarnation of our Lord Jesus Christ . . . and of all the Saints—the Sacred Martyrs, and of all the Saints—the sacred images of all these, I salute, and venerate."[83]

Further, it pronounced "anathema to those who do not salute the holy and venerable images" and "anathema to those who call the sacred images idols."[84] And in a zealous overkill it declared, "To those who have a doubtful mind and do not confess with their whole heart that they venerate the sacred images, anathema!"[85] It encouraged prayer to Mary and the saints, saying, "I ask for the intercession of our spotless Lady the Holy Mother of God, and those of the holy and heavenly powers and those of all the Saints."[86]

In theory the council distinguished between worship of God and veneration of images, saying, "The worship of adoration I reserve alone to the supersubstantial and life-giving Trinity."[87] However, in practice there is no real way to tell the difference between the two. Further the Bible forbids making any graven images of God or heavenly beings and of even bowing down before them (Ex. 20:4–5).

79. Ibid., 350.
80. Ibid., 347.
81. Ibid., 350.
82. Ibid., 353.
83. Ibid.
84. Ibid.
85. Ibid.
86. Ibid., 533, Session 1.
87. Ibid., 539, Session 3.

The contemporary iconoclasts' objections to the council's decisions are expressed in another council claiming to be the true seventh ecumenical council. They declared flatly that "Satan misguided men, so that they worshipped the creature instead of the Creator."[88] They argued that the only admissible figure of the humanity of Christ, however, is "bread and wine in the holy Supper."[89] They cited Exodus 20:4: "Thou shalt not make thee any graven image, or any likeness of anything that is in heaven . . ."[90] and concluded, "Supported by the Holy Scriptures and the Fathers, we declare unanimously, in the name of the Holy Trinity, that there shall be rejected and removed and cursed out of the Christian Church every likeness which is made out of any material and colour whatever by the evil art of painters."[91] The council concluded, "If anyone does not accept this our Holy and Ecumenical Seventh Synod, let him be anathema."[92] They condemned Emperor Germanus of Constantinople, calling him "the double-minded worshiper of wood."[93]

The canons forbade the secular appointment of bishops, thus solidifying the independent authority of the church over against the state. Further, the primacy of Peter and of apostolic succession were emphasized: "For the blessed Peter himself, the chief of the Apostles, who first sat in the Apostolic See, let the chiefship of his Apostolate, and pastoral care, to his successors who are to sit in his most holy seat for ever."[94] They further spoke of "the holy Roman Church which has prior rank, which is the head of all the Churches of God."[95]

8) The Fourth Council of Constantinople (AD 869) was the last council to be called by the emperor. It explicitly affirmed the Second Council of Nicea and condemned the schism of Photius, patriarch of Constantinople. Photius challenged the *Filioque* clause in the creed—a clause that affirmed the Holy Spirit also proceeded from the Son. That clause later became a bone of contention between the Western and Eastern churches in 1054, which resulted in the Eastern church rejecting any councils after the seventh.

9) The First Lateran Council (AD 1123) was the first one called by Pope Callistus, which signaled a further step in the development of the

---

88. Schaff, 543.
89. Ibid., 544.
90. Ibid.
91. Ibid., 545.
92. Ibid., 546.
93. Ibid., 547.
94. Henry Percival, ed., "Seventh Ecumenical Council," Session 2 in ibid., 537.
95. Ibid.

Roman Church. It confirmed the Concordat of Worms (AD 1122), which granted the pope, not the emperor, the sole right to invest a bishop-elect with a ring and staff and to receive homage from him before his consecration.

10) *The Second Lateran Council (AD 1139)* was convoked by Pope Innocent II for the reformation of the church. It condemned the schism of Arnold of Brescia, a reformer who spoke against confession to a priest in favor of confession to one another.

11) *The Third Lateran Council (AD 1179)* was convened by Pope Alexander III to counter antipope Callistus III. It affirmed that the right to elect the pope was restricted to the College of Cardinals, and a two-thirds majority was necessary for the election of a pope.

12) *The Fourth Lateran Council (AD 1215)* was called by Pope Innocent III. It pronounced the doctrine of transubstantiation, the primacy of the bishop of Rome, and seven sacraments. Many consider this a key turning point in the development of Roman Catholicism in distinction from non-Catholic forms of Christianity. It gave the church (Dominicans) authority to set the Office of the Inquisitors, which gave authority to the church to investigate heresy and turn over heretics to the state for punishment.

13) *The First Council of Lyons (AD 1245)* was convened by Pope Innocent IV to heal the "five wounds" of the Church: (1) moral decadence of the clergy; (2) the danger of the Saracens, Arab Muslims against whom the Crusaders fought; (3) the schism with the Eastern church; (4) the invasion of Hungary by the Tartars; and (5) the rupture between the church and the emperor Frederick II. The council condemned and formally deposed Emperor Frederick II for his imprisonment of cardinals and bishops on their way to the council. It instituted minor reforms but left the main issues of the Reformation untouched.

14) *The Second Council of Lyons (AD 1274)* was called by Pope Gregory X to bring about union with the Eastern church, to liberate the Holy Land, and to reform morals in the church. It unsuccessfully demanded affirmation of the double procession of the Holy Spirit from the Father and the Son, which the Eastern church rejected. Albert the Great and Bonaventure attended, but Aquinas (d. 1274) died on the way to the council. The council approved some newly founded orders including the Dominicans and the Franciscans. It defined the procession of the Holy Spirit (the *Filioque* clause). The union with the East was short-lived, ending in 1289.

15) *The Council of Vienne (AD 1311–1312)* was convoked by Pope Clement V to deal with the Templars, a military order of the Church, who were accused of heresy and immorality. The council announced reforms, suppressed the Templars, provided assistance for the Holy Land, encouraged missions, and made decrees concerning the Inquisition that were instituted formally in 1232 by Frederic II but were claimed for the church.

16) *The Council of Constance (AD 1413–1418)* was convened by Pope John XXIII in order to end the Great Schism of three simultaneous popes, to reform the church, and to combat heresy. It condemned over two hundred propositions of John Wycliffe. Reformer John Hus, who held similar doctrines to those of Wycliffe, refused to recant and was burned at the stake. The council proclaimed the superiority of an ecumenical council over the pope, declaring (in *Haec Sancta*) that "this Council holds its power direct from Christ; everyone, no matter his rank of office, even if it be papal, is bound to obey it in whatever pertains to faith."[96] This was the culmination of a long history of increased authority for the bishop of Rome, which had begun gradually in the second century with the emergence of one fallible bishop in each church and ended with one infallible bishop over all the churches. And it was later contradicted by the decision of Vatican I that the pope alone had the right to make infallible pronouncements on his own.

17) *The Council of Basel-Ferrara-Florence (AD 1431–1445)* was called by Pope Martin V. It was a series of councils beginning in Basel (1431), moving to Ferrara (1438–1439), then to Florence (1439–1443), and lastly to Rome (1443–1445). Its chief objective was union with the Eastern church, which sought support from the West against the Turks who were nearing Constantinople. The controversy centered on double procession of the Holy Spirit, purgatory, and the primacy of the pope. By July 1439 there was agreement on "the Decree of Union" between East and West. Subsequently many bishops recanted, and the union ceased when the Turks captured Constantinople in 1453. The Council of Basel and its members were pronounced heretical.

18) *The Fifth Lateran Council (AD 1512–1517)* was called by Pope Julius II to invalidate the decrees of the antipapal council of Pisa convened by Louis XII of France. The council began a few minor reforms but did not treat the main issues of the Reformation. An Augustinian

96. Cross, *Oxford Dictionary*, 336–37.

monk named Luther did. He tacked up his ninety-five theses on October 31, 1517, which started the great Protestant Reformation.

19) The Council of Trent (AD 1545–1563) was called to counter the Reformation. This council declared many of the characteristic doctrines of Roman Catholicism, including the equal validity of tradition with Scripture, the seven sacraments, transubstantiation, good works as necessary for justification, purgatory, indulgences, the veneration of saints and images, prayers for the dead, prayers to the dead (saints), and the canonicity of eleven apocryphal books. Many Protestants believe Rome apostatized at this point by a denial of the true gospel. Others see what was declared at this council as a significant deviation from biblical and historic orthodoxy but not as a total apostasy.[97]

20) The First Council of the Vatican (AD 1869–1870) called by Pope Pius IX denounced pantheism, materialism, and atheism. Pope Pius IX pronounced papal infallibility. The council rejected Saint Antonio of Florence's formula that the pope, "using the counsel and seeking for help of the universal Church," cannot err. Instead it ruled that the pope's definitions are "irreformable of themselves, and not from the consent of the Church" when speaking *ex cathedra*, that is, as pastor and doctor of all Christians.

21) The Second Council of the Vatican (AD 1962–1963) attempted ecumenicity with Eastern Orthodox and Protestant observers, instituted ritualistic changes such as mass in local languages, pronounced reforms, and declared inclusivism of "separated brethren" and salvation of sincere non-Christians.

The Nature and Authority of the Church Councils

Comments on the nature of these councils are now in order, with general comments on the nature of the councils first. Many consider the first seven councils as ecumenical since they occurred before the East-West split between Eastern orthodoxy and Roman Catholicism. However, even some of these did not have strong representation from both sections of Christianity. And some affirmed doctrines that many consider

---

97. At the center of the debate is whether the total sufficiency of Christ's sacrifice and complete *necessity* of God's grace (which Trent confesses) are sufficient to merit the label "orthodox" or whether the Reformation doctrine of the *exclusivity* of faith (*sola fidei*) is necessary for orthodoxy on salvation (see discussion in Geisler and MacKenzie, *Roman Catholicism and Evangelicals*, chap. 12).

contrary to biblical teaching, such as the perpetual virginity of Mary and the veneration of images.[98]

Further, many pronouncements of later councils did not attain to the standard of orthodoxy as stated at the Roman Catholic Council of Trent, which demanded "the universal consent of the Fathers" as a test for orthodoxy. Some later councils pronounced doctrines that have little or no consent, let alone universal consent, of the early Fathers whose views, one would have thought, should have, by virtue of their proximity with the apostles, been considered of great value in determining apostolicity.

The Roman Catholic View

The Roman Catholic view is that all twenty-one of these councils are ecumenical and binding on the whole Christian church. They insist that it is inconsistent to accept some of these councils and reject others. However, there are serious problems with this view.

First, it entails the claim that the Roman Catholic Church is the only true church on earth. This exclusivistic claim is implausible on the face of it, since there was a church in the East before there was one in the West. Why, then, should Eastern orthodoxy be excluded from the true church?

Second, it assumes wrongly that the true universal church must be identified with a single visible organization rather than with a general category of all individual churches that confess historic biblical Christianity, including Eastern Orthodox, Anglican, Lutheran, Presbyterian, Reformed, Methodist, Baptist, and others.

Third, some of the councils accepted by Rome had inconsistent pronouncements. For example, the sixteenth council proclaimed the superiority of an ecumenical council over the pope, declaring in *Haec Sancta* that "this Council holds its power direct from Christ; everyone, no matter his rank of office, even if it be papal, is bound to obey it in whatever pertains to faith."[99] Yet, the twentieth council claimed that when speaking *ex cathedra*, the pope's definitions alone are "irreformable of themselves, and not from the consent of the Church." Or, as Vatican I put it, "such definitions of the Roman Pontiff *from himself, but not from the consensus of the Church, are unalterable.*"[100] Clearly, both cannot be

98. See ibid., chap. 15.
99. Cross, *Oxford Dictionary*, 336–37.
100. Henry Denzinger, *The Sources of Catholic Dogma*, trans. Roy J. Deferrari (London: Herder, 1957), 1840, emphasis added.

true; for either the pope can make infallible proclamations alone or he cannot without the aid of the council.

Fourth, there are good biblical reasons to reject the teachings of many of these councils, beginning with the fifth one.[101] These objectionable doctrines include the perpetual virginity of Mary (council 5), the veneration of images (council 7), the authority of the pope (councils 8 and 9), condemnation of those not confessing sin to a priest (council 10), the authority of the College of Cardinals to elect a pope (council 11), the primacy of the bishop of Rome, seven sacraments, and transubstantiation (council 12), and condemnation of reformers Wycliffe and Hus (council 13). This is to say nothing of the additional errors pronounced by Trent and later councils, including adding the Apocrypha to the Bible, approving of prayers for the dead, veneration of saints, worship of the consecrated host, the necessity of works as a condition for salvation, the infallibility of the pope, and the bodily assumption of Mary.[102]

Fifth, there are no logical reasons why all twenty-one councils must be accepted. The history of many organizations reveals the same pattern as Rome, namely, they start out well and then deviate from their founders' teachings somewhere along the line. The United States Supreme Court's interpretations of the United States Constitution are a case in point, particularly on its interpretation of the First Amendment, which does not even contain the words "separation of church and state." This amendment has been taken out of context due to a private letter concerning a revision of the framers' intention of Congress (the federal government) about making "no law respecting the establishment of religion." Knowing it is not an uncommon occurrence within organizations to stray from their original intentions, explanations other than the Roman claim of the councils must be examined.

The Eastern Orthodox View

The Eastern church is sometimes called "the church of the seven councils" since it agrees with Rome on the first seven councils, which are believed to be infallible in their pronouncements. While they reject as heretical some of the pronouncements of Rome—for example, the infallibility of the pope—this does not tell the whole story. Tradition for them embraces the continuing presence of the Holy Spirit in the church. Whereas the Bible is considered the inspired Word of God, it is also seen as part of

---

101. See Geisler and MacKenzie, *Roman Catholicism and Evangelicals*, part 2.
102. See ibid.

the larger concept of tradition. As Timothy Ware put it, the Bible "must not be regarded as something set up *over* the Church, but as something that lives and is understood *within* the Church."[103] Thus, the Bible is not over the church or the church over the Bible. The Bible is understood within the church and her traditions.

Protestants reject this view for several reasons. First, councils five through seven accept some unbiblical teachings, such as the perpetual virginity of Mary and the veneration of images, which is a violation of the second commandment. Second, it is a rejection of the doctrine of *sola Scriptura*, which was affirmed by early Fathers and reaffirmed by Reformers (see Keith Mathison, *The Shape of Sola Scriptura*). Eastern Orthodoxy considers these seven councils as infallible whereas Protestants do not, pointing to errors in them.

Third, the Eastern view is highly mystical, setting forth no objective criteria by which the voice of the Holy Spirit is discerned in the traditions of the church. Fourth, contrary to the Eastern Orthodox view the church did not create the canon.[104] It simply recognized the prophetic books that God, by his inspiration, determined to be canonical. Fifth, there are no objective criteria by which an ecumenical council is distinguished from a non-ecumenical one. Even Eastern Orthodox theologian Timothy Ware admits that "what it is that makes a council ecumenical is not so clear."[105]

Sixth is the orthodox view that the Fathers are an inspired source of apostolic tradition. But neither the Bible—nor the Fathers themselves—consider them to be inspired. Finally, their justification of the mind of the Fathers is circular, using the mind of the Fathers to justify what is the mind of the Fathers on Scripture.

The Protestant View

Most Protestants demur on the authority of any council after council four, since council five speaks of Mary's perpetual virginity and council seven of venerating images, to say nothing of all the unbiblical pronouncements by the Council of Trent and beyond. Thus, according to Protestants and many Anglicans, only the first four ecumenical councils are binding in the Christian church. Beginning with the fifth council, which pronounced the perpetual virginity of Mary, most Protestants

103. Timothy Ware, *The Orthodox Church* (London: Penguin, 1997), 199.
104. Keith Mathison, *The Shape of Sola Scriptura* (Moscow, ID: Canon Press, 201), 227.
105. Ware, *The Orthodox Church*, 252.

reject the ecumenicity and catholicity of the councils, though they may agree with many things said by later councils.

The Free Church View (Including Anabaptist)

Many churches in Christendom deny the authority of any council, though they agree with many things stated by them, particularly in the early ones. This they do by insisting strongly that only the Bible has binding authority. All creeds and confessions are man-made. Thus, no authority is attached to any church councils, whether they be local or so-called universal councils. This view is called *solo Scriptura* by Keith A. Mathison[106] in contrast to the Reformed view of *sola Scriptura*, since the latter read the Bible in the light of the early Fathers and creeds whereas the former do not.

By holding a free church view, as we do, one does not need to deny there is any *value* to the creeds and councils. It is simply that there is no *authority* in them, either divine or ecclesiastical. In fact, all orthodox Christians, Catholics and non-Catholics, agree with the basic doctrines affirmed in the earlier so-called ecumenical councils, such as the Trinity, virgin birth, deity of Christ, and Christ's hypostatic union of two natures in one person. The main concern of orthodox Christians is with attributing any divine or even ecclesiastical authority to creedal and conciliar pronouncements.

Plymouth Brethrenism (Darbyism)

An even more radical view is found in John Nelson Darby, the founder of the Plymouth Brethren movement. Darby not only rejected any authority for church councils, but he also denied that there was any church over which they could have authority. He held that the church Christ announced (in Matthew 16) was ruined.[107] In short, the apostles failed

---

106. Mathison, *Shape of Sola Scriptura*, 331.

107. Darby wrote: "It is not my intention to enter any great detail, but to shew simply, in every instance there was total and complete failure as regarded man, however the patience of God might tolerate and carry on by grace the dispensation in which man has thus failed in the outset" ("ASD," www.biblecentre.org). He points to the fact that the apostles failed to keep the Great Commission, so "the church which was gathered has departed from the faith of the gospel, and gone backward, so as to be as bad or worse than the heathen" (ibid.). This total and complete apostasy of the church from the very beginning leaves us with only the possibility of gatherings and assemblies during the rest of this dispensation. Elsewhere, he said, "The church is in a state of ruin, immersed and buried in the world—invisible, if you will have it so; whilst it ought to hold forth, as a candlestick, the light of God" (Darby, "OFC"). Further, it cannot be restored from this state. "What remains? The Holy Spirit is in our midst whenever two or three are gathered together." Nowhere are we authorized to choose elders or pastors. Only God can give these gifts and they are effective whether there are organized churches or not"

in their mission. Hence, there is no visible church of Christ. Instead, there are merely assemblies of believers to break bread and edify each other.

But no organization that exists on earth can be identified as the visible church. Hence, so-called church councils are not binding. However, it is difficult to reconcile this view with Jesus' prediction that the gates of hell would not prevail against the church (Matt. 16:18). This is to say nothing of other Scriptures that indicate the church would continue after the time of the apostles (John 17:20–21; 2 Tim. 2:2). Further, the fact is that there are still churches founded on the doctrine of Christ and the apostles that exist today all over the globe. These are living proof that the New Testament church is still alive.

The Development of Roman Catholicism

In view of the above discussion, one can see the gradual development of Roman Catholicism, with its imperial governmental structure and the doctrinal beliefs it controls. It can also be observed that the claim that only the Catholic view—that all councils should be accepted—is based on an equivocal use of the term *Roman Catholic*. Roman Catholicism as it is known today is not the same as the Catholic Church before 1215. Even though the split between East and West occurred in 1054, most non-Catholics today would have been able to belong to the Catholic Church before the thirteenth century. Regardless of certain things the church permitted, none of its official doctrinal proclamations regarding essential salvation doctrines were contrary to orthodoxy.

While the development of Roman Catholicism from the original church was gradual, beginning in early centuries, one of the most significant turning points came in 1215, when one can see the beginning

---

(ibid.). In brief, "The children of God have nothing to do but to meet together in the name of the Lord" (ibid.). "In speaking of the ruin of the church, we speak of it as down here, set to manifest Christ's glory in unity on the earth" ("PRC"). "As regards the purpose of God the church cannot be ruined, but as regards its actual condition as a testimony for God on earth it is in ruin" (ibid.). "The church of the living God is the body of saints formed on earth in unity with Christ in heaven as the Head, by the Holy Ghost sent down from heaven to form them into unity with Christ at the right hand of God" (ibid.). "What do I find people talking about? A visible and invisible church. Now this is Satan's lie" (ibid.). "The so-called visible church is in fact the world, and cannot give any testimony at all for Christ" (ibid.). "Now what do I mean by the ruin of the church? A simple question will answer this. Who will show me the manifestation of the unity of the body of Christ? . . . But the church as a manifested body on the earth is ruined" (ibid.). "Some years after the conversion of my soul I looked around to find where the church was, but I could not find it. I could find plenty of saints better than myself, but not the church as it was set up with power on the earth. Then I say the church as thus set up is ruined, and I cannot find a better word for it" (ibid.).

of Roman Catholicism as it is subsequently known. It is here that the seeds of what distinguishes Roman Catholicism were first pronounced as dogma. It is here that they pronounced the doctrine of transubstantiation, the primacy of the bishop of Rome, and seven sacraments. Many consider this a key turning point in the development of Roman Catholicism in distinction from non-Catholic forms of Christianity.

The evolution of the doctrine of infallibility of the pope, a central doctrine of Roman Catholicism, illuminates the development of the Roman Church in general. It stands in stark contrast to the apostolic teaching recorded in the New Testament. As we have shown elsewhere,[108] the visible New Testament church had no hierarchy, but each church was independent and congregational in form. There was no episcopal form of government where a bishop was distinct from and had authority over elders. The New Testament had a plurality of elders and deacons in each church (Acts 14:23; Phil. 1:1). And the terms *bishop* and *elder* refer to the same office (Acts 20:17, 28; 1 Tim. 3:1; Titus 1:5, 7).

As we have noted, this episcopal form of government continued into the subapostolic period at the end of the first century and into the early second century. Later the term *bishop* came to refer to a single leader among the elders in each church. A plausible explanation of how this happened has been proposed: as time went on a leading elder assumed more and more authority so that he was eventually exalted to a higher position and called a "bishop" in distinction to an "elder."

The Emergence of One Bishop Over a Church

The placement of one bishop over a church "came about almost naturally, and certainly informally, as special status and responsibility in each church came to be assigned to an elder who regularly chaired meetings of what Ignatius calls 'the presbytery.'"[109] He offers several lines of evidence for his conclusion. First, "even after the development of the monarchial episcopate, bishops seem often to have been referred to as 'elders.'" Second, "the third-century church order known as the *Didascalia Apostolorum* identifies the chief pastor of a local church as 'bishop and head among the presbytery.'" Third, "for a long time elders were regarded not as the bishop's representatives or delegates but as his colleagues." Fourth, "at least for a while the two different structures must have existed simultaneously."[110]

---

108. See Geisler, *The Church and Last Things*, chap. 3.
109. Walker, 48–49.
110. Ibid., 49.

The Appearance of One Bishop Over a Region

This informal and local episcopate gave way eventually to regional bishops and then to one bishop who was prime among the bishops, namely, the bishop of Rome. Eusebius speaks of "Silvanus, bishop of the churches about Emesa" during the wicked reign of Emperor Diocletian (ca. AD 303). It is understandable that the growth of one church in an area might lead to many churches over which the bishop of the mother church would remain in charge. And Rome being the largest and capital city of the empire would naturally have a powerful and influential bishop.

The Inception of One Bishop Over the Whole Church

Irenaeus seems to have served as a transition in this process, for he took a key step toward the position of authoritative bishop, namely, the bishop of bishops, in Rome. In doing so he referenced:

> That tradition derived from the apostles, of the very great, the very ancient, and universally known Church founded and organized at Rome by the two most glorious apostles, Peter and Paul; as also by pointing out the faith preached to men, which comes down to our times by means of the succession of the bishops. . . . It is a matter of necessity that *every Church should agree* [Lat. *convenire*] *with this Church*, on account of its preeminent authority, that is, the faithful everywhere, inasmuch as the apostolic tradition has been preserved continuously by those faithful men *who exist everywhere*.[111]

While Irenaeus is probably not stressing the *authority* of the medium but the *accuracy* of it in transmitting the message of the apostles who alone possessed the God-given authority, nonetheless, he did believe that each church had a single bishop over it, for he spoke of Polycarp as "bishop of Smyrna" (cf. *Haer.* 3.3.4) and that there was a line of bishops in Rome beginning with Linus.[112] Likewise, he believed there was some sense of primacy in the bishop of Rome, whether it was merely reflective or authoritative.

Irenaeus aside, at least by the time of Cyprian the evolution of a more monarchial episcopate had occurred. Cyprian insisted, "There is one God, and Christ is one, and there is one chair [episcopate] founded upon the rock by the word of the Lord."[113]

111. *Haer.* 1.415–416, emphases added.
112. Ibid., 1.416.
113. Cyprian, *Epistles* 39, 5.

The Emergence of the Coercive Authority of the Bishop of Rome

Saint Augustine added to the developing doctrine of the authority of the episcopacy when he concluded that heretics could be coerced by the church to deny their unorthodox doctrine and accept the authority of the church. In his book *On The Correction of the Donatists* he wrote: "Whence it appears that great mercy is shown toward them, when by the force of those very imperial laws they are in the first instance rescued against their will from that sect . . . so that afterwards they might be made whole in the Catholic Church, becoming accustomed to the good teaching and example which they find in it."[114]

In his *Against the Epistle of Manichaeus* he wrote:

> The consent of peoples and nations keeps me in the Church; so does her authority, inaugurated by miracles. . . . The succession of priests keeps me, beginning from the very seat of the Apostle Peter, to whom the Lord, after His resurrection, gave it in charge to feed His sheep, down to the present episcopate. . . . For my part, I should not believe the gospel except as moved by the authority of the Catholic Church.[115]

Thus, the church presided over by the bishop of Rome, as the successor of Saint Peter, has authority to coerce people to believe in its truth. Indeed, Augustine added, "The Catholic Church alone is the body of Christ, of which He is the Head and Saviour of the body. Outside this body the Holy Spirit giveth life to no one. . . . Therefore they have not the Holy Ghost who are outside the Church."[116]

The Appearance of Monarchial Papal Authority to Formulate Creeds

Another step was taken in the emergence of the doctrine of the bishop of Rome in the late Middle Ages, at the time of Thomas Aquinas. He held that "*there must be one faith for the entire Church*. . . . This norm could not be followed unless every question arising out of faith were resolved by one having care over the whole Church. A new version of the creed, then, falls to the sole authority of the Pope, just as do all other matters affecting the whole church."[117] However, Aquinas believed in

---

114. Augustine, "On Christian Doctrine," 3.13, in Schaff, *Nicene and Post-Nicene Fathers of the Christian Church*, vol. 2.

115. Augustine, "Against the Epistle of Manichaeus," in Schaff, *Nicene and Post-Nicene Fathers of the Christian Church*, 4:130–31.

116. Augustine, "On Christian Doctrine," 11.50.

117. Thomas Aquinas, *Summa Theologica* (New York: McGraw-Hill, 1974), 2a.2a1.10, 1, reply, emphasis added.

the primacy of Scripture, for he affirmed that "the truth of faith is sufficiently plain in the teaching of Christ and the apostles."[118]

Further, "The truth of faith is contained in sacred Scripture, in diverse ways and, sometimes, darkly. . . . That is why there was a need to draw succinctly together out of the Scriptural teachings, some clear statements to be set before all for their belief. The symbol [i.e., creed] is not added to Scripture, but drawn from Scripture."[119] Indeed, Aquinas never repudiated his earlier statement: "We believe the successors of the apostles only in so far as they tell us those things which the apostles and prophets have left in their writings."[120] Likewise, the pope does not have the authority to set forth new doctrines not found in Scripture but only to restate in clear form (e.g., by creeds) what the Scriptures teach.

However, even given this authority of the pope, noted Roman Catholic authority Yves Congar admitted, "It is a fact that St. Thomas has not spoken of the infallibility of the papal magisterium. Moreover, he was unaware of the use of *magisterium* in its modern sense."[121] He goes on to say that it is not certain that Aquinas would even have said that the pope is without error "in his role of supreme interpreter of Christ's teaching."[122]

Congar cites several texts in support of this conclusion (see *On Truth* 14.10–11). One reads, "The simple have implicit faith in the faith of their teachers only to the degree that these hold fast to God's teaching. . . . Thus the knowledge of men is not the rule of faith but God's truthfulness."[123] Further, Congar refers to this text: "Note, however, that where there is real danger to the faith, subjects must rebuke their superiors even publicly. On this account Paul, who was subject to Peter, publicly rebuked him when there was imminent danger of scandal in a matter of faith."[124]

So, while Aquinas believed in the authority of the Bishop of Rome to promulgate a creed based on apostolic truth,[125] it is evident from the

---

118. Ibid., ad. 1.
119. Ibid., 2a.2a2.1.9.
120. Thomas Aquinas, *On Truth*, trans. Anton C. Pegis (New York: Image, 1955), 14.10 and 11.
121. Yves M. J. Congar, "St. Thomas Aquinas and the Infallibility of the Papal Magisterium," in *The Thomist* (January 1974) vol. 38, no. 1, 102.
122. Ibid.
123. Of course, Congar affirms papal infallibility and believes that it is "possible" to deduce it from what Thomas said, but he admits it is not necessary, nor did Thomas ever do so himself.
124. Ibid., 2a.2ae 33.4, ad 2.
125. Aquinas also held that the pope was "the vicar of Christ" (*Summa Theologiae*, 2a2ae.39, 1), the "visible head of the Church" (*Summa Theologiae*, 31.8, 7), and the one "who has the care of

foregoing quotation that he also held to *sola Scriptura*, a doctrine later repudiated by the Council of Trent, which proclaimed the sole and infallible authority of the bishop of Rome as Peter's successor, saying, "I acknowledge that the holy Catholic and apostolic Roman Church as the mother and teacher of all churches; and the Roman Pontiff, the successor of the blessed Peter, chief of the Apostles and vicar of Jesus Christ, I promise and swear true obedience."[126] Further, the faithful must confess "this true Catholic faith, outside of which no one can be saved (and) which of my own accord I now profess and truly hold."[127]

The Pronouncement of Infallible Authority of the Pope over the Whole Church

The final step in the evolution of the primacy of the Roman episcopacy, however, awaited the pronouncement of Pope Pius IX that the bishop of Rome is infallible when speaking from Peter's chair (*ex cathedra*) on matters of faith and practice. This occurred at the First Vatican Council (1870). The Roman dogma declared:

> We, adhering faithfully to the tradition received from the beginning of the Christian faith . . . teach and explain that the dogma has been divinely revealed, that the Roman Pontiff, when he speaks *ex cathedra*, that is, when carrying out the duty of pastor and teacher of all Christians in accord with his supreme apostolic authority he explains a doctrine of faith or morals to be held by the universal Church, through the divine assistance promised him in blessed Peter, operates with that infallibility with which the divine Redeemer wished that His church be instructed in defining a doctrine on faith and morals; and so such definitions of the Roman Pontiff from himself, but not from the consensus of the Church, are unalterable.[128]

This declaration of papal infallibility, without the other bishops, was the climax of centuries of increasing authority for the bishop of Rome and his successors. This represents a macro leap from the role of a bishop/elder in the New Testament as one among many leaders in a local church to one God-appointed vicar of Christ over all Christian

---

the whole Church" (*Summa Theologiae*, 2a2a3.89, 9 ad 3). But Aquinas never affirmed papal infallibility. Indeed, to the everlasting embarrassment of Roman Catholics, their greatest theologian, St. Thomas Aquinas, even called the immaculate conception, later pronounced true by papal authority, "unintelligible" (*Summa Theologiae*, 3a.27.4).

126. Denzinger, *The Sources of Catholic Dogma*, no. 999, 303.
127. Ibid.
128. Ibid., no. 1840, 457.

churches. As we have shown (chapter 3), there is no real foundation for this teaching in the New Testament or in the earliest fathers. Rather, it came as a result of a long process whereby more and more authority was given to fewer and fewer persons until at last it rested in one person, the alleged bishop of all bishops, the bishop of Rome.

There is here a great gulf between the New Testament and papal infallibility. For there is an essential difference between the form of government in the New Testament and that of the post-Vatican I Roman Catholic Church. From its original independent, autonomous, local congregational church with a plurality of elders (bishops) to a monolithic hierarchy of bishops headed by a bishop of bishops who is infallible in his official pronouncements is a gigantic evolutionary leap. In fact, it is an entirely new creation not genetically related to the original New Testament church in governmental structure. And, as a consequence, this produced serious doctrinal deviations as well.

Conclusion

In summary, it took many centuries for the episcopal form of government to gradually emerge from the simple self-governing independent New Testament churches with a plurality of elders to the monolithic episcopalism of the Roman Catholic Church. This evolution can be traced in several steps.

First the unorthodox seeds were found in New Testament times when John the apostle spoke of it in his third epistle where he warned: "I wrote to the church, but Diotrephes, who loves to have the preeminence among them, does not receive us" (3 John 9 NKJV).

Second, even in apostolic times false traditions began, and if false traditions could spring up even during the time of the apostles, it is easy to see how quickly they could spread with no apostles there to squelch them.

Third, by the mid-second century apocryphal gospels were emerging. Indeed, Irenaeus wrote decades after the time of the apocryphal *Gospel of Thomas* (ca. AD 140). So there was plenty of time for false views to emerge, even among those who were otherwise orthodox.

Fourth, considering the attacks on Christianity during the second century, there was strong motivation to develop an ecclesiology that would provide a united front against divergent heretical groups, which is reflected in Irenaeus's episcopal view of church government—a view that achieved a more mature form in Cyprian by the mid-third century.

Fifth, even if it can be shown that some second-century writers fa-vored the primacy of Rome as the center of Christianity, this does not support the later Roman Catholic pronouncements on the infallibility of the pope. The early fathers constantly appeal to the original apostles (plural) as the God-established authority. Further, the early fathers did not single out Peter as superior to other apostles.

Sixth, even if the disputed text of Irenaeus (*Haer.* 3.3.2) be understood as saying that "every Church should agree with this Church [at Rome]" in his day, it does not follow that Rome could not later deviate from the truth and be an unreliable source for all essential Christian truth.

Finally, the conversion of Constantine and his use of imperial power to influence the emergence of an imperial church structure were most significant catalysts in the formation of the monolithic episcopal form of government. This, combined with the natural penchant for power, pro-duced the Roman Church with its claim to papal infallibility and other unbiblical teachings. This was well under way by 1215 (Fourth Lateran Council) and culminated in the doctrinal deviations of the Council of Trent and the disastrous dogma of papal infallibility of Vatican I.

In short, there was no Roman Catholic kind of authoritative episco-palism in the New Testament or in the early church where one bishop had authority over all other bishops and churches, to say nothing of infallible authority. Thus, the argument for the primacy of Peter lacks a biblical and early structure in which Peter could fill the role. It is not only a question of whether Peter had primacy but whether there was any primacy for Peter to have. There is no evidence in the New Testa-ment or early fathers that there was even a general episcopalism, let alone a universal or authoritative one such as Rome claims for Peter and his successors.

CHAPTER 3

THE ROMAN ARGUMENT
FOR THE PRIMACY OF PETER:
STATED AND EVALUATED

There are several links in the Roman Catholic claim to being the true church of Christ on earth. First, Roman Catholics believe in the primacy of Peter, that he was chief among the apostles. Second, they hold to the infallibility of Peter, that he cannot err when making official pronouncements on doctrine and morals. Third, they believe in apostolic succession, that the divine authority granted to Peter was passed on to his successors. Therefore, Roman Catholics contend that the current pope of the Roman Church is Peter's successor, the rightful head of the church.

According to Roman Catholic tradition, all other groups, lacking apostolic authority as they do, are at best defective "ecclesial communities" with "separated brethren" who need to repent, receive forgiveness for their sin, and be restored to Rome sweet home. Those who do not are under the anathema of infallible pronouncements of Rome that, if not heeded, will lead to hell. This anathema of Rome includes all who knowingly reject this teaching, including the authors of this book. Clearly, this Catholic teaching is a cause for concern, for if it is true, then those who knowingly reject it will forever be lost. And if it is not true, then it is a fearful and false claim made by an organization that is not the true church of Christ, regardless of how much other truth may be housed in it.

Being the first link in the chain of argument, the doctrine of Peter's primacy is a crucial one. As is true of any chain of reasoning, the argument is no stronger than its weakest link. Hence, if one link is false, then the whole argument crumbles. Further, in this kind of chain of reasoning the argument builds so that the truth of the first link is the condition of the second, and the truth of the second is the condition of the third, and so on. This means that the primacy of Peter is a precondition for his infallibility. In other words, without primacy Peter and his successors have no infallibility. Therefore, this is not only a logical but a crucial place to begin our analysis.

An Exposition of Peter's Primacy

The Roman Catholic Church holds to the belief that Jesus Christ appointed the apostle Peter as the church's earthly head. Further, it believes that Peter's office has been occupied by the papacy in an unbroken chain since the first century. Saint Peter, then, stands as the "rock" of the church promised by Christ (Matt. 16:17–19) to prevail till the end of time. Christ, of course, is the spiritual and invisible head of the spiritual body of Christ. But in his absence he has appointed first Peter and then Peter's successors to head up his body, the church of Christ, on earth.

The Primacy of Peter Defined

Yet, before we can properly analyze the Roman argument for Peter's primacy, we must first understand it. Renowned Catholic authority Ludwig Ott explains the nature of primacy as it is ascribed to Peter: "Christ made Peter the foundation of His Church, that is, the guarantor of her unity and unshakable strength, and promised her duration that will not pass away" (Matthew 16:18).

As chief of the apostles, Peter stood over the other apostles in his authority. Ott contends, "It follows from the dogma of the Primacy that Paul, like the other Apostles, was subordinate to Peter as the supreme head of the whole Church."[1] That is to say, although Paul was one of the chief apostles (given his prominence in the New Testament), he was still subject to Peter's authority and in no way diluted it.

The doctrine of Peter's primacy teaches that the pope is "first in rank" among his fellow bishops, and that he has jurisdiction over the whole

1. Ludwig Ott, *Fundamentals of Catholic Dogma* (Rockford, IL: Tan, 1960), 281.

Christian church. Ott explains, "Christ appointed the Apostle Peter to be the first of all the Apostles and to be the visible Head of the whole Church, by appointing him immediately and personally to the primacy of jurisdiction."[2] In response to the Protestant Reformation, the Council of Trent in 1546 declared:

> The Church has but one ruler and one governor, the invisible one, Christ, whom the eternal Father *hath made head over all the Church, which is his body*; the visible one, the Pope, who, as legitimate successor of Peter, the Prince of the Apostles, fills the Apostolic chair. It is the unanimous teaching of the Fathers that this visible head is necessary to establish and preserve unity in the Church. This St. Jerome clearly perceived and as clearly expressed when . . . he wrote: "*One is elected that, by the appointment of a head, all occasion of schism may be removed.*" . . . Should anyone object that the Church is content with one Head and one Spouse, Jesus Christ, and requires no other, the answer is obvious. For we deem Christ is not only the author of all the sacraments, but also their invisible minister—He it is who baptizes, He it is who absolves, although men are appointed by Him the external ministers of the Sacraments—so has He been placed over His Church, which He governs by His invisible head; therefore the Saviour appointed Peter head and pastor of all the faithful, when He committed to his care the feeding of all His sheep, in such ample terms that He willed the very same power of ruling and governing the entire Church to descend to Peter's successors.[3]

Likewise, the Council of Trent declared:

> All the faithful of Christ *must believe* that the Apostolic See and the Roman Pontiff hold *primacy over the whole world*, and that the Pontiff of Rome himself is the successor of the blessed Peter, the chief of the apostles, and is the true vicar of Christ and head of the whole Church and faith, and teacher of all Christians. . . . To him was handed down in the blessed Peter, by our Lord Jesus Christ, full power to feed, rule, and guide the universal Church, just as also contained in the records of the ecumenical Councils and in the sacred canons.[4]

---

2. Ibid., 279.
3. *The Catechism of the Council of Trent*, 2nd rev. ed., trans. J. A. MacHugh and C. J. Cullan (Rockford, IL.: Tan, 1982), 103–4, quoted in Stephen Ray, *Upon This Rock: St. Peter and the Primacy of Rome in Scripture and the Early Church* (San Francisco: Ignatius Press, 1999), 245, emphases added.
4. Henry Denzinger, *The Sources of Catholic Dogma*, trans. Roy J. Deferrari (Fitzwilliam, NH: Loreto Publications, 1955), no. 1826, 454, emphases added. The doctrine of the papacy had become binding on all at this point. The warning of anathematization was given for those who denied the doctrine.

So, the primacy of Peter "represents the position of Christ in the external government of the militant Church, and it is to this extent 'the representative of Christ' on earth."[5] Ott describes the *nature* of papal primacy when he says, "The Pope possesses full and supreme power of jurisdiction over the whole Church, not merely in matters of faith and morals, but also in Church discipline and in the government."[6] The pope, then, possesses primacy over the whole church; that is, he is the supreme pastor of Christ's visible church whom all must obey, since he has not equals or rivals.

The Primacy of Peter Defended

Even before the arguments for primacy are offered, Catholic scholars try to establish the need also for an authoritative teacher in the church. They offer biblical, historical, and theological arguments.

Biblical Arguments

Rome insists that a pope is needed to preserve the unity and solidarity of the church. Ott writes, "The Church . . . is to continue substantially unchanged until the end of time for the perpetuation of the work of salvation; the Primacy also must be perpetuated." That is, "Peter, like every other human being, was subject to death (John 21:19); consequently his office must be transmitted to others. For, "the structure of the Church cannot continue without the foundation which supports it (Matt. 16:18): Christ's flock cannot exist without shepherds."[7]

The three main passages in support of papal infallibility traditionally have been Matthew 16:18, John 21:15–17, and Luke 22:32.

Matthew 16:18

Ott, utilizing the classic passage in Matthew, argues, "Christ made Peter the foundation of His Church, that is, the guarantor of her unity and unshakable strength, and promised her duration that will not pass away (Matt. 16:18)" Again, "the unity and solidarity of the Church is not possible without the right Faith. Peter is, therefore, also the supreme teacher of the Faith. As such he must be infallible in the official promulgation of Faith, in his own person and in his successors."[8] Catholic scholars point to the following support of their understanding of this test. First, the name Peter (*Petra*) means "rock." Second, in Aramaic his name Cephas

5. Ott, *Fundamentals*, 279.
6. Ibid., 285.
7. Ibid., 282.
8. Ibid., 287.

(*Kepha*) leaves no room for distinguishing between *petra* and *petros* in Matthew 16:18. Third, only Peter is given the "keys" to the kingdom, not the other apostles. Ott contends that Christ handed to Peter the gift of "the keys," which implies stewardship and responsibility of his kingdom on earth. Fourth, Ott claims that "in view of the universal term [whatever you bind on earth], the plenary power promised to Peter is not limited to his teaching power, but it extends to the whole sphere of jurisdiction. [Therefore,] God in heaven will confirm whatever obligations Peter will impose or dispense from on earth."[9]

John 21:15–17

> So when they had finished breakfast, Jesus said to Simon Peter, "Simon, son of John, do you love Me more than these?" He said to Him, "Yes, Lord; You know that I love You." He said to him, "Tend my lambs."
>
> He said to him again a second time, "Simon, son of John, do you love Me?" He said to Him, "Yes, Lord; You know that I love You." He said to him, "Shepherd My sheep."
>
> He said to him the third time . . . "do you love Me?" . . . And he said to Him, "Lord, You know all things; You know that I love You." Jesus said to him, "Tend My sheep." (NASB)

According to the First Vatican Council this text shows why Peter was the "chief of apostles . . . the true vicar of Christ and head [shepherd] of the whole Church and faith, and of all Christians."[10] It proves that "Christ installed Peter (and his successors) as the supreme pastor over the whole flock." The reasons given by Catholic scholars are these: first, Jesus was speaking only to Peter, not to the other apostles. Second, Jesus told Peter three times to "feed my sheep" or "lambs." By this he made Peter the chief shepherd over the church. Ott says, "Christ installed Peter (and his successors) as supreme pastor over the whole flock" (John 21:15–17). The word translated as "feed" and "tend" literally means "to feed," which taken figuratively teaches and promotes the spiritual welfare of the members of the Church."[11] Catholic commentator W. Leonard writes the following: "The whole flock (all the sheep of the Good Shepherd) are committed to Peter's care. . . . The passage has been dogmatically interpreted in this traditional sense by the Vatican Council."[12]

9. Ibid., 280.
10. Denzinger, *The Sources of Catholic Dogma*, 1837–40, 454.
11. Ray, *Upon This Rock*, 49, n. 65.
12. W. Leonard, "The Gospel of Jesus Christ according to St. John," in *ACCHS*, 1017.

Luke 22:31–32

Here Christ tells Peter, "I have prayed for thee, that thy faith fail not; and thou, being once converted, confirm thy brethren" (AT). According to Ott, "The reason for Christ's praying for Peter especially was that Peter, after his own conversion, should confirm his brethren in their faith, which clearly indicates Peter's position as head of the Apostles."[13] With these three classic passages, Ott concludes the following:

> Peter's leading position in the primitive community shows that he fulfilled the Lord's mandate. Now, if these words are directed to Peter personally, then they must, in accordance with Matt. 16:18, be also understood as referring to those in whom Peter is perpetuated as Head of the Church; for the endangering of faith, which exists at all times, makes the protection of the faith a pressing task of the Head of the Church in all times.[14]

Evidence to support this interpretation comes, Catholics claim, from the fact that, first, Jesus speaks only to Peter, not to the other disciples. Otherwise, "Why, then, does Jesus only pray for Peter and not for the other eleven disciples at this point?"[15] Steven K. Ray, Catholic apologist and theologian, says the fact that Jesus prayed exclusively for Peter in this verse is a confirmation "that Christ had made [him] the leader, the rock [of the church], and had invested him with the keys." Thus, "Luke was not ignorant of the authority invested in Peter by our Lord. The whole apostolic band would be strengthened by the one for whom the Lord prayed—the one whom the Lord appointed as shepherd of his flock."[16] Second, Peter's faith is said to be unfailing. This is essential to his primacy as head of the church.

Interestingly, according to its index, *The Catechism of the Catholic Faith* makes only one direct passing comment on this text relating to the role of Peter, saying, "Peter had been called to strengthen the faith

13. Ibid., 288.
14. Ibid. Also, "John 11:49–52 is used by some Catholics to defend papal infallibility. Caiaphas, in his official capacity as high priest, made an unwitting prophecy about Christ dying for the nation of Israel so they would not perish. Since in the Old Testament the high priest has an official revelatory function connected with his office, Catholics claim it's to be expected that the same would be true in the New Testament, and that this is indeed manifest in the bishop of Rome"; Norman L. Geisler, *Systematic Theology*, vol. 4: *The Church and Last Things* (Grand Rapids, MI: Bethany, 2005), 75.
15. Ray, *Upon This Rock*, 48, n. 63.
16. Ibid. Ray also mentions the fact that Jesus spoke directly to Simon, uttering his name twice for emphasis. Again, the prayer offered for the strengthening of Simon's faith was singular and not plural, which would have included the other apostles had it been plural.

of his brothers" (No. 641 cf. 643). It makes no attempt to build a case for Peter's primacy from the text.

Other Texts Used by Catholics to Support Peter's Primacy[17]

Even many Catholics admit that the following texts do not explicitly refer to Peter's primacy. Nevertheless, some use them indirectly to supplement and support the preceding texts in upholding that doctrine.

Isaiah 22:22

It is reasoned by analogy that the "key" in the Old Testament refers to the stewardship of the house of David by Eliakim. Thus Ray argues that "the parallels between Peter and [Eliakim] are striking. The physical kingdom of Israel has been superseded by the spiritual kingdom of God. The office of steward in the old economy is now superseded by the Petrine office with the delegation and handing on of the keys. The office of steward was successive, and so is the Petrine office in the new kingdom."[18]

Matthew 7:24

Jesus speaks of the wise man building his house on the "rock." Peter is the rock of the church from which she finds her unity and unshakable strength.

Matthew 10:2

Peter is named first in the list of the apostles. This attests to the veracity of his superior position among the Twelve.

Mark 3:16

Again Simon is listed here first among the twelve apostles. Ott says that "the constant placing of Peter's name at the head of the list of the Apostles indicates dignity of office."[19] Further, Simon is said to have been given the name Peter, which again means "rock."

Matthew 17:1

Peter, James, and John were taken with Jesus to witness his transfiguration. Peter seems to have taken the most active role of the three apostles throughout this glorious event, a fitting role for the leader of the apostles.

17. Unless otherwise noted, all scriptural texts in favor of supporting the papacy have been taken from Ott, *Fundamentals*, 280–81.
18. Ray, *Upon This Rock*, 274.
19. Ott, *Fundamentals*, 280.

Matthew 17:27
Jesus had Peter pay the temple tax for both of them with the shekel Jesus miraculously provided from the fish's mouth.

Matthew 26:37
Jesus came with Peter and the two sons of Zebedee, James and John, to the garden of Gethsemane, the place where Jesus wept.

Mark 5:37
Peter, along with James and John, witnessed the awakening of Jairus's daughter. None of the other apostles were allowed to accompany them. What is more, Peter's name is listed first.

Luke 5:3
Jesus taught the crowd from Peter's boat. Peter's prominent role is indicated from the fact that there were other boats present, which presumably belonged to other apostles.

John 10:16
Jesus mentioned that he has other sheep elsewhere (the Gentiles) and that there would be one shepherd over his entire fold (both Jew and Gentile), namely Peter.

John 11:49–52
It is argued that Caiaphas the high priest, in his official capacity as high priest, "unwittingly prophesied about Christ dying for the nation of Israel so that they would not perish."[20] So, just as in the Old Testament the high priest possessed an official revelatory function connected with his office, it is argued *a fortiori* (with greater force) that the same would be true in the New Testament with respect to Peter and his successors.[21]

Acts 1:12–16, 20–26
Peter was recognized as the leader of the apostles, one whose judgment was never questioned when he applied the Scriptures to a contemporary situation. Further, Jesus left no alternate apostle to fill Judas's office, although he certainly could have done so. That decision, says Ray, was left to Peter.[22]

20. Norman L. Geisler and Ralph E. MacKenzie, *Roman Catholics and Evangelicals: Agreements and Differences* (Grand Rapids, MI: Baker, 1995), 206.
21. Ibid., 206–7.
22. Ray, *Upon This Rock*, 51, n. 68.

Acts 2:14

Peter again was recognized as the leader of the church and of the apostles. Peter spoke on their behalf as they stood next to him when he addressed the crowd.[23]

Acts 15:7

Peter "is the first to speak at the Council of the Apostles."[24]

1 Corinthians 15:5

Paul, in his discourse of the resurrection of Christ, said that Jesus appeared to Cephas first, then to the Twelve.

Galatians 1:16–19

Upon Paul's contact with the church, it was Peter whom he saw first. Further, Paul referred to Peter as "Cephas," meaning "Rock" in Aramaic.[25] The reference Paul used is absolutely consistent with the data found in the Gospels.

Revelation 1:18; 3:7

Though these verses do not speak of Peter directly, they do, however, express the idea that the keys are a symbol of power and dominion. Taken with Matthew 16:17–19 and 18:18, the "power of binding and loosing, in the sense of the exclusion from or acceptance into the community, is bestowed on all the Apostles, and in view of the universal term ('whatever'), the plenary power promised to Peter is not limited to his teaching power, but it extends to the whole sphere of jurisdiction. God in Heaven will confirm whatever obligations Peter will impose or dispense from on earth."[26]

These above verses taken together form Rome's case for the primacy of Peter.

Historical Arguments for the Primacy of Peter

This need for an authoritative teacher, Ott argues, was not only manifest in Scripture, but "early on the Fathers expressed the thought that Peter

---

23. Simon Kistemaker and William Hendriksen, *Acts*, New Testament Commentary (Grand Rapids, MI: Baker, 1990), 87–88; cited by Ray, *Upon This Rock*, 51, n. 68. Ray cites a prominent Reformed scholar to suggest that even learned Protestant scholars have conceded the point that Peter was first in dignity.

24. Ott, *Fundamentals*, 281.

25. Ray, *Upon This Rock*, 52, n. 69.

26. Ott, *Fundamentals*, 280.

lives on and works through his successors."[27] This shows they believed there was a need for the primacy of Peter.

Tertullian (ca. AD 60–225)
Ott says, "Tertullian speaks of the Church: 'which was built on him' (De monog. 88)."[28] The *him* referred to here is none other than Saint Peter, according to Ott and many other Catholic theologians.

Saint Cyprian (ca. AD 300)
Saint Cyprian, commenting on Matthew 16:18 said, "He builds the Church on one person (De monog. 8)."[29] Again the *one person* mentioned in Cyprian's commentary is a reference to Saint Peter.

Saint Cyril of Jerusalem (ca. AD 315–386)
Saint Cyril of Jerusalem calls Peter "'the head and the leader of the Apostles' (Cat. 2, 19)."[30] Thus, Saint Cyril is another early voice that attested to the primacy of Peter and, consequently, to subsequent popes as well.

The Council of Ephesus (AD 431)
According to Ott, the papal legate Phillipus, at the Council of Ephesus, declared, "'This (Peter) lives and passes judgment up to the present day, and for ever, in his successors (Denzinger 112, 1824).'"

Saint Peter Chrysologous (ca. AD 400–450)
In his letter to Eutyches, "St. Peter Chrysologous says of the Roman Pontiff: 'The blessed Peter who on his Bishop's Chair lives on and leads the council, offers true Faith to those that seek it.'"[31]

Saint Leo the Great (d. AD 461)
Ott appeals to Saint Leo the Great's declaration of papal primacy, which was to be a perpetual institution: "As that which Peter believed in Christ lives for ever, so also that which Christ instituted in Peter lives for ever."[32] Leo further states, "Only Peter was chosen out of the whole world to be the Head of all called peoples, of all Apostles, and of all the Fathers of the Church."

27. Ibid. Ott cites other biblical passages as well: Acts 1:15; 2:14; 15:7, Gal. 1:18.
28. Ibid., 281.
29. Quoted in ibid.
30. Quoted in ibid.
31. Quoted in ibid.
32. Cited in ibid.

Ott concludes that the Fathers assert the decisive teaching authority of the Roman Church and of its pontiff.[33] For example, "St. Ignatius of Antioch recognizes of the Christians of Rome that they 'are purified of every foreign colour,' that is, are free from every false doctrine."[34] Ott further argues that Ignatius probably had the letter of Saint Clement, whom the Catholic Church considers to be the third successive pope, in mind when he wrote, "You have taught others."

Perhaps this is, at least to the Catholic observer, an appeal to Clement's authority as the bishop of Rome. Next, St. Irenaeus of Lyons supposedly recognizes the faith of the Roman Church as the norm for the whole Church. Irenaeus writes, "With this Church on account of its special eminence, every other Church must agree . . . in her the apostolic tradition has always been kept pure."[35]

Ott further argues, "The freedom of the Roman Church from error in faith presupposes the Infallibility of her episcopal teachers of faith. St. Cyprian characterized the Roman Church 'as the teaching chair of Peter' (*cathedra Petri*), as 'the starting point of the episcopal unity' and . . . pride in the purity of faith." Ott rests his case on the fact that "the teaching Primacy of the Pope from the earliest times was expressed in the practice of the condemnation of heretical opinions."[36]

Theological Arguments

Roman scholars offer several theological arguments in favor of the primacy of Peter. Most of them fall into two basic categories. First, there is the need for an official interpreter of the teachings of Christ. The reasoning goes like this: the Bible is not self-interpreting. Therefore, there is a need for an interpreter. Further, to preserve the teachings of Christ from corruption, there must be a divinely authorized interpreter. Christ chose Peter to fit this role.

The second argument is that without an authoritative interpretation, there will be a proliferation of sects, cults, and heresies—all laying claim to the truth of Christ. In order to avoid this, God set up a magisterium (in the apostles) for his visible church, over which he placed Peter. In this way, the unity and perpetuity of the church of Christ can be preserved on earth.

33. Ott, *Fundamentals*, 288.
34. Ibid.
35. Irenaeus, *Haer.*; quoted by Ott, *Fundamentals*, 288.
36. Ibid.

An Evaluation of the Roman Catholic Arguments for the Primacy of Peter

As already noted, the primacy of Peter is the first and fundamental step in the Catholic chain of argument used to support its claim to be the true church of Christ. Also, the primacy of Peter is the basis for the Catholic dogma of the infallibility of the pope.

If the primacy of Peter is firmly founded in Scripture, history, and reason, then there is a basis on which to build the rest of their argument for the infallibility of the pope and the claim to exclusivity. If, on the other hand, there is no solid basis for the primacy of Peter, then the whole castle of Catholicism crumbles. With this in view, let's carefully analyze their arguments for primacy.

The Biblical Arguments for Primacy Evaluated

The three main texts used to support primacy are crucial to the whole Roman argument. If the support they provide is not sound, then the Roman Church is built on sand, not rock.

Matthew 16:18

The important statement here is found in Jesus' words to Peter: "I also say to you that you are Peter, and *upon this rock I will build My church*"[37] (NASB). Two basic things must be noted in response to the Catholic argument for the primacy of Peter based on this text. First, even if it could be shown that Peter is the "rock" on which Christ said he would build his church, the Catholic claim for the primacy of Peter would not necessarily follow. Second, there are good reasons to believe Peter was not the "rock" to which Christ referred.

Peter could have been the rock in the sense that he was part of the apostolic rocklike foundation on which the church was built. As the apostle Paul declared, the church is "built on the foundation of the apostles [plural] and prophets, Jesus Christ Himself being the chief cornerstone" (Eph. 2:20 NKJV). Indeed, the same power to bind and loose given here (in Matt. 16:19) was given to all the apostles (Matt. 18:18). And the fact that Jesus is speaking only to Peter in Matthew 16 is understandable since he is responding to Peter's confession about Jesus' being the Son of God. What is more, making Peter a rock in the foundation of the church does not thereby endow him with all of the magisterial authority Rome loads into the term "primacy." It may indicate no more than spiritual leadership, which Peter certainly did exercise in the early

37. Emphasis added.

church, as both Protestants and Catholics agree. Additionally, there are good reasons to believe that Peter was not the rock to which Christ referred in Matthew 16.

First, Peter's confession that Jesus was the Son of God was the occasion for Christ's statement.

Second, Jesus used two different words in the inspired text: "You are Peter [*petros*, a little rock] and on this rock [*petra*, a big rock] I will build my church."

Third, Peter is referred to in this passage in the second person, "you"; however, it is noted that the statement "this rock" is in the third person.

Fourth, *Peter* (Gk. *petros*) is a masculine singular term, while *rock* (*petra*) is a feminine singular term, thus pointing out that the two terms do not have the same referent.[38]

Fifth, this text does not bestow a unique authority on Peter, since the same power to bind and loose was given later to *all* of the apostles (see Matt. 18:18) as well.

Sixth, nowhere else in Scripture is Peter singled out as the rock foundation of the church. Instead, Christ is said to be the "chief cornerstone" (Eph. 2:20).

Seventh, even Peter himself refers to Christ as the "chief cornerstone" (1 Pet. 2:7 NKJV).

Eighth, many early Fathers deny this is a reference to Peter, including Augustine who wrote, "The Rock (*Petra*) was Christ; and on this foundation was Peter himself also built. For other foundation can no man lay than that is laid, which is Christ Jesus."[39] This is all the stronger since Augustine believed in the primacy of Peter. So he would have been more than happy to use this verse if he thought it would support his belief, but he did not. George Salmon asks the pointed question: "If Christ established Peter as 'the rock' of the Church, then why did most of the prominent leaders [before the Middle Ages] of this very Church fail to see this interpretation of this all-important passage?"[40]

---

38. Geisler and MacKenzie, *Roman Catholics and Evangelicals*, 207. Catholic theologians are quick to point out that Jesus probably spoke Aramaic here, which, in point of fact, does not make a distinction between genders, thus allegedly providing a counter example to the Protestant claim. However, as Geisler and MacKenzie rightly point out, "The *inspired* Greek original does make such distinctions."

39. Augustine, "On the Gospel of John," in *Nicene and Post-Nicene Fathers*, ed. Philip Schaff (Peabody, MA: Hendrickson, 2004), 7:450.

40. George Salmon, *The Infallibility of the Church* (rprt., Grand Rapids, MI, Baker, 1959), 334.

Ninth, as for the "keys," these too may have been shared by the other apostles in the sense that they had the power to bind or loose (Matt. 18:18). Or Peter may very well have had a unique historic role that he used in opening the door of the gospel to Jews (Acts 2) and later to the Gentiles (Acts 10).[41] But there was no indication of a perpetual use of the keys by either Peter or his successors.

Tenth, Salmon asked pointed questions: "If our Lord meant all this [concerning Peter], we may ask, why did he not say it? Who found out that He meant it? The Apostles did not find out at the time; for up to the night before [Jesus'] death the dispute went on, which should be the greatest."[42] In short, if Peter was already appointed as the greatest in Matthew 16, then why did Christ not say so later when the disciples asked who would be the greatest in his kingdom (Matt. 18:1–4)?

Eleventh, a dogma like this should not be established apart from the "unanimous consent" of the Fathers. The First Vatican Council and numerous other Catholic decrees unequivocally insisted that one *must* interpret the Scriptures according to *the unanimous consent of the Fathers*. Trent proclaimed that the faithful should confess: "I shall never accept nor interpret [the Bible] otherwise than in accordance with the *unanimous consent of the Fathers*."[43] Similarly, the First Vatican Council stated, "No one is permitted to interpret Sacred Scripture itself contrary . . . to the *unanimous agreement of the Fathers*."[44] But even as Catholic authority Ludwig Ott admits, some of the Fathers themselves took "the rock on which the Lord built the Church as meaning the faith of Peter in the Divinity of Christ."[45] Hence, by their own infallible standard, the Roman Catholic interpretation of their primary text on Peter's primacy fails!

Twelfth, while Catholic commentators insist that Matthew 16 proves Peter's primacy, no Catholic commentator is willing to assign Peter primacy in evil when he was rebuked by Jesus just a few verses later: "Get behind Me, Satan! You are a stumbling block to Me; for you are not

---

41. Again, the terms "bind" and "loose" were common rabbinic terms for "forbidding" and "allowing" and the "keys" was a metaphor explaining the authority to do this; Geisler, *The Church and Last Things*, 77.

42. Salmon, *The Infallibility of the Church*, 334.

43. Denzinger, *The Sources of Catholic Dogma*, no. 996, p. 303, emphasis added.

44. Ibid., no. 1788, p. 444, emphasis added. For another similar statement concerning the unanimous consent of the Fathers, see Pope Leo XIII's encyclical, "Providentissimus Deus," (November 1893) quoted in ibid., no. 1944, p. 489.

45. Ott, *Fundamentals*, 280.

setting your mind on God's interests, but man's (v. 23 NASB)."[46] Salmon recognized this inconsistency and wrote:

> If Peter were the foundation of the Church [referred to in Matt. 16] . . . it would have shaken immediately afterwards when our Lord said unto him: "Get thee behind me, Satan," and tottered to its base when he denied his Lord. *Immediately after Peter had earned commendation by his acknowledgment of Jesus as the Messiah, the doctrine of a crucified Messiah was proposed to him and he rejected it.* . . . [So if] the Apostles had believed that the words "On this rock I will build my Church" constituted Peter their infallible guide, the very first time they followed his guidance they would have been led to miserable error.[47]

So it is inconsistent of Catholic scholars to apply primacy to Peter in one instance but not in the other. Since Peter was representing the group of the apostles, it is only natural that Jesus would single him out for affirming Jesus' divine messiahship. Why, then, should one conclude that Peter was given the charism of infallibility when he was merely speaking out in response to Jesus' question?[48] To be sure, "Rome has read much more into the text than can be found here."[49]

D. A. Carson summarized the thrust of the Matthew 16 passage as follows:

> The name *Peter* means "Rock," and Jesus played on this meaning to designate Peter as the foundation of the new people of God. His leadership would involve the authority of the steward, whose *keys* symbolized his responsibility to regulate the affairs of the household. Peter would exercise his leadership by his authority to declare what is and is not permissible in the *kingdom of heaven* (to *bind* and to *loose* have this meaning in rabbinic writings). The story of the early years of the church in Acts shows how Peter fulfilled this role. But the same authority was shared with the other disciples in 18:18 (where *you* is plural; here it is singular). He was thus a representative leader rather than an overlord.[50]

In brief, no matter whether Peter is the "rock" to which Christ referred, the Roman concept of the papacy cannot be legitimately derived from it. What is more, the evidence is very strongly in favor of the passage

---

46. Ibid.
47. Salmon, 343, emphasis added.
48. Geisler, *The Church and Last Things*, 77.
49. Keith A. Mathison, *The Shape of Sola Scriptura* (Moscow, ID: Canon Press, 201), 186.
50. D. A. Carson, *New Bible Commentary: 21st Century Edition*. 4th ed. (Downers Grove, IL: InterVarsity, 1994); available from Logos Bible Software ED 3.0; emphases added.

not referring to Peter as the "rock" on which the church is built. Thus, the primary verse of the foundational doctrine of the Roman Church is found not to support the Roman claim. This places their whole case in serious jeopardy.

John 21:15–17

This text is used by Roman Catholics to prove that "Christ installed Peter (and his successors) as the supreme pastor over the whole flock." Carson writes, "The task of teaching Christian truth and of protecting it from error is part of the function of the supreme pastor. But he could not fulfill this task if, in exercise of his supreme teaching office, he himself were subject to error."[51] In response, several observations are relevant.

First, in both the immediate and more remote contexts it is not authority but pastoral care that is in view. Noted New Testament commentator Leon Morris made the point well:

> This passage must be taken in conjunction with Peter's threefold denial of his Lord. Just as he had a short time ago [John 18:25–27] in the presence of the enemy denied all connection with the Lord, so now in the presence of his friends he affirms three times over that he loves his Lord. . . . There can be little doubt but that the whole scene is meant to show us Peter as completely restored to his position of leadership. He has three times denied his Lord. Now he has three times affirmed his love for Him, and three times he has been commissioned to care for the flock. This must have had the effect on the others of a demonstration that, whatever had been the mistakes of the past, Jesus was restoring Peter to a place of trust.[52]

Second, the context of the passage demonstrates Jesus' restoration of Simon to properly administer pastoral care to the flock. But nowhere does this text suggest that this leadership role involved a charism of primacy. One does not need to have these special powers in order to tend the flock of Christ. In point of fact, "feeding is a God-given pastoral function that even non-apostles had in the New Testament."[53]

Third, what is more, Peter did not demonstrate an exemplar primacy in faith and practice, even in the New Testament times where the apostle Paul had to rebuke him for his fallible practice (Gal. 2:11–12) that was contrary to the gospel. So serious was what Peter exhibited by his life that

51. Ibid., 287–88.
52. Leon Morris, *The Gospel According to John*, New International Commentary on the New Testament (Grand Rapids, MI: Eerdmans, 1995), 767.
53. Geisler, *The Church and Last Things*, 80.

Paul called it hypocrisy and a denial of the straightforward truth of the gospel. This was not an ordinary inconsistency that any mortal person, including a pope, might fall into. In short, Peter's denial was a *de facto* denial of the gospel. This is seriously inconsistent with the Roman claim that he is the primary teacher of faith and practice in the church.

Finally, the fact that Jesus singled out Peter does not show so much his primacy as his fallibility. After all, he was the one who denied Christ three times and needed to be restored by a threefold affirmation. If anything, the passage implies Peter's primacy in evil, for he alone, not the other apostles, denied his Lord outright on three occasions. If Peter was going to be used as a leader in the future, he needed to be restored. Thus, the focus here is on Peter because he alone had committed these serious sins.

Luke 22:31–32

The third major passage used for direct support of the Roman dogma of Peter's infallibility is in Luke 22. It is argued that since Christ prayed only for Peter's faith not to fail, this indicates that he alone held primacy as teacher over all other apostles. However, such an interpretation is scarcely found in this scant reference.

A careful examination of this text and its parallel passage in Mark's Gospel reveals that it is not a unique reference to Peter's powers but to the other apostles as well.[54] Mark's Gospel provides additional information not found in Luke. Peter said to Jesus, "Even though all may fall away, yet I will not" (Mark 14:29 NASB). Mark follows with Jesus' prediction of Peter's denial.[55] Mathison provides a clear explanation of these series of circumstances that unfold in Mark:

> All of the Apostles are told they will stumble. Peter alone informs His Lord that He is wrong. Peter claims that even if everyone else falls away, he will not. It is more likely, then, that the reason Jesus singled Peter out for a special prayer was because of Peter's special arrogance in this situation. Peter dramatically overestimates his own faith despite Jesus' warning. . . . Therefore Jesus, because of His love for Peter, prays especially for him.[56]

So, this text shows nothing about Peter's primacy.

54. Mathison, *Shape of Sola Scriptura*, 192.
55. Ibid.
56. Ibid., 192–93.

Additionally, Catholic theologian Hans Küng, whom the Catholic Church censored for his pointed critiques of the papacy, pointed out that the Catholic proof-texts in no way support the doctrine of the papacy. Küng wrote, "In Luke 22:32 (and in Matthew 16:18 and John 21:15) . . . *there is not a word here about infallibility.*"[57]

In short, Catholic commentators have to read back into the text their peculiar interpretation in order to yield their papal conclusions.

Also, if Peter were the prime teacher among the apostles, why does the apostle Paul play a much greater role in the New Testament, both in spreading the gospel and in writing inspired Scripture? While Peter wrote only two short epistles, Paul wrote nearly half of the New Testament (13 of 27 books) and maybe more, if he wrote Hebrews. Further, Peter was not the primary agent for the spread of the gospel. Little is heard of him after the first several chapters of Acts. Instead, it is the apostle Paul who is attempting to fulfill Jesus' command to take Christ's message to the end of the earth (cf. Col. 1:23).

To be sure, Peter did have a significant role in the early church, which no Protestant can deny, but, again, this is not the same thing as affirming that Peter had an infallible office of authority in the New Testament church or that his successors have the same. Other than the possible historic use of the "keys" for Jews (Acts 2) and Gentiles (Acts 10), Peter was not given any unique authority that was not later assigned to the rest of the apostles; all were given the *same* authority to bind and loose (see Matt. 18:18 cf. John 20:21–23). He was one of the "eminent apostles" (plural, 2 Cor. 12:11 NASB), but not the "chief apostle."[58]

In spite of the Catholic claim that Peter was positionally superior to Paul, Paul under the guidance of the Holy Spirit revealed the contrary, namely, that no other apostle was superior to him—including Peter! Paul says, "For I was not at all inferior to these super apostles" (2 Cor. 12:11).[59] When reading the epistles of Paul, e.g., Galatians, it is difficult to come away with the impression that any of the apostles were superior to Paul, since, as Paul himself says, he received his revelation independently of the other apostles. The revelation that Paul received came from the original source, namely, from the risen, glorified Christ (see Gal. 1:12). Paul, then, was on equal footing with Peter by virtue of his receiving revelation from Christ; thus Peter and Paul shared the

57. Hans Küng, *Infallibility? An Inquiry*, trans. Edward Quinn (Garden City, NY: Doubleday, 1971), 109, emphasis added.
58. Geisler, *The Church and Last Things*, 78.
59. Ibid.

same status. Indeed, as seen above, Paul used that revelation to rebuke Peter when Peter vacillated between his association with the Gentiles and his unbelieving Jewish kinsmen (Gal. 2:11ff.), thus engaging in a practical denial of the gospel.[60]

If Peter enjoyed primacy as the first pope, it is strange that he and John were commissioned (sent) by the other apostles on a mission to Samaria. The fact that they were commissioned suggests that Peter was not the superior apostle as Catholics claim (see Acts 8:14). Indeed, if Peter were the God-ordained superior apostle, it would be strange that more attention is given to the ministry of Paul than to that of Peter in Acts. Peter is the focus in chapters 1 to 12; Paul is the dominant figure in chapters 13 to 28.[61]

It is true that Peter addressed the church's first council in Jerusalem (see Acts 15); however, it is also true that Peter exercised no primacy over the others.[62] As the text demonstrates, the final decisions of the council were carried out by *all* of the apostles and the elders, as well as with the consent of the entire church (15:22), thus at once demonstrating more of a collegial or conciliar model rather than a Petrine Roman model. Moreover, it has been observed by some scholars that it was *not* Peter who presided over the council, but it was James instead (15:13–21).[63]

Additionally, Peter never refers to himself as *the chief* pastor of the church but only as a *"fellow* elder" (1 Pet. 5:1–2), which would be a strange admission for one who allegedly possesses primacy.[64] In fact, in

---

60. Ibid.
61. Ibid.
62. Some might take verse 7 as implying Peter's primacy; however, the *context* of the entire passage reveals that the decisions were carried out by all of the apostles and not by Peter alone; see Mathison, *Shape of Sola Scriptura*, 196–98.
63. Ibid. Concerning Petrine and Collegial models, at the First Vatican Council (1870) there were two schools of thought present, the majority party called the "ultramontanists" (for they sought authority "beyond the mountain," that is, the Alps), and the minority party (led by John Henry Newman) who held to a form of "conciliarism." Concerning the former, the minority group wished to see infallibility linked to all of the bishops and not to the pope alone. Out of the some seven hundred bishops present at Vatican I, one hundred of them opposed the doctrine of papal infallibility (Geisler and MacKenzie, *Roman Catholics and Evangelicals*, 460). In fact, Gregory the Great (pope from AD 590–604) reproached Patriarch John the Faster of Constantinople for calling himself the universal bishop. In Gregory's mind, this universal claim of supreme authority in a bishop was a sure identification of the corruption of the church, or even the work of the Antichrist. Thus Gregory reacted in such a way to defend the rights of all bishops, and not simply because he sought the title for himself; see Harold O. J. Brown, *Protest of a Troubled Protestant* (New Rochelle: Arlington House, 1969), 122.
64. Stephen Ray attempts to counter this point by arguing that Peter was simply manifesting the humility he was exhorting his readers to practice. In addition, Ray asserts that Peter

his epistle addressed to the dispersed Christians throughout the Roman Empire, he salutes them by addressing himself as "*an* apostle" (1:1). Since Peter was one of the church's "pillars" (plural) nowhere does Peter ever write that he was "*the* apostle," nor does he ever write that he was "*the* bishop of Rome."[65]

Also, if Peter were the first bishop of Rome, it is strange that he is listed as only a cofounder of the church there along with the apostle Paul by one of our earliest sources on the topic. Irenaeus, who knew Polycarp, the disciple of the apostle John, affirmed "that tradition derived from the apostles, of the very great, the very ancient, and universally known Church founded and organized at Rome by the two most glorious apostles, Peter and Paul" (*Haer.* 3). If Irenaeus had known and believed Peter had primacy over Paul, then surely he would have mentioned it here.

Irenaeus repeatedly speaks of "the apostolic tradition" *(Haer.* 3.3.2) and "the blessed apostles" who "founded and built up the Church" (3.3.3), "the doctrine of the apostles" (3.12.4), and "the tradition from the apostles" (3.5.1). He wrote, "*These [apostles] are the voices of the Church from which every Church had its origin* . . . these are the voices of the apostles; these are the voices of the disciples of the Lord, the truly perfect, who after the assumption of the Lord, were perfected by the Spirit" (3.12.4, emphasis added). For "[God] sent forth His own apostles in the spirit of truth, and not in that of error, He did the very same also in the case of the prophets" (4.35.2). No primacy is given to Peter by Irenaeus.

Most commentators recognize that Peter had a significant role as the initial leader in the early church, as the book of Acts records (chaps. 1–12). Yet, the biblical data suggest that Peter did not have any superiority over the other apostles; he was simply one of *many* pillars of the church.[66] It may be a *necessary* condition for Peter to have been the leader of the apostles to fit the papal description, but it is not a *sufficient* condition for

---

never denies the primacy bestowed upon him by Jesus. Ray attempts to use the analogy of a presidential address whereby the president refers to himself as a "fellow American" when addressing the nation, even though he holds the highest office in the nation (Stephen Ray, *Upon This Rock: St. Peter and the Primacy of Rome in Scripture and the Early Church* [San Francisco: Ignatius Press, 1999], 59, n. 79). This analogy does not work since the power claimed for the presidency and the power claimed for the papacy are not the same—the pope is said to possess a charism of *infallibility* as the vicar of Christ; the president is simply recognized as the national leader to whom neither infallibility nor absolute jurisdiction is ascribed. To answer Ray's second question, Peter never denies his primacy because he *never* had it to begin with (as the biblical evidence demonstrates)—Ray's assertion simply begs the question.

65. Geisler, *The Church and Last Things*, 78.
66. Ibid., 78–79.

primacy; that is, there are other ways Peter could have been the leader of the apostles without requiring him to be the first pope. He could simply have been the leader of the twelve apostles, nothing more, nothing less. As noted before, all the apostles were given the same authority to bind and loose (Matt. 18:18), even though Peter was given this authority first (Matt. 16:19). As for the other verses offered by Rome in support of the primacy of Peter, all of them fail to support the claim of primacy. All of them are indirect inferences at best, and most do not really apply to the issue of Peter's primacy as conceived by Rome.

In Isaiah 22:22, the "key" refers to the stewardship of the house of David that would be placed in the hands of Eliakim. It has nothing to do with Peter or the New Testament church.

Matthew 7:24 refers to a wise man building his house on the rock and has absolutely nothing to say about Peter being the rock for the church.

Matthew 10:2 and Mark 3:16 list Peter's name first because he was a leader among the apostles. But these verses say nothing about Peter's being *the* leader among them, to say nothing of his being the divinely authoritative leader.

In Matthew 17:1 Peter's active role among the three apostles reveals his leadership abilities as well as his impetuous nature, something that led Jesus to say to him, "Get behind me, Satan!" (Matt. 16:23). The fact that in Matthew 17:27 Peter did a miracle does not show his primacy, since the other apostles had the same power (Matt. 10:8; 2 Cor. 12:12; Heb. 2:3–4), as did some laypersons (Acts 8:6).

In Matthew 26:37 Peter came with Jesus to the garden, but so did James and John. This proves nothing of Rome's claim that primacy uniquely belonged to Peter. The same is true when these same three witnessed the awakening of Jairus's daughter in Mark 5:37 and Jesus' transfiguration in Luke 9:28ff.

Luke 5:3 tells us about the availability of Peter's boat from which Jesus could preach. It says nothing about Peter's primacy. Likewise, John 10:16 says nothing about Peter but merely about Jesus' other sheep, Gentiles, whom he will bring into the fold.

Using John 11:49–52 as an analogy to show "the high priest possessed an official revelatory function" is a false analogy that, if true, would prove too much. It proves that Israel had a divinely authoritative magisterium too—something both Rome and Jesus rejected (Matt. 5:31–32, 38–39, 43–44; 15:1–6).

The use of Acts 1:12–16, 20–26; 2:14 to show leadership in the early church is accepted by all, but it tells us nothing about Peter's being the first pope.

In Acts 15:7 Peter was the first to speak at the council, but James was apparently the leader there since he spoke last and summed up the whole matter (15:13–21) leading to the decision of all the "apostles and elders" present (vv. 22–29).

In 1 Corinthians 15:5 Peter is listed as the first of the apostles to see the resurrected Christ, but the Gospels tell us that the women saw Jesus before Peter. Why then would not Rome take that as proof of the primacy of women over men?

In Galatians 1:16–19 it was Peter whom Paul saw first because Peter was one of many "pillars" of the church (Gal. 2:9), not because he had primacy over the others. Indeed, Paul even had to rebuke Peter for his denial of the gospel he taught (Gal. 2:11f.).

Revelation 1:18 and 3:7 do not speak of Peter directly but only that keys are a symbol of power and dominion, but all the apostles had this power (Matt. 18:18). It was not limited to Peter.

In summation, there is no direct evidence for Peter's primacy in any New Testament text. Further, some Roman Catholic arguments employ false analogy. Others show only Peter's leadership in the early church, not his infallibility. And some verses prove absolutely nothing. All in all, it is a futile attempt to give indirect justification for a doctrine that has no direct justification in the New Testament.

The Historical Arguments for Primacy Evaluated

Roman Catholics also support their argument for primacy by their appeal to the teachings of the early fathers. Protestants reject the use of this as an authoritative argument, since they believe that the Bible, not the fathers, is the only authoritative source for faith and practice. So we must first address the issue of the authority of the fathers.

The Fathers Had No Divine Authority as Individuals

The first thing to note is that the fathers held many contrary views on Christian doctrine and practice and, hence, they cannot all be right. So, any alleged divine authority there may be in one father's writings would be canceled by the fact that the same authority would exist in an opposing father's view. In short, their alleged authority as individuals is self-canceling and nonexistent.

"The Universal Consent of the Fathers" Principle

Roman Catholics attempt to bolster the above argument by appealing to the so-called universal consent of the fathers. They claim that such universal agreement of the fathers makes their view true. But there are at least three major problems with this view: definitional, logical, and historical.

The very principle of universal consent of the fathers is problematic *definitionally.* How do we know who qualifies as a father and by what standard do we judge? We cannot use orthodox Christian teaching as the standard, for that presupposes that we already know from some other source what qualifies as orthodox. And if it can be known independently from the fathers—say, by the Bible alone—then it defeats the Catholic argument that the fathers are needed to know it is true. In short, if the Catholic view is correct that we cannot know what the Bible means apart from the fathers, the argument is circular. It would be using orthodoxy known from the fathers to test which of the fathers are orthodox. But if we can't know who a father is, then we cannot use the universal consent of the fathers to know if a proposed doctrine is true.

There is also a *logical* problem with the Roman principle of universal consent of the fathers; namely, it is actually possible that all the fathers were wrong on a given doctrinal point of universal agreement. After all, neither Catholic nor non-Catholic Christians believe their writings were divinely inspired and infallible. But if they are fallible, then it is logically possible that all of them could be wrong on a given point. So, even universal consent could be no more than consent to err. Even the great Roman Catholic theologian Thomas Aquinas affirmed, "We believe the prophets and apostles because the Lord has been their witness by performing miracles. . . . And we believe the successors of the apostles and the prophets *only in so far as they tell us those things which the apostles and prophets have left in their writings.*"[67]

The *historical* problem is that even given the validity of the criterion of universal consent, still many of the disputed areas do not have universal consent. In fact, depending on who qualifies as a father, there is no universal consent among the fathers. Even if universal consent of the fathers were a solid principle in theory, nevertheless, in practice there are few disputed areas on which it is useful. And the primacy of Peter is not one. So the Roman Catholics' appeal to this principle of universal consent to support many of their dogmas fails. This is true, for example,

---

67. Thomas Aquinas, *On Truth*, 10, 14.10, 11, emphasis added.

on the immaculate conception of Mary, which even the greatest Catholic theologian of all time, Thomas Aquinas, rejected.[68] The same is true of the bodily assumption of Mary (proclaimed a dogma in 1950), the veneration of the host, and the infallibility of the pope. So, there is no practical purpose for the principle of universal consent.

The fact is that there is no universal consent for Peter's primacy Yet Rome insists that there must be for any of its dogmas. As seen earlier, the First Vatican Council and numerous Catholic decrees unequivocally insisted that one *must* interpret the Scriptures according to *the unanimous consent of the fathers*. Trent proclaimed that the faithful should confess: "I shall never accept nor interpret [the Bible] otherwise than in accordance with the unanimous consent of the Fathers."[69] Similarly, the First Vatican Council stated, "No one is permitted to interpret Sacred Scripture itself contrary . . . to the unanimous agreement of the Fathers."[70] But even as Catholic authority Ludwig Ott admits that some of the fathers themselves took "the rock on which the Lord built the Church as meaning the faith of Peter in the Divinity of Christ,"[71] so, by Rome's own criterion, the primacy of Peter fails to qualify for a Roman dogma!

One final point needs to be made. Even if one modifies the criterion to "many early fathers" agree (which would not be an adequate criterion), we would still run into a serious problem with Peter's primacy for several reasons. For there are not many early, undisputed references to Peter's primacy. There are only a few even relatively early references, and most of them are disputable.

Tertullian. For example, Catholics cite Tertullian speaking of the "the Church, [which was] built upon him [Peter]" (*Mon.* 8).[72] But the reference is oblique and non-didactic with no explanation of what it means. And what Ott omits is informing us of a clear didactic passage where Tertullian affirms teaching contrary to the primacy of the Roman hierarchy. In addressing Matthew 16:19, Ott says clearly:

> You therefore [wrongly] presume that the power of binding and loosing has derived to you, that is, to every Church akin to Peter, what sort of man are you, subverting and wholly changing the manifest intention of

---

68. Aquinas affirmed, "The sanctification of the blessed Virgin before her animation is unintelligible" (*Summa Theologica* 3a, 27, 4).
69. Denzinger, *Sources of Catholic Dogma*, no. 996, p. 303.
70. Ibid., 444, 1788. For another similar statement concerning the unanimous consent of the Fathers, see Pope Leo XIII's encyclical, "Providentissimus Deus" (November 1893), quoted in ibid., no. 1944, p. 489.
71. Ott, *Fundamentals*, 280.
72. Philip Schaff, *Ante-Nicene Fathers* (Grand Rapids, MI: Eerdmans, 1885), 4:65.

the Lord, conferring (as that intention did) this (gift) personally on Peter? 'On thee,' He says and "I will give *to thee* the keys," not to the Church. . . . Accordingly, "the Church," it is true, will forgive sins: but (it will be) the Church of the Spirit, by means of a spiritual man; not the Church which consists of a number of bishops. (*Pud.* 21)[73]

But this is directly contrary to what the Roman church claims about the gift given to Peter in Matthew 16.

Cyprian could be called the first Roman Catholic, though his view on Peter is more Eastern Catholic than Western (Roman) Catholic. He speaks of "the foundation of the one Church which was based by Christ upon the rock [Peter]" (*Epistles* 74.16).[74] But he also held: "The Church is founded upon the bishops, and every act of the Church is controlled by these same rulers" (*Epistles* 26.1).[75] The way Cyprian reconciled these divergent thoughts was to point out that while the gift was given to Peter alone, nonetheless, all the other apostles participated in it in an undivided partnership (*Epistles* 74.16).[76] In short, Peter is first among equals. But Roman Catholics teach that Peter (and thus the popes following him) had primacy over the other apostles and could act independently of them, even in an ecumenical council (Vatican I).[77]

But the fact that there is a primitive primacy teaching in Cyprian is not surprising. He came two hundred years after the apostles. That was more than enough time for a false teaching to develop. Indeed, there were heresies like Docetism (1 John 4) and incipient kinds of Gnosticism (Colossians 2) right in the New Testament. Again, even an incipient primacy practice is implicit in 3 John 9 in "Diotrephes, who loves to have the preeminence among them" (AT). What Roman Catholic scholars must find—but which is conspicuously absent—is the primacy of Peter in the apostolic fathers.

The doctrine of Peter's primacy, however, is more explicit in the writings of the subsequent fathers, such as Augustine and Cyprian, since they, too, had received a more developed view of Peter's leadership. It is observed that during the middle of the second century, as the city of Rome went, so went the church at Rome. What seems to have happened was that Peter's rank, as the leader of the Twelve, was *transferred* to the Roman congregation (i.e., the church at Rome), but, as Jaroslav Pelikan

73. Ibid., 99–100.
74. Ibid., 394.
75. Ibid., 305.
76. Ibid., 394.
77. See Denzinger, *The Sources of Catholic Dogma*, no. 1830.

observes, "only after *considerable time* had elapsed."[78] By the time of the first pro-Christian emperor, Constantine, the Roman hierarchical imprint had firmly implanted itself on the church, and it is understandable that there would be more fathers cited on the side of Peter's primacy, such as Cyril of Jerusalem, and Augustine. Even the Council of Ephesus was on the side of Peter's primacy, and Leo the Great.

But as often noted, Rome was not built in a day and neither was the Roman Catholic Church. It developed gradually from New Testament churches with a plurality of bishops or elders (Phil. 1:1; Acts 14:23) in each church to one bishop over elders in each church (by the second century), to one bishop over an area of churches, to one bishop over all the churches—which is the Roman teaching of Peter's primacy.

More important than the late, sparse, and misapplied fathers who are cited in favor of Peter's primacy is the universal silence of all the earlier fathers in support of Peter's primacy. As we have seen, the absence of Peter's primacy in apostolic times was followed by the same in sub-apostolic times. The truth is that there is no real support for it for some two hundred years after the time of Christ. This silence is deafening. The people who should have known this best seemed most oblivious of it.

The most important link with the apostles is Irenaeus, since he knew Polycarp, the disciple of John the apostle. Irenaeus never spoke of the primacy of Peter. Instead, he repeatedly referred to "the apostolic tradition" *(Haer.* 3.3.2) and "the blessed apostles" who "founded and built up the Church" (*Haer.* 3.3.3), "the doctrine of the apostles" (*Haer.* 3.12.4), and "the tradition from the apostles" (*Haer.* 3.5.1). As cited earlier, no primacy is given to Peter by Irenaeus (*Haer.* 3.1.24; 4.35.2).

Theological Arguments for Peter's Primacy Evaluated

Roman scholars offer several theological arguments in favor of the primacy of Peter. Most of them boil down to two categories. First, some argue that there is the need for an official interpreter of the teachings of Christ because, they reason, the Bible is not self-interpreting. Further, to preserve the teachings of Christ from corruption, there must be a divinely authorized interpreter. Christ chose Peter to fit this role.

The second argument is that without an authoritative interpretation, there will be a proliferation of sects, cults, and heresies—all laying claim to the truth of Christ. In order to avoid this, God set up a magisterium (in the apostles) for his visible church over which he placed

---

78. Jaroslav Pelikan, *The Riddle of Roman Catholicism* (New York: Abington, 1959), 36, emphasis added.

Peter. In this way, the unity and perpetuity of the church of Christ can be preserved.

Non-Catholics and Eastern Orthodox Catholics have different responses to this criticism. The Eastern church believes that reliable (non-infallible) tradition is sufficient to accomplish this task. Protestants appeal to *sola Scriptura* (the Bible alone) and the doctrine of perspicuity (clarity) as a solution. In other words, the main message of the Bible alone is sufficient and has no need for an authoritative interpretation other than the Holy Spirit who can enlighten the reader's mind to the central teachings of the Bible.

As for the alleged proliferation of sects and cults without a Roman magisterium, such a magisterium did not keep the Roman Church from two major splits of its own: one with Eastern orthodoxy and the other with Protestantism at the Reformation. Further, its magisterium has not kept itself from numerous divisions within its own ranks in (a) anti-popes, (b) heretical popes, and (c) religious orders, and (d) in the influence of religious liberalism. What is more, evangelical Protestants who hold to the infallibility of Scripture and the historical-grammatical means of interpreting Scripture have retained essential orthodoxy without any kind of authoritative tradition or Roman magisterium.

Conclusion

The Roman Catholic Church offers scriptural, historical, and theological support for her doctrine of the papacy. It offers the doctrine of papal primacy as the ground for the notion that the Roman pontiff is inherently infallible, e.g., when expounding upon doctrines related to faith and morals. Vatican I stated that the pope's authority stands alone apart from the consent of the whole church. Vatican II reaffirmed the notion of the infallibility of the church's magisterium, including that of the bishops. Of course, there are limits on the doctrine; infallibility only extends to official (*ex cathedra*) pronouncements for the whole church made on doctrine or morals.

The overall argument came about through three basic steps. First was the step arising from the belief that Jesus appointed Peter and endowed him with the authority to be the visible head of the church on earth and promised the same to his successors. The second step was Peter and his successors being recognized as church head(s) by the early church. The third step was subscribing to belief in the infallibility of Peter and his successors in all their official pronouncements to the church on matters of doctrine and morals.

Thus, the claim of the Roman Church to being the true church is confirmed, as are all of its other official pronouncements made *ex cathedra*. If their claim is true, then any who knowingly oppose this are anathema. If it is false, then regardless of what actual truth may be found in the Roman Church, it is not the true church of Christ.

We have examined the biblical, historical, and theological evidence for the Roman Catholic doctrine of the primacy and have found it wanting. Our finding is fatal to the Roman position, for, as we have seen, the primacy of Peter is the foundation for the infallibility of Peter and his successors. And the infallibility of the pope is fundamental to the church's claim to being the only true church. Rather than being built on a solid rock, it is erected on sinking sand.

We have found that nowhere in the New Testament is it affirmed that Peter has any special divinely authoritative role not given to the rest of the apostles. In the books of Acts, after the first few chapters, Peter is no longer even the central apostolic figure. James, our Lord's brother, appeared to be in charge of the council held in Jerusalem (Acts 15). Paul is the dominant figure from Acts 13 to 28, where Peter is scarcely mentioned.

In his epistles Peter speaks of Christ as the "chief cornerstone" of the church (1 Pet. 2:6 NKJV). He introduces himself as just "an apostle of Jesus Christ," not the chief among the apostles (1 Pet. 1:1). Indeed, he speaks of himself as a "fellow elder" (1 Pet. 5:1), all of whom should "shepherd the flock" (1 Pet. 5:2), not being "lords over" them (5:3), and all of whom were subject, not to him, but to the Chief Shepherd, Christ, whose coming they awaited (1 Pet. 5:4). In his second epistle Peter speaks only of the authority of the apostles (plural), not of any unique authority of his own (2 Pet. 3:2). Indeed, he speaks with deference of the unique revelation given to Paul the apostle, which Peter, though he found it hard to understand, accepted as inspired Scripture (2 Pet. 3:15–16). Just how this allegedly infallible interpreter of God's revelation could not himself understand it fully is not compatible with the Roman Catholic view of Peter's primacy.

One thing is clear: the New Testament view of Peter is a far cry from the Roman Catholic description of the unique primacy and power that Christ is alleged to have given Peter as head of the visible church. Other than his temporary apostolic and leadership roles as one of the early pillars of the faith (Gal. 2:9) and his collegiate role with the other apostles as part of the foundation of the church (Eph. 2:20), one looks in vain to the inspired New Testament for anything close to what Rome claims for Peter. Nor do the earliest Christians following the apostles indicate his primacy. In short, no real support is found in the New Testament for the primacy and authority of Peter as the visible head of the church. Nor is there any such evidence in the earliest fathers of the church. As with other false doctrines, unless one resorts to proof-texting, one has to look outside the Bible in the human penchant for power and authority to find the source of this unbiblical teaching.

Likewise, the historical and theological arguments are no better. At best they show a scattered, sparse, and late support for Peter's primacy. They fail totally to make any real apostolic or sub-apostolic link to the real Peter. Likewise, theologically they provide no definite argument that there must be a single primate endowed with such authority.

CHAPTER 4

THE ROMAN ARGUMENT
FOR THE INFALLIBILITY
OF PETER: STATED

In this chapter we will address more specifically the claim of Peter's infallibility and thus that of succeeding popes. Since the primacy of Peter is a prerequisite for his infallibility, the argument for infallibility can be no stronger than that for primacy. In a chain of argument, such as this is, the chain is no stronger than its weakest link.

The strength of the infallibility link will be determined by the biblical, historical, and theological arguments provided for it. We will begin with the biblical arguments offered by Rome in favor of its infallibility.

Papal Infallibility Defined

Before attempting to defend infallibility, it must first be defined. Roman Catholics have carefully set forth what the term *infallible* means and does not mean as it applies to the pope.

The First Vatican Council (AD 1870)

The doctrine of papal infallibility became official dogma at the First Vatican Council when Pope Pius IX declared it as such. Ironically, it was the first time a pope had ever defined a dogma on his own without

90

the support of a council.[1] The council went to great pains in preparing the statement to explain when and how the pope spoke infallibly. The council made this declaration:

> [T]his gift of truth and a *never failing* faith [i.e., infallibility] was divinely conferred upon Peter and his successors in this chair, that they might administer their high duty for the salvation of all; that the entire flock of Christ, turned away by them from the poisonous food of error, might be nourished in the sustenance of heavenly doctrine, that with the occasion of schism removed the whole Church might be saved as one, and relying on her foundation might stay firm against the gates of hell. But since in this very age, in which the salutary efficacy of the apostolic duty is especially required, not a few are found who disparage its authority. We deem it most necessary to assert solemnly the prerogative which the Only-begotten Son of God deigned to enjoin with the highest pastoral office. Of course, the Council declared the Pope infallible only when he speaks *ex cathedra* ("from the chair") of St. Peter.

Infallibility is defined in the paragraph that follows:

> [We] teach and explain that the dogma has been divinely revealed: that the Roman Pontiff, when he speaks *ex cathedra*, that is, when carrying out the duty of the pastor and teacher of all Christians in accord with his supreme apostolic authority he explains a doctrine of faith or morals to be held by the universal Church, through the divine assistance promised him in blessed Peter, operates with infallibility with which the divine Redeemer wished that His church be instructed in defining doctrine on faith and morals; and so such definitions of the Roman Pontiff from himself, but not from the consensus of the Church, are unalterable.

The council concluded with this solemn warning: "But if anyone presumes to contradict this definition of ours, which may God forbid: let him be anathema."[2] Given this definition, it can be concluded that the pope's authority is irreformable as such; that is, his authority rests without the intervention of any further authority, i.e., an ecumenical council. The council stated, "Those who say that it is permitted to appeal to an ecumenical council from the decisions of the Roman Pontiff (as to an

1. Justo Gonzáles, *The Story of Christianity*, rev. ed. (Peabody, MA: Prince Press, 2004), 297.
2. Henry Denzinger, *The Sources of Catholic Dogma* (St. Louis, MO: Herfer, 1957), 457.

authority superior to the Roman Pontiff) are far from the straight path of truth."[3]

Conversely, the pope does not have the absolute authority to unilaterally undo or override a previous *ex cathedra* statement given by a previous pope. Yet, as Dulles notes, "Vatican I firmly rejected one condition . . . as necessary for infallibility, namely, the consent of the whole church."[4] Still, and as it stands today, the Church as a *whole* is considered infallible, i.e., the magisterium alongside the pope.

The Second Vatican Council (AD 1962–1965)

This council picked up where the first one almost one hundred years earlier had left off. Particular attention was paid to the nature of the church itself, especially the relationship between the college of bishops and the pope.[5] With this in mind Vatican II, in the spirit of pastoral concern for the modern church, restated the doctrine of papal infallibility this way:

> This infallibility, however, with the divine redemption wished to endow his Church in defining doctrine pertaining to faith and morals, is co-extensive with the deposit of revelation, which must be religiously guarded and loyally and courageously expounded. The Roman Pontiff, head of the college of bishops, enjoys this infallibility in virtue of his office, when, as supreme pastor and teacher of all the faithful—who confirms his brethren in the faith (cf. Lk. 22:32)—*he proclaims in an absolute decision a doctrine pertaining to faith and morals*. For that reason his definitions are rightly said to be *irreformable by their very nature and not by reason of assent of the Church*, in as much as they were made with the assistance of the Holy Spirit promised to him in the person of blessed Peter himself; and as a consequence they are *in no way in need of approval* of the others, and do

3. "The Vatican Council (1869–70)" as cited in *The Church Teaches: Documents of the Church in English Translation*, ed. John F. Clarkson, et al. (Rockford, IL: Tan, 1973), 99, 210.

4. Avery Dulles, "Infallibility: The Terminology," in *Teaching Authority*; ed. Paul C. Empie, et al. (Minneapolis: Augsburg, 1980), 79. I [Norman Geisler] point out that "in contrast to Vatican I, many (usually liberal or progressive) Catholic theologians believe that the pope is *not* infallible independently of the bishops but only infallible as he speaks in one voice with and for them in collegiality; infallibility 'is often attributed to the bishops as a group, to ecumenical councils, and to popes,'" Geisler, *Systematic Theology*, vol. 4: *The Church and Last Things* (Bloomington, MN: Bethany House, 2005), 74. For a progressive Catholic treatment of these issues, see Luis Bermejo, S. J., *Towards a Christian Reunion: Vatican I: Obstacles and Reunion* (Lanham, MD: University Press of America, 1984); *Infallibility on Trial* (Westminster, MD: Christian Classics Inc., 1992).

5. Alister McGrath, *The Future of Christianity* (Malden, MS: Blackwell, 2002), 104. McGrath observes that "after the Second Vatican Council the Catholic Church increasingly came to see itself more as a community of believers than as a divinely ordained and hierarchically ordered society" (ibid.).

not admit of appeal to any other tribunal. For in such a case the Roman Pontiff does not utter a pronouncement as a private person, but rather does he *expound* and defend the teaching of the universal Church, in whom the Church's charism of infallibility is present in a singular way.[6]

So the Second Vatican Council in no way abrogated what Vatican I proclaimed, that when the pope proclaims dogmas of faith and morals, he does so *without* the consent of the whole church. It was also affirmed at Vatican II that the pope does not utter pronouncements as a "private person" but rather expounds on what was already taught and believed by the universal church, though Vatican II appears to have articulated this stipulation with more caution than in previous statements.[7]

The Catechism of the Catholic Church

In the recent authoritative and widely acclaimed *Catechism of the Catholic Church* we read a reaffirmation of the Second Vatican Council on papal infallibility as follows:

> The Roman Pontiff, head of the college of bishops, enjoys this infallibility in virtue of his office, when, as supreme pastor and teacher of all the faithful . . . he proclaims by a definitive act a doctrine pertaining to faith or morals. . . . The infallibility promised to the Church is also present in the body of bishops when, together with Peter's successor, they excise the supreme Magisterium, above all in an ecumenical council. . . . This infallibility extends as far as the deposit of divine Revelation itself.[8]

The Ex Cathedra Qualification

The doctrine of papal infallibility claims to be unquestionable as is indicated by the anathemas the Catholic Church pronounces on those who oppose it. Nonetheless, it is subject to certain qualifications of its

6. Austin Flannery, "Lumen Gentium," in *Vatican Council II*, vol. 1, rev. ed. (Boston: St. Paul's Books and Media, 1992), 380, emphasis added.
7. McGrath reports that "most observers are convinced that Catholicism will remain the dominant and most successful form of Christianity in the next century. One of the reasons for this is the achievement of the Second Vatican Council (1962–5), especially the reforming and renewing agenda which it imposed upon a hesitant church." For example, "one of the most radical (and some would say, most overdue) decisions taken at Vatican II was that the Roman Catholic worship should now take place in the vernacular, rather than the traditional Latin" (McGrath, *Future of Christianity*, 90, 103).
8. *Catechism of the Catholic Church: Libreria Editrice Vaticana* (Washington: United States Catholic Conference, 1994), 235 (Sect. 891).

own. Not all papal statements are deemed infallible; only those made *ex cathedra* of doctrine of morals.[9]

The status of infallibility applies only when the pope is said to speak *ex cathedra*. *Ex cathedra* statements are identified, according to noted Catholic authority Avery Dulles, when all four of the following qualifications are either stated or implied: (1) the pope speaks to fulfill his office as supreme pastor and teacher of all Christians; (2) the pronouncement is in accord with his supreme apostolic authority, i.e., as successor of Peter; (3) the statement determines a doctrine of faith and morals, i.e., a doctrine expressing divine revelation; and (4) the pope imposes a doctrine to be held definitively by all.[10]

The Biblical Evidence Offered by Rome for Papal Infallibility

As we have seen, the word *infallibility*, when applied to the papacy, is understood as the pope's immunity from error when defining dogmas of faith and morals, i.e., *de fide* doctrines.[11] Peter, by virtue of his office as the vicar of Christ's church, was allegedly endowed with this gift of primacy and infallibility. Thus, from the very beginning Christ *distinguished* the apostle Peter from the other apostles. It follows, therefore, that Peter—and Peter alone—was the supreme leader among Christ's apostles. Even Christ changed Peter's name from Simon to *Cephas*, meaning "rock." As we have noted, the first classic passage in support of the doctrine of the papacy is Matthew 16:17–19.[12]

Matthew 16:17–19

In giving the names of the apostles, Matthew says that the first disciple was Simon who was later called Peter (Matt. 10:2). However, Catholic theologians claim that though Peter was not first in *time* (since Andrew preceded him), he was the first in *dignity*. Peter was made the foundation (the "rock") of Christ's church for the preservation of her perpetual unity and existence. He was made the supreme teacher of the faith as he is given the unique power to bind and loose, which is understood as rabbinical speech in giving the authentic declaration of the law. In this

---

9. The last infallible pronouncement made by Pope Pius XII in 1950 being the bodily assumption of Mary.

10. Dulles, "Infallibility," 78–79.

11. Dulles, "Infallibility," 71.

12. Again, the Catholic Church condemns the view that Peter and Paul were joint heads of the church. Pope Innocent X rejected this view as heretical in 1647. This heresy was propagated by the Jansenist Anton Arnauld. "The Primacy of power belongs to Peter alone; to Paul belongs a leadership in the promulgation of the faith," says Ott (Ludwig Ott, *Fundamentals of Catholic Dogma* [Rockford, IL: Tan, 1960], 282).

case it would be the declaration of the law of the new covenant, the gospel.[13] Ludwig Ott says, "God in heaven will confirm the Pope's judgment. This supposes that, in his capacity of supreme Doctor of Faith, he is preserved from error."[14]

God will confirm the pope's judgment on earth as it is in heaven, just as he revealed Christ's messiahship and divinity to Peter (Matt. 16:16–17). So, based on Peter's confession of Christ as "the Son of the living God," God has set him apart to be the natural foundation of the Son's society, that is, the church militant.[15] It is in this passage where Christ reveals what is meant elsewhere in Scripture, in John 1:42, when Christ told Peter that the apostle's name would be changed to *Cephas* (cf. Matt. 4:18 and 10:2)—the name *Cephas* in Aramaic literally means "rock" or "stone."[16] On the basis of this text Catholics argue not only for Peter's primacy (see chap. 3) but also for his infallibility. Briefly stated, they argue as follows:

1) The text clearly shows Peter's primacy since he is singled out as the "rock" in which Christ will build his church.
2) Peter is given "the keys." This means "Simon [Peter] is to be the ultimate authority on earth of this society, which is itself the hierarchical body described in [Matthew] 18:15–18."[17] Ott comments:

[Peter] is to be the holder of the keys, that is the steward of the Kingdom of God on earth (cf. Is. 22:22; Apoc. I, 18:3, 7; the keys as a symbol of power and dominion). He is to bind and loose, that is, following Rabbinical language, impose the ban or loose from the ban, and also interpreting the law, pronounce a thing to be forbidden (bound) or permitted (loosed). . . . The plenary power promised to Peter is not limited to his teaching power, but it extends to the whole sphere of jurisdiction. [Therefore,] God in heaven will confirm whatever obligations Peter will impose or dispense from in earth.[18]

13. Ibid., 280–81
14. Ibid., 281.
15. Dom B. Orchard, "The Gospel of Jesus Christ According to St. Matthew," in *A Catholic Commentary on Holy Scripture*, ed. Dom Bernard Orchard, et al. (London: Thomas Nelson, 1955), 881.
16. Stephen Ray notes that "in the Torah and in Jewish tradition, a name changed meant a change in status. . . . We see Simon's name changed by Jesus from Simon to *Kepha*, Peter, signifying a new designation, a new commission, and a new status" (Stephen Ray, *Upon This Rock: St. Peter and the Primacy of Rome in Scripture and the Early Church* [San Francisco: Ignatius Press, 1999], 24).
17. Orchard, "The Gospel of Jesus Christ," 881, emphasis added.
18. Ott, *Fundamentals*, 280.

3) Since "the gates of hell" (Matt. 16:18) are helpless against the church for which Peter has the authoritative keys, it follows that Peter must be infallible. Otherwise, Rome argues, Peter could not prevail in defining and defending the truth over against the errors of the Evil One.

4) Since Christ said he would build his church through Peter, it follows that Peter must share in the infallible authority of Christ in his function as head of Christ's church. The *Catechism of the Catholic Church* comments, "The Lord made Simon alone, whom he named Peter, the 'rock' of his Church. He gave him the keys of his Church and instituted him shepherd of the whole flock. 'The office of binding and loosing which was given to Peter was also assigned to the college of apostles united to its head [i.e., the Magisterium].' This pastoral office of Peter and the other apostles belongs to the Church's very foundation and is continued by the bishops under the primacy of the Pope."[19] Implied in this, Rome argues, is the concept of infallibility. The church and its head are unfailing in their magisterial role of teacher of Christ's truth.

Luke 22:31–32

Another text we have already considered that is often used to support the doctrine of the papacy is Luke 22:31–32. Though the text is relatively short, it supposedly contains an implicit truth about Peter—his infallible position as Christ's representative on earth. As we noted earlier, Steven K. Ray, Catholic apologist and theologian, says that the fact that Jesus prayed exclusively for Peter in this verse is a confirmation "that Christ had made [him] the leader, the rock [of the church], and had invested him with the keys." Thus, "Luke was not ignorant of the authority invested in Peter by our Lord. The whole apostolic band would be strengthened by the one for whom the Lord prayed—the one whom the Lord appointed as shepherd of his flock."[20]

John 21:15–17

Perhaps the second most cited text used to establish the notion that Christ appointed Peter to the *office* of the papacy and that he alone was

19. *Catechism of the Catholic Church*, 233, 881.
20. Ray, *Upon This Rock*, also mentions the fact that Jesus spoke directly to Simon, uttering his name twice for emphasis. Again, the prayer offered for the strengthening of Simon's faith was singular and not plural, which would have included the other apostles had it been plural.

given infallible *authority* to shepherd the flock of Christ is John 21:15–17. On the basis of this text, Catholic scholars claim:

1) Jesus appointed Peter alone to be the shepherd of the whole church, of all God's "sheep" and "lambs." So, Christ is the Chief Shepherd, the prime pastor of the Christian church. As Catholic commentator W. Leonard writes: "The whole flock (all the sheep of the Good Shepherd) are committed to Peter's care. So, Catholics claim that to understand this commission as anything less than a primacy of authority over the universal church is to falsify the text. The passage has been dogmatically interpreted in this traditional sense by the Vatican Council."[21]

2) Christ as shepherd of the whole church cannot accomplish the task of "feeding" all God's sheep without the gift of infallibility. Apart from infallibility, he could err and unwittingly lead the sheep astray. The words *feed* and *tend* when taken figuratively teach and promote the spiritual welfare of the members of the church.[22] Since this is the case, it stands to reason that if Christ was and is infallible, then so was Peter by virtue of his office as Christ's earthly vicar.

Indeed, the First Vatican Council affirmed that Peter was the "chief of apostles . . . the true vicar of Christ and head [shepherd] of the whole Church and faith, and of all Christians."[23] But again, Rome insists that Peter cannot accomplish this without unerring authority from God which is given to Peter alone. The *Catechism of the Catholic Church* emphasizes this point when it states the following:

> Jesus entrusted a specific authority to Peter: "I will give you the keys of the kingdom of heaven, and whatever you bind on earth shall be bound in heaven, and whatever you loose on earth shall be loosed in heaven." The "power of the keys" designates authority to govern the house of God, which is the Church. *Jesus, the Good Shepherd, confirmed this mandate after his Resurrection: "Feed my sheep."* The power to "bind and loose" connotes the authority to absolve sins, to pronounce doctrinal judgments, and to make disciplinary decisions in the Church. Jesus entrusted this authority to the Church through the ministry of Peter, the only one to whom he specifically entrusted the keys of the kingdom.[24]

21. W. Leonard, "The Gospel of Jesus Christ According to St. John," in *ACCHS*, 1017.
22. Ray, *Upon This Rock*, 49, n. 65.
23. Denzinger, *The Sources of Catholic Dogma*, no. 1837–40, p. 454.
24. *The Catechism of the Catholic Church*, 142, 553, emphasis added.

Other Biblical Texts[25]

Catholic scholars have offered many other biblical texts in support of the pope, but most of them apply, at best, only to the question of Peter's primacy and were discussed in chapter 3. There are some, however, that have been used to imply infallibility.

Isaiah 22:22. We already noted that the "key" refers to the steward-ship of the house of David that would be placed in the hands of Eliakim; thus, this text substantiates *a fortiori* what would be later true of Peter and the "keys" in reference to the kingdom of God. Thus Steven Ray argues, "The parallels between Peter and Eliakim are striking. The physical kingdom of Israel has been superseded by the spiritual kingdom of God. The office of steward in the old economy is now superseded by the Petrine office with the delegation and handing on of the keys. The office of steward was successive, and so is the Petrine office in the new kingdom."[26] From this one may imply the superior need for infallibility for the one who holds the keys to God's spiritual kingdom on earth.

Matthew 7:24. Jesus spoke of the wise man building his house on the "rock." Peter was the rock of the church for which she found her unity and unshakable strength. This, it can be reasoned, is possible only with an endowment of infallibility from God.

Matthew 10:2 (Mark 3:16). Peter was named first in the list of the apostles. This attests to the veracity of his superior position among the Twelve.

Matthew 17:1. In the inner circle of apostles, Peter, James, and John, Peter is listed first. And it was Peter who spoke on this glorious occasion of Christ's transfiguration.

John 11:49–52. It is argued that Caiaphas the high priest, in his official capacity as high priest, "unwittingly prophesied about Christ dying for the nation of Israel so that they would not perish."[27] So, just as in the Old Testament the high priest possessed an official revelatory function connected with his office, it is argued *a fortiori* that the same would be true in the New Testament with respect to Peter and his successors.[28]

Acts 1:12–16, 20–26. As with the doctrine of papal primacy, this passage is also utilized to support Peter's infallibility since his judgments

---

25. Unless otherwise noted, all scriptural texts in favor of supporting the papacy have been taken from Ott, *Fundamentals of Catholic Dogma.*
26. Ray, *Upon This Rock,* 274.
27. Norman L. Geisler and Ralph E. MacKenzie, *Roman Catholics and Evangelicals: Agreements and Differences* (Grand Rapids, MI: Baker, 1995), 206.
28. Ibid., 206–7.

were never questioned when he applied the Scriptures to a contemporary situation. This implies that his decisions could have been carried out infallibly. Again, the decision to replace Judas's office was carried out by Peter and not Jesus (who could have easily done so as Jesus was still physically present with the apostles).[29]

Acts 15:7. Peter "[was] the first to speak at the Council of the Apostles."[30] This supposedly indicated his authority over it.

In addition to the biblical argument, Catholic scholars also offer historical arguments for the infallibility of the pope. These, they believe, support the biblical arguments and provide further reason to believe in this crucial Catholic dogma.

Historical Evidence Offered by Rome for Papal Infallibility

There are several steps in the historical argument for the infallibility of Peter and the other bishops of Rome after him. The first part of the argument is that Peter went to Rome. The second argument is that he was a bishop there. The third is that the bishop of Rome had universal authority over the whole church. Arising from the first three arguments is the fourth—that this authority was infallible authority.

Peter's Presence in Rome

This is the first step of the historical argument for Peter's infallibility. Surprisingly, the New Testament has no explicit reference to Peter's ever being in Rome, whereas it clearly references Paul being there (Acts 28).

1 Peter 5:13. The only passage that could apply is a possible covert reference in Peter's first epistle where it refers to his being in Babylon (1 Pet. 5:13). Babylon is alleged by many scholars to be a symbolic word for Rome that Peter used to protect his identity from persecution from the Roman authorities.

While this is possible (cf. Rev. 17:5), it is by no means necessary. The reference here could be to a literal city of Babylon either in Egypt or in ancient Babylon where Peter had fled.

Clement of Rome (ca. AD 95)

Clement alleges to be a contemporary of Peter and Paul. Some claim that Clement is the person Paul referred to in Philippians 4:3. Rome claims that Clement was the third pope (after Peter and Linus). This claim is based on a fourth-century statement of Eusebius that "Clem-

29. Ray., *Upon This Rock*, 51, n. 68.
30. Ott, *Fundamentals*, 281.

ent also, who was appointed third pope of the church at Rome, was, as Paul testifies, his co-laborer and fellow-soldier [Phil. 4:3]."[31] However, Clement does not mention Peter's being in Rome, nor does he attribute any primacy or infallibility to Peter.

Ignatius (ca. AD 35–ca. 107)
Ignatius does speak of Peter, but he does not say Peter was in Rome. Neither is Peter given primacy by Ignatius but merely mentioned by him along with Paul. Ignatius wrote, "Not like Peter and Paul do I issue any order to you. They were Apostles, I am a convict; they were free, I am until this moment a slave."[32]

Origen (ca. AD 185–ca.254)
Origen writes the following: "Now Phlegon, in the thirteenth or fourteenth book, I think, of his Chronicles, not only ascribed to Jesus a knowledge of future events (although falling into the confusion about some things which *refer to Peter*, as if they referred to Jesus), but also testified that the result corresponded to His predictions."[33] But Origen does not place Peter in Rome.

Irenaeus of Lyons (ca. AD 130–ca. 200)
The first clear reference to Peter's being in Rome comes over a century after the time of Peter. Irenaeus wrote, "Matthew also issued a written Gospel among the Hebrews in their own dialect, while Peter and Paul were preaching at Rome, and laying the foundation of the Church"[34]

Clement of Alexandria (AD 190–210)
By the third century Peter is not only placed in Rome but given prominence there. Clement wrote, "Therefore on hearing those words, the blessed Peter, the chosen, the pre-eminent, the first of the disciples, for whom alone and Himself the Saviour paid tribute [Matt. 17:27], quickly seized and comprehended the saying."[35]

31. Eusebius, "Church History," in *The Nicene and Post-Nicene Fathers*, vol. 1, 3:137.
32. Ignatius of Antioch, "The Epistle of Ignatius to the Romans," in *The Ante-Nicene Fathers*, vol. 1, ed. Alexander Roberts, et al. (Peabody, MA: Hendrickson, 1994), 1, emphasis added; "The Epistle of St. Clement of Rome and St. Ignatius of Antioch," trans. James A. Kleist, Ancient Christian Writers (New York: Newman Press, 1946), 1:82; quoted in Ray, *Upon This Rock*, 72, n. 17
33. Origen, "Against Celsus," in *The Ante-Nicene Fathers*, vol. 4, *xiv*, 437.
34. Irenaeus, *Haer.* 3.1.1.
35. Clement of Alexandria, "Who is the Rich Man that Shall be Saved?" in *The Ante-Nicene Fathers*, vol. 2, *xxi*, 597.

Tertullian (ca. AD 160–ca. 225)

Tertullian challenged the heretics, saying:

> Let them produce the original records of their churches; let them unfold the roll of their bishops, running down in due succession from the beginning. . . . For this is the manner in which the apostolic churches transmit their registers: as the church of Smyrna, which records that Polycarp was placed therein by John; also the church of Rome, which makes Clement to have been ordained by Peter.[36]

He adds, "Peter, who is called 'the rock on which the church should be built,' who also obtained 'the keys of the kingdom of heaven,' with the power of 'loosing and binding in heaven and on earth.'"[37] From this they conclude that Peter was not only in Rome, but that he had a primary apostolic role there.

Eusebius (ca. AD 325)

By the time of the first pro-Christian emperor, Constantine, in the fourth century, the tradition of Peter being in Rome was firmly in place. He wrote: "[Peter] having come to Rome . . . was crucified head-downwards; for he had requested that he might suffer in this way."[38] Further, Eusebius says concerning the apostolic succession of the episcopate that "after the martyrdom of Paul and of Peter, Linus was the first to obtain the episcopate of the church of Rome. Paul mentions him, when writing to Timothy from Rome, in the salutation at the end of the epistle [2 Tim. 4:21]."[39] From this point on there are numerous references to Peter being in Rome. These include references by Chrysologous (ca. 400–450), Pope Innocent I (402), Leo the Great (440), and others.

Peter Was a Bishop in Rome

Having presented the evidence that Peter went to Rome, it remains to show that he was the first bishop of Rome, that the bishop of Rome had universal authority over the whole church, and, finally, that the bishop of Rome had infallible authority over the entire church. For the first two points Roman Catholics point to the following evidence:

36. Tertullian, "On Prescription Against Heretics," in *The Ante-Nicene Fathers*, vol. 3, *xxii*, 1–3.
37. Ibid., *xxii*.
38. Eusebius, "Church History," in *The Nicene and Post-Nicene Fathers*, vol. 1, III:132–33.
39. Ibid.

Eusebius

Eusebius says, concerning the apostolic succession of the episcopate, "After the martyrdom of Paul and of Peter, Linus was the first to obtain the episcopate of the church of Rome. Paul mentions him, when writing to Timothy from Rome, in the salutation at the end of the epistle [2 Tim. 4:21]."[40]

Clement of Rome

There is no direct reference from Clement of Rome to Peter's being bishop of Rome. Nor is there any affirmation of his having universal authority over the church. Clement simply refers to Peter's prominence in the church alongside the apostle Paul and to the martyrdom of both.[41]

Ignatius

Ignatius wrote seven important letters containing ecclesiastical information, five of which were addressed to the Christian communities of Ephesus, Magnesia, Tralles, Philadelphia, and Smyrna; the other two were addressed to Polycarp and to the "Christian community residing at his destination—Rome."[42] In his letter addressed to the Romans he makes no reference to Peter's being bishop there, and he places Peter and Paul on the same authoritative level, saying, "Not like Peter and Paul do I issue any order to you. They were Apostles, I am a convict; they were free, I am until this moment a slave."[43]

Ludwig Ott writes that "St. Ignatius of Antioch recognizes of the Christians of Rome that they 'are purified of every foreign colour,' that is, are free from every false doctrine (Rom. Insc.)."[44] Ott suggests that Ignatius probably had Clement's letter (the Catholic Church considers

40. Ibid.

41. Clement, "The First Epistle of Clement to the Corinthians," in *The Ante-Nicene Fathers*, vol. 1, 5:1–6.

42. Ibid., 72, n. 15. Ray states that Ignatius's "letters are an important source of information about the beliefs and organization of the early Christian Church. Ignatius wrote them as warnings against heretical doctrines, thus providing his readers with detailed summaries of Christian doctrine. He also gave a vivid picture of church organization as a community of love gathered around a presiding bishop assisted by a council of presbyters (elders) and deacons. In his writings he stressed the virgin birth of Christ, the threefold hierarchy of the Church (bishop, priests, and deacons), the Eucharist as a sacrifice, and the Real Presence of Christ; and he was the first person known to have used the term *catholic* to describe the universal Church" (ibid.).

43. Ignatius of Antioch, "The Epistle of Ignatius to the Romans," in *The Ante-Nicene Fathers*, vol. 1, *i*, emphasis added; "The Epistle of St. Clement of Rome and St. Ignatius of Antioch," 1:82; quoted in Ray, *Upon This Rock*, 72, n. 17.

44. Ott, *Fundamentals*, 281.

Clement as the third successive pope) in mind when Ignatius wrote, "You have taught others." Perhaps this is, at least to the Catholic observer, an appeal to Clement's authority as the bishop of Rome.

Origen

Catholic scholars claim that in Origen's treatise *Against Celsus* he writes of a person named Phlegon, presumably the emperor Hadrian writing under a pseudonym, which, according to Catholic apologist Ray, "is very significant as implying that Peter must have been well known in Rome."[45] This, some Catholic scholars claim, reveals that Peter had spiritual authority in the church throughout the Roman domain. Origen wrote of Peter: "Upon whom is built the Church of Christ, against which the gates of hell shall not prevail, left only one Epistle of acknowledged genuinity. Let us concede also a second, which however, is doubtful."[46] He added, "Look at the great foundation of the Church, that most solid of rocks, upon whom Christ built the Church! And what does the Lord say to him? 'O you of little faith,' He says, 'why did you doubt!'"[47]

Irenaeus of Lyons

Catholic scholars appeal to Irenaeus as an early and clear example of one who held to the universal authority of the Catholic Church from Rome, where Peter is said to have been bishop. In *Against Heresies* Irenaeus referred to

> that tradition derived from the apostles, of the very great, the very ancient, and universally known Church founded and organized at Rome by the two most glorious apostles, Peter and Paul; as also by pointing out the faith preached to men, which comes down to our times by means of the succession of the bishops. . . . It is a matter of necessity that *every Church should agree with this Church*, on account of its preeminent authority, that is, the faithful everywhere, inasmuch as the apostolic tradition has been preserved continuously by those faithful men who exist everywhere.[48]

Clement of Alexandria

Clement of Alexandria claimed that Matthew 17:27 clearly favors the primacy of Peter who was bishop of Rome.

45. Ray, *Upon This Rock*, 73, n. 19.

46. Origen, "Commentaries on John," in *The Faith of the Early Fathers*, vol. 1, ed. Jurgen A. Williams (Collegeville, MN: Liturgical Press, 1976), 3, 5; quoted by Ray, *Upon This Rock*, 177, n. 58.

47. Origen, "Homilies on Exodus," in *The Faith of the Early Fathers*, vol. 1, 4–5.

48. Irenaeus, *Haer.* 3.3.2, emphasis added.

Tertullian

The early apologist Tertullian is claimed by Rome in its support of the papacy. Ludwig Ott wrote that Tertullian "speaks of the Church: 'which was built on him'" (De monog. 8).[49] The "him" referred to by Tertullian is none other than Peter, says Rome. He also cites him claiming there is a line of succession that goes back to Peter. Tertullian said:

> For this is the manner in which the apostolic churches transmit their registers: as the church of Smyrna, which records that Polycarp was placed therein by John; also the church of Rome, which makes Clement to have been ordained by Peter. In exactly the same way the other churches likewise exhibit (their several worthies), whom, as having been appointed to their episcopal places by apostles, they regard as transmitters of the apostolic seed.[50]

Cyprian, Bishop of Carthage (AD 248–258)

Commenting on Matthew 16:18, Cyprian said, "He builds the Church on one person" (De monog. 8).[51] Again the *one person* mentioned in Cyprian's commentary is a reference to Peter. He wrote:

> The Lord says to Peter, "I say unto thee that thou art Peter," etc. (Matt. xvi. 18, 19). . . . He builds his church on *one man* . . . ordained by his authority the source [and system] of unity *beginning from one man.* . . . Our Lord, whose precepts and admonitions we are bound to observe, ordered the high office of bishop and the system of his Church when he speaks in the Gospel and says to Peter, "Thou art Peter," etc. (Matt. xvi. 18, 19).[52]

Cyril of Jerusalem (b. AD 315–d. 386)

Cyril calls Peter, "'The head and the leader of the Apostles' (Cat. 2, 19)."[53] Thus, Catholics believe Cyril is another early voice that attested to the primacy of Peter as the "rock" and, consequently, to the validity of the apostolic authority built on him.

49. Quoted in Ott, *Fundamentals,* 281.
50. Tertullian, "On Prescription Against Heretics," in *The Ante-Nicene Fathers,* vol. 3, *xxii,* 1–3.
51. Ott, *Fundamentals,* 281.
52. Cyprian of Carthage, "On the Unity of the Church," in *Documents of the Christian Church,* rev. ed., ed. Henry Bettenson and Chris Maunder (Oxford: Oxford University Press, 1999), 78–80.
53. Ott, *Fundamentals,* 281.

Athanasius (c. AD 296–373)

Rome also claims the great defender of orthodoxy against Arianism in favor of the authority of Rome over the church. Athanasius is said to have been quoting Pope Julius in defense of his own orthodoxy[54] when he wrote, "When I left Alexandria, I did not go to your brother's headquarters, or to any other persons, but only Rome; and having laid my case before the Church (for this was my concern), I spent my time in the public worship."[55]

Basil the Great (AD 330–379)

Basil the Great, known as one of the great Cappadocian Fathers, writes, "When we hear the name of Peter, that name does not cause our minds to dwell on his substance, but we figure to our minds the properties that are connected with him. For at once, on hearing that name, think of the son of him that was called from amongst fisherman unto the ministry of the Apostleship; him who on account of the pre-eminence of his faith received upon himself the building of the Church."[56]

Gregory of Nyssa (ca. AD 330–395)

Gregory was the younger brother of Basil the Great. Concerning Peter he writes: "Peter, with his whole soul, associates himself with the Lamb, and by means of the change of his name, he is changed by the Lord into something more divine; instead of Simon being both called and having become a rock (Peter)."[57] Thus, "the memory of Peter, the head of the Apostles, is celebrated" and magnified indeed with him are the other members of the Church; but (upon him) is the Church of God firmly established. For "he is, agreeably to the gift conferred upon him by the Lord, that *unbroken* and most firm rock upon which the Lord built His Church."[58]

Gregory of Nazianzen (ca. AD 329–389)

Another Cappadocian father says this concerning Peter: "Seest thou that of the disciples of Christ, all of whom were great and deserving of the choice, one is called rock, and is entrusted with the foundations of the Church; whilst another is the beloved, and reposed on the breast

54. Ray, *Upon This Rock*, 201.
55. Athanasius, "In Defense before Constantius," in *The Nicene and Post-Nicene Fathers*, vol. 4, 4.
56. Basil the Great, "Adv. Eunom.," in *Faith of Catholics*, vol. 2, comp. Joseph Berington and John Kirk, ed. T. J. Capel (New York: Pustet, 1885), 22; quoted by Ray, *Upon This Rock*, 206.
57. Gregory of Nyssa, "Homily," in *Faith of Catholics*, vol. 2, 20–21.
58. Gregory of Nyssa, "Alt. Or. De. S. Steph.," in *Faith of Catholics*, 2:21, emphasis added.

of Jesus; and the rest bear with the prior honor (thus bestowed)."[59] Further, "neither does a man know, though he be the parent of an evil unto Judas, whether his offspring shall be called the godlike Paul, or be like unto Peter—Peter who became the unbroken rock, and who had the keys delivered to him."[60]

Pope Innocent I (AD 402)
One would expect that Pope Innocent I, who was crowned pope in 402, would make substantial claims for the papacy, and he did. He wrote:

> In your pursuit of the things of God ... following the examples of ancient tradition ... you have made manifest by your proper course of action ... when you agreed to have recourse to our judgment, knowing what is due to the apostolic See, since all of us placed in this position wish to follow the apostle [Peter], from whom have come this episcopate and all the authority belonging to this dignity.

He added:

> They decreed, not with human but with divine judgment, that no deci-sion (even though it concerned the most remote provinces) was to be considered final unless this See were to hear of it, so that all the authority of this See might confirm whatever just decision was reached. From this See the other Churches receive the confirmation of what they ought to ordain, just as all waters proceed from their source and through diverse regions of the world remain pure liquids of an uncorrupted source.[61]

Peter Chrysologous (ca. AD 400–450)
Chrysologous says of the Roman pontiff: "'The blessed Peter who on his Bishop's Chair lives on and leads the council, offers true Faith to those that seek it' (with Leo, Ep. 25, 2)."[62] Again, this is another voice from antiquity in defense of the papacy.

Augustine (d. AD 430)
This great teacher of the Catholic faith is used in favor of the primacy of Peter and the authority of the Catholic Church. Augustine wrote: "For my part, I should not believe the gospel except by the authority

59. Gregory of Nazianzen, "Oration," in *Faith of Catholics*, vol. 5, 20–21.
60. Gregory of Nazianzen, "Carm" in *Faith of Catholics*, vol. 2, 20–21.
61. J. Neuner, S. J. and J. Dupuis, S. J., *The Christian Faith: In the Doctrinal Documents of the Catholic Church* (New York: Alba, 1996), 279, 801.
62. Quoted in Ott, *Fundamentals*, 288.

of the Catholic Church." Again, speaking of the Scripture (in Acts), he said, "Which book I must needs believe if I believe the gospel, since both writings alike Catholic authority commends to me."[63] Elsewhere he added, "The Catholic Church alone is the body of Christ, of which He is the Head and Saviour of His body. Outside this body the Holy Spirit giveth life to no one."[64] Significantly, however, Augustine did not believe Peter was the "rock" Christ referenced in Matthew 16.

Leo the Great (d. AD 461)

Leo assumed his reign in AD 440 wherein he perpetuated the Roman claims for the papacy, saying, "For the solidity of that faith which was praised in the chief of the Apostles is perpetual: and as that remains which Peter believed in Christ, so that remains which Christ instituted in Peter. . . . The dispensation of Truth therefore abides, and the blessed Peter preserving in the strength of the Rock, which he has received, has not abandoned the helm of the Church, which he undertook."[65] Leo further states that "'Only Peter was chosen out of the whole world to be the Head of all called peoples, of all Apostles and of all the Fathers of the Church' (Sermo 4, 2)."[66]

So, according to Roman Catholic scholars, the Fathers form a strong argument for the authority of Peter, Bishop of Rome, and his successors and to the claim of universal authority over the whole Christian church. Likewise, the church councils add to this growing claim.

The Council of Nicea (AD 325)

Almost all sections of Christendom accept the doctrinal pronouncements of this great ecumenical council. The Nicene Creed they produced is recognized almost universally. Lesser known is the fact that the Roman Catholic Church claims Nicea to support its authority through Christendom as well. Canon VI declares: "Let the ancient customs in Egypt, Libya and Pentapolis prevail, that the Bishop of Alexandria have jurisdiction in all these, since the like is customary for the Bishop of Rome."[67] It is claimed that Rome is here set as the standard for all churches.

---

63. Augustine, *Against the Epistle of the Manichaens*, 5.5.6, in Schaff, *Nicene and Post-Nicene Fathers*, 4:131.
64. Augustine, *The Correction of the Donatists* (11.50), in Schaff, *Nicene and Post-Nicene Fathers*, 651.
65. Leo the Great, "Sermons," in Schaff, *Nicene and Post-Nicene Fathers*, 12:iii, 2, 3.
66. Quoted in Ott, *Fundamentals*, 281.
67. "The First Ecumenical Council: The Council of Nicea," in Schaff, *Nicene and Post-Nicene Fathers*, 14:15.

The Council of Ephesus (AD 431)

This ecumenical council declared, "No one doubts, in fact, it is obvious to all ages that holy and most Blessed Peter, head and Prince of the Apostles, the pillar of faith, and the foundation of the Catholic Church, received the keys of the kingdom from our Lord Jesus Christ, the savior and the redeemer of the human race. Nor does anyone doubt that the power of forgiving and retaining sins was also given to this same Peter who, in his successors, lives and exercises judgment even to this time and forever."[68]

The Council of Chalcedon (AD 451)

The second session opens by declaring that "Peter has spoken thus through Leo."[69] The council went on to say, "Wherefore the most holy and blessed Leo, archbishop of the great and elder Rome, through us, and through this present most holy synod together with the thrice blessed and all-glorious Peter the Apostle, who is the rock and foundation of the Catholic Church, and the foundation of the orthodox faith . . ."[70] In short, the primacy of Peter is reaffirmed here.

The Second Council of Lyons (AD 1274)

The council declared:

> The holy Roman Church possesses the supreme and full primacy and authority over the universal Catholic Church, which she recognizes in truth and humility to have received with fulness of power from the Lord himself in the person of Blessed Peter, the Prince or head of the apostles, of whom the Roman Pontiff is the successor. And, as she is bound above all to defend the truth of faith, so too, if any questions should arise regarding the faith, they must be deciding by her judgement.[71]

The Council of Trent (AD 1566)

In response to the Protestant Reformation, the Council of Trent stated that "a visible Church requires a visible head; therefore the Saviour appointed Peter head and pastor of all the faithful, when He committed to his care the feeding of all His sheep."[72] This growing papal authority, tracing itself back to Peter, all came to a climax at the First Vatican

---

68. Clarkson, S. J., et al., *The Church Teaches*, 69, 146.
69. "The Fourth Ecumenical Council: The Council of Chalcedon," in Schaff, *Nicene and Post-Nicene Fathers*, 14:259.
70. Ibid., 259–60.
71. Neuner, *The Christian Faith*, 296, 833.
72. *The Catechism of the Council of Trent*, rev. ed., trans. J. A. MacHugh and C. J. Cullan (Rockford, IL: Tan, 1982), 103; quoted in Ray, *Upon This Rock*, 246.

Council where not only was Peter recognized as the first pope but also both he and his successors were recognized as infallible.

The First Vatican Council (AD 1870)
This council declared: "The Roman Pontiff, when he speaks *ex cathedra* ['from the chair'], that is, when carrying out the duty of the pastor and teacher of all Christians in accord with his supreme apostolic authority, he explains a doctrine of faith or morals to be held by the universal Church, through the divine assistance promised in blessed Peter, [who] operates with that infallibility [given by] . . . the divine Redeemer."[73]

The Second Vatican Council (AD 1962–1965)
At this council the claim to infallibility was repeated one hundred years later: "The Roman Pontiff, as the successor of Peter, is the perpetual and visible source and foundation of the unity both of the bishops and the whole company of the faithful."[74]

Catechism of the Catholic Church (AD 1994)
The most recent *Catechism of the Catholic Church* caps off the Roman claim to papal supremacy and infallibility in these words: "When Christ instituted the Twelve, 'constituted [them] in the form of a college or permanent assembly, at the head of which he placed Peter, chosen from among them.'" Just as "by the Lord's institution, St. Peter and the rest of the apostles constitute a single apostolic college, so in like fashion the Roman Pontiff, Peter's successor, and the bishops, the successors of the apostles, are related with and united to one another."[75] It added, "The body of bishops has no authority unless united with the Roman Pontiff, Peter's successor, as its head" (No. 883). And this authority includes "infallibility" (No. 889) because the magisterium "unfailingly adheres to this faith" (No. 890).

Thus ends the claim to growing authority for general jurisdiction by Rome over all the churches to infallible pronouncements by it on doctrine and morals. It remains now to examine the theological argument in favor of this claim for papal infallibility.

The Theological Arguments Offered by Rome for Papal Infallibility
Even granting that Peter was recognized as the first bishop of Rome, which by no means all scholars do, and even granting universal juris-

73. Denzinger, *The Sources of Catholic Dogma*, 457.
74. Flannery, "Lumen Gentium," 380.
75. *Catechism of the Catholic Church* (Vatican City: Libreria Editrice Vaticana, 1994), 880.

diction of Rome over the whole church, which all other sections of Christendom deny, there is another important link in the chain that is necessary to establish, namely, the infallibility of the pope.

The Argument for Infallibility from the Nature of Causality

It is of the nature of causality that every effect must have a cause. It is also true that the effect cannot be greater than the cause. Using these principles, contemporary Catholic philosopher Peter Kreeft argued that "the church must be infallible if the Bible is [infallible], since the effect cannot be greater than the cause and the church caused the canon."[76] The argument can be stated in this way:

1) For every effect there is a cause.
2) The effect is never greater than its cause.
3) The Bible came into existence (was caused by another).
4) The church ratified (caused) the canon of Scripture.
5) If the Bible is infallible, then the church must be infallible, too (since the effect is never greater than its cause).
6) Therefore, the church is infallible and is thus logically prior to the Bible as its cause.

In short, an infallible Bible, which orthodox Protestants accept, demands an infallible church to produce it. Hence, granted what even Protestants believe about the Bible, there must have been an infallible church to produce it.

The Argument for Infallibility from the Nature of Truth

The infallibility of the church is also deduced from the nature of truth. For one cannot know something is true unless it is without error.[77] The argument can be formally stated as follows:[78]

---

76. Kreeft, as summarized by Geisler and Mackenzie in *Roman Catholics and Evangelicals*, 173. Utilizing the principle of causality against the Protestant principle of *sola Scriptura*, Kreeft writes, "It violates the principle of causality: that an effect cannot be greater than its cause. The Church (the apostles) wrote Scripture; and the successors of the apostles, i.e., the bishops of the Church, decided on the canon, the list of books to be declared scriptural and infallible. If Scripture is infallible, then its cause, the Church, must be infallible"; as quoted by Philip Blosser, "What Are the Philosophical and Practical Problems with *Sola Scriptura*," in *Not By Scripture Alone*, ed. Robert Sungenis (Santa Barbara, CA: Queenship, 1997), in Keith A. Mathison, *The Shape of Sola Scriptura* (Moscow, ID: Canon Press, 2001), 291.

77. The Principle of Non-contradiction; see Geisler, "First Principles," in *BECA*, 250–52.

78. Norman L. Geisler, "Arguments for the Infallibility of the Roman Catholic Church" (unpublished paper, 2005).

1) We cannot know truth unless we know it without error (otherwise it would not be truth).
2) But to know truth without error is to know infallibly.
3) Hence, we cannot know the truth of Scripture without knowing it infallibly.
4) But we do not know the truth of Scripture.
5) Hence, we must know it infallibly.
6) But we know the truth of Scripture only through the teaching of the church.
7) Hence, the magisterium of the church must be infallible.

The Argument for Infallibility from the Self-defeating Nature of Its Denials

Catholic apologists often charge evangelicals with making self-defeating statements in their denial of an infallible authority because evangelicals elevate a certain authority or tradition of their own. And just as it is self-defeating to assert that there are no absolutes, Catholic apologists argue that it is equally self-defeating to assert that no authority is needed to interpret the Bible, because when someone seeks to understand Scripture, he actually is providing an authority—himself. The Catholic argument can be stated as follows:

1) The statement "there is no infallible authority for the church" is self-defeating.
2) Self-defeating statements are false.
3) Therefore, there is an infallible authority for the church.
4) The Roman Catholic Church has rightful claim to be that authority.
5) Therefore, the Roman Catholic Church is the infallible authority for the universal church.

The Argument for Infallibility from the "Self-contradictory" Nature of Sola Scriptura

Protestants have opposed the Roman view of papal authority by stressing the authority of the Bible alone without the need for an infallible interpreter of it. But Roman Catholic scholars insist that the concept of *sola Scriptura* is self-contradictory.[79] Why? Because "unqualified biblicism is not biblical." In short, Rome's argument can be summarized as follows:

79. Wladimir D'Ormesson, *The Papacy* (New York: Hawthorne Books, 1959), 36.

The Protestant principle of *sola Scriptura* teaches that one ought to believe only what the Scriptures say about faith and practice, but the Bible never states this principle. It couldn't state it because it is a statement about the whole Bible, which the Bible can't make about itself. Only another source could make it. Therefore, the principle of *sola Scriptura* is self-defeating.

The Argument for Infallibility from the Alleged Self-clarity of the Bible

Protestants claim that the essential message of the Bible is sufficiently clear (perspicuous), that it needs no interpreter. But one cannot know what the essential message is without the help of an interpreter. Hence, the Bible needs an interpreter to be understood. The argument can be stated more fully in this form:

1) Protestants claim that the essential message of the Bible is sufficiently clear so that it needs no interpreter.
2) It is impossible to know what the essential message is without an interpreter.
3) In order to know that an interpreter's interpretation is true, it must be known infallibly; otherwise, it could be wrong.
4) Therefore, the only way to know for sure what is the essential message of the Bible, is to have an infallible interpreter.

The Argument for Infallibility from the Nature of the Canon

Both Catholics and Protestants agree that there is a fixed and closed canon of Scripture. But the canon did not fix and close itself. Therefore, there must be some entity outside the canon that fixed and closed it. This argument breaks down this way:

1) The canon of Scripture is fixed and closed.
2) The canon cannot fix and close itself.
3) Therefore, some other entity fixed and closed the canon.
4) The entity that fixed and closed the canon is the church.
5) The canon can be closed with finality only by infallibility.
6) Thus, an infallible church was needed to fix and close the canon.

In short, the Bible has no inspired table of contents. Someone else had to do that. Historically, Catholics argue, it was the Roman Church that composed the table of contents of the Bible.

The Argument for Infallibility Based on Historical Improbability

Roman Catholic apologist Philip Blosser objects to *sola Scriptura* when he says:

> The doctrine that Scripture *alone* is sufficient to function as the *regula fidei*—the infallible rule for the ongoing faith and life of the Church—is of highly improbable orthodoxy since . . . it had no defender for the first centuries of the Church. It does not belong to historic Christianity. . . . It wasn't until the theologians of the Protestant Reformation elevated the notion into a principle in the sixteenth century that it became widespread.[80]

Broken down the argument looks like this:

1) Whatever is highly improbable is not true.
2) *Sola Scriptura* is highly improbable since it had no defenders for the first sixteen centuries of the church.
3) Hence, *sola Scriptura* is not true.

The second premise is defended by the historical claim that *sola Scriptura* had no defender for the first sixteen centuries. If it had been true, there would have been proponents of it earlier than this.

The Argument for Infallibility Based on the Inconsistency of Its Opposition with the New Testament Church

It is argued that since the church did not have a universally available copy of the entire New Testament for several centuries, the early church could not have functioned under the notion of *sola Scriptura*. Logically stated:

1) *Sola Scriptura* demands that the Bible alone is sufficient for faith and practice.
2) The church universal had only an incomplete copy of the Bible for many centuries.
3) Hence, the Bible-alone principle was not necessary for the church to operate.

The Argument for Infallibility Based on Protestant Failure to Recognize Extrabiblical Influences

Others have argued that "a certain disdain for history and lack of historical consciousness fostered by *sola Scriptura* can make its adherents

---

80. Philip Blosser, "What Are the Philosophical and Practical Problems of Sola Scriptura?" in *Not by Scripture Alone*, ed. Robert Sungenis (Santa Barbara, CA: Queenship, 1997), 66; cited by Keith A. Mathison, *The Shape of Sola Scriptura* (Moscow, ID: Canon Press, 2001), 294.

particularly vulnerable to extra-biblical historical influences on their own thinking."[81] This being the case, it is alleged that evangelicals unwittingly "read their philosophical assumptions into Scripture."[82] The argument dissected appears this way:

1) Trusting the Bible-alone premise makes one vulnerable to danger-ous extrabiblical influences.
2) Protestants trust the Bible-alone principle.
3) Hence, Protestants are more vulnerable to extrabiblical influences than Catholics, who do not trust that principle.

Indeed, Catholics claim to have an infallible guide to ward off such influences. Hence, only Catholics have a sure guarantee of ward-ing off dangerous extrabiblical influences. This, they claim, can be supported by the history of splintering in Protestantism vs. that of Catholicism.

The Argument for Infallibility from the Failure of the Opposing View to Provide a Proper Context for Interpretation

Briefly stated, it is argued by Catholic apologists, "*Sola Scriptura* assumes no ultimate need for the larger context of the Church's tradition and teaching."[83] Thus Scripture becomes removed from her ancient context and becomes an isolated book with no certain foundation or community of faith to insure the fidelity of its interpretation. Rome claims that an infallible interpreter provides a proper context and removes this difficulty. Thus,

1) It is dangerous to the faith to remove the Bible from its proper context in order to interpret it.
2) Protestants remove it from its context by their principle of *sola Scriptura*.
3) Hence, Protestant use of this principle is dangerous to the faith.

Blosser gives many reasons for this. First, it fails to distinguish matters of dogma from matters of discipline; second, it fails to understand the principle of doctrinal development; third, it fails to distinguish official teachings from private opinion; fourth, it fails to reckon history; fifth, and last, it fails to translate Scripture accurately.[84]

81. Ibid., 70.
82. Ibid.
83. Ibid.
84. Ibid., 66.

The Argument for Infallibility from the Consent of the Church Fathers

Blosser argues:

> Protestant adherents of *sola Scriptura* misinterpret the Church fathers because, while they are able to find fathers who affirm the unique inspiration of Scripture, they cannot find "a Church Father who affirms that the whole content of God's revelation for the ongoing instruction of His Church was committed wholly to Scripture without residue, so that it serves in that capacity as a text, *apart* from the larger tradition and ongoing community of memory of which it is a part."[85]

Stated succinctly,

1) What is not in accord with the consent of the Fathers is false.
2) The Protestant principle of *sola Scriptura* is not in accord with the consent of the Fathers.
3) Therefore, the Protestant principle of *sola Scriptura* is false.

The Argument for Infallibility from the Hermeneutical Anarchy That Results without It

Many evangelicals who have converted to Catholicism have offered reasons for their departure from Protestantism related to what Catholic apologists have called "hermeneutical anarchy." Blosser writes:

> The fact that hundreds of denominations, each professing to derive its teaching by means of the Holy Spirit's guidance from "Scripture alone," cannot even agree on the fundamentals of that faith, such as the meaning of baptism or the Lord's Supper or even the means of salvation, constitutes a powerful *prima facie* case against it. The principle itself becomes impracticable and self-undermining—a recipe for anarchy.[86]

The basic argument can be formed this way:

1) Without an infallible interpreter, hermeneutical anarchy results.
2) Non-Catholics reject an infallible interpreter.
3) Therefore, hermeneutical anarchy results from rejecting an infallible interpreter.

85. Ibid., 78.
86. Ibid., 91–93.

As Blosser put it, "As a result of its hermeneutical anarchy, *sola Scriptura* has splintered into denominational factionalism. It has spawned thousands of denominations, and sects and conventicles." Alister McGrath reported that there exist some twenty thousand Christian denominations worldwide—a number Catholic writers exploit in their critique of Protestantism, as seen above.[87]

The Argument for Infallibility from the Fact That Opposing It Undermines Pastoral Authority and Discipline

Blosser writes, "What does it mean for *him* to 'submit' to his spiritual leaders? Clearly the Bible enjoins him to do so. But to which leaders? And what does it mean for him to *submit*, if spiritual leaders are to gain his submission only in so far as their leadership and teaching agree with (his own interpretation of) Scripture?"[88] Clearly for Rome, it is impossible even to be a faithful Christian without having the proper authority to guide his or her walk with God. In brief, the reasoning goes like this:

1) Pastoral authority is undermined without an infallible authority.
2) Non-Catholics do not have an infallible authority.
3) Hence, the non-Catholic view (of no infallible authority) undermines pastoral authority.

The Argument for Infallibility from the Need for Ecumenical Councils

The Roman argument from the ecumenical councils can be stated in this way:[89]

1) There must be a divinely appointed authority to settle doctrinal and moral disputes.
2) The ecumenical councils of the church are the proper authority for settling doctrinal and moral disputes because this is the church as a whole operating in unison.
3) One cannot accept some of the ecumenical councils without accepting the others.
4) If all are accepted, then the Roman Catholic Church is that divinely appointed doctrinal authority.

87. McGrath, *Future of Christianity*, 83.
88. Blosser, "What Are the Philosophical and Practical Problems?" 102.
89. Geisler, "Arguments for the Infallibility of the Roman Catholic Church."

Conclusion

There are several links in the Roman Catholic claim to being the true church of Christ on earth. First, Catholics believe in the primacy of Peter. Their conviction that he was chief among the apostles provides the second link, that of Peter's infallibility. In this chapter we have set forth the biblical, historical, and theological bases for this link. Together these bases make the claim for the infallibility of Peter as the first bishop of Rome. In the next chapter we will evaluate that claim.

CHAPTER 5

THE ROMAN ARGUMENT FOR THE INFALLIBILITY OF PETER: EVALUATED

As the earlier chapters have shown, several crucial steps exist in the Roman Catholic argument for the infallibility of Peter. To review, first, he had primacy over the other apostles. Second, this primacy necessarily involved infallibility. Third, the infallibility was passed on to Peter's successors. Fourth, the present pope is the successor of Peter.

We have already examined the primacy of Peter and found no real basis for the teaching in Scripture or in the earliest fathers of the church. Thus, a fundamental pillar of infallibility has already proven false. So in a basic sense this chapter is unnecessary since Peter did not even have primacy, which is the prerequisite of infallibility. Nonetheless, in this chapter we will examine the biblical, historical, and theological basis for infallibility to show that both the first and second links of the Roman argument are broken. If any one of them proves to be without sufficient grounds, then the castle of Catholicism crumbles. So, not only is the chain of argument broken because the first link is broken, but the second link is also broken. Thus, even if the first link were good, the argument would still be broken.

An Evaluation of the Biblical Evidence for the Infallibility of Peter

The three main texts used to support primacy are crucial to the whole Roman argument. If they are not sound, then the Roman Church is built on sand, not on rock.[1]

Matthew 16:18

The important statement here is found in Jesus' words to Peter: "I also say to you that you are Peter, and *upon this rock I will build My church*" (NASB). Two things must be noted in response to the Catholic argument for the primacy of Peter based on this text. First, even if it could be shown that Peter is the "rock" on which Christ said he would build his church, the Catholic claim for the infallibility of Peter would not necessarily follow. For Peter was part of the apostolic rock-like foundation on which the church was built. As the apostle Paul declared, the church is "built on the foundation of the apostles [plural] and prophets, Jesus Christ Himself being the chief cornerstone" (Eph. 2:20 NKJV). Indeed, the same power to bind and loose given in Matthew 16:19 was given to all the apostles (Matt. 18:18). And the fact that Jesus is speaking only to Peter in Matthew 16 is understandable, since he is responding to Peter's confession about his being the Son of God. What is more, making Peter a rock in the foundation of the church does not thereby endow him with all of the magisterial authority Rome loads into the term "infallibility" (see chap. 4). It may indicate no more than spiritual leadership, which Peter certainly did exercise in the early church, as both Protestants and Catholics agree.

Furthermore, there are good reasons to believe that Peter was not the "rock" to which Christ referred in Matthew 16.

First, Peter's confession that Jesus was the Son of God was the occasion for Christ's statement.

Second, Jesus used two different words in the inspired text: "You are Peter [*petros*, a little rock] and on this rock [*petra*, a big rock] I will build my church."

Third, Peter is referred to in this passage in the second person ("you"); however, the statement "this rock" is in the third person.

---

1. The reasoning here is parallel to that on Peter's primacy (see chap. 3), only it is specifically the infallibility of Peter in question here. He could have been chief of the apostles without being infallible, as a head pastor could be in a local Baptist church. But it is hard to see how Peter could have unique and infallible authority without thereby having primacy over the other apostles. So, infallibility is dependent on primacy but not the reverse.

Fourth, "Peter" (*petros*) is a masculine singular term, while the term "rock" (*petra*) is feminine singular, so the two terms do not have the same referent.[2]

Fifth, it does not bestow a unique authority on Peter, since the same power to bind and loose was given later to *all* of the apostles (see Matt. 18:18) as well.

Sixth, nowhere else in Scripture is Peter singled out as the rock foundation of the church. Instead, Christ is said to be the "chief cornerstone" (Eph. 2:20 NKJV).

Seventh, even Peter himself refers to Christ as the "chief cornerstone" (1 Pet. 2:7 NKJV).

Eighth, any early fathers deny this is a reference to Peter, including Augustine who wrote, "The Rock (*Petra*) was Christ; and on this foundation was Peter himself also built. For other foundation can no man lay than that is laid, which is Christ Jesus."[3] This is all the stronger since Augustine believed in the unique authority of Peter. So, he would have been more than happy to use this verse, if he thought it could support his belief, but he did not. George Salmon asks the pointed question: "If Christ established Peter as "the rock" of the church, then why did most of the prominent leaders (before the Middle Ages) of this very church fail to see this interpretation of this all-important passage?"[4]

Ninth, as for the "keys," these too may have been shared by the other apostles in the sense that they had the power to bind or loose (Matt. 18:18). Or, Peter may very well have had a unique historic role that he used in opening the door of the gospel to Jews (Acts 2) and later to the Gentiles (Acts 10).[5] But there was no indication of a perpetual use of the keys by either Peter or his successors.

Tenth, Salmon asked pointed questions: "If our Lord meant all this [concerning Peter], we may ask, why did He not say it? Who found out that He meant it? The Apostles did not find out at the time; for up to

2. Norman L. Geisler and Ralph E. MacKenzie, *Roman Catholics and Evangelicals: Agreements and Differences* (Grand Rapids, MI: Baker, 1995), 207. Catholic theologians are quick to point out that Jesus probably spoke Aramaic here, which, in point of fact, does not make a distinction between genders, thus allegedly providing a counter-example to the Protestant claim. However, the *inspired* Greek original does make such distinctions).

3. Augustine, "On the Gospel of John," in the *Nicene and Post-Nicene Fathers*, ed. Philip Schaff (Peabody, MA: Hendrickson, 2004), 7:450.

4. George Salmon, *The Infallibility of the Church*, repr. (Grand Rapids, MI: Baker, 1959), 185.

5. Again, the terms *bind* and *loose* were common rabbinic terms for "forbidding" and "allowing" and "keys" was a metaphor explaining the authority to do this; Norman L. Geisler, *Systematic Theology*, vol. 4: *The Church and Last Things* (Bloomington, MN: Bethany, 2005), 77.

the night before His [Jesus'] death the dispute went on, which should be the greatest."[6]

Eleventh, a dogma like this should not be established apart from the "unanimous consent" of the Fathers. The First Vatican Council and numerous other Catholic decrees unequivocally insisted that one *must* interpret the Scriptures according to *the unanimous consent of the Fathers*. Trent proclaimed that the faithful should confess: "I shall never accept nor interpret it [the Bible] otherwise than in accordance with *the unanimous consent of the Fathers*."[7] Similarly, the First Vatican Council stated, "no one is permitted to interpret Sacred Scripture itself contrary . . . to the *unanimous agreement of the Fathers*."[8] But even as Catholic authority Ludwig Ott admits, some of the Fathers themselves took "the rock on which the Lord built the church as meaning the faith of Peter in the Divinity of Christ . . ."[9] Hence, by their own infallible standard, the Roman Catholic interpretation of their primary text on Peter's infallibility fails!

Twelfth, while Catholic commentators insist that Matthew 16 proves Peter's infallibility, no Catholic commentator is willing to assign Peter infallibility in evil when he was rebuked by Jesus just a few verses later: "Get behind Me, Satan! You are a stumbling block to Me; for you are not setting your mind on God's interests, but man's"[10] (v. 23 NASB). Salmon recognized this inconsistency and wrote: "If Peter were the foundation of the Church in any other sense than I have explained, it would have shaken immediately afterwards when our Lord said unto him: 'Get thee behind me, Satan,' and tottered to its base when he denied his Lord. *Immediately after Peter had earned commendation by his acknowledgment of Jesus as the Messiah, the doctrine of a crucified Messiah was proposed to him and he rejected it*." So if "the Apostles had believed that the words 'On this rock I will build my church' constituted Peter their infallible guide, the very first time they followed his guidance they would have been led to miserable error."[11]

6. Salmon, *The Infallibility of the Church*, 334.
7. Henry Denzinger, *The Sources of Catholic Dogma*, trans. Roy J. Deferrari (Fitzwilliam, NH: Loreto Publications, 1955), no. 995, p. 303.
8. Ibid., no. 1788, p. 444, emphasis added. For another similar statement concerning the unanimous consent of the Fathers, see Pope Leo XIII's encyclical, "Providentissimus Deus" (November 1893), quoted in Denzinger, no. 1944, p. 489.
9. Ludwig Ott, *Fundamentals of Catholic Dogma* (Rockford, IL: Tan, 1960), 280.
10. Ibid.
11. Salmon, *The Infallibility of the Church*, 343.

It is inconsistent of Catholic scholars to apply infallibility to Peter in one instance but not in the other. Since Peter was representing the group of the apostles, it is only natural that Jesus would single him out for affirming Jesus' divine Messiahship. Why, then, should one conclude that Peter was given the charism of infallibility when he was merely speaking out in response to Jesus' question? To be sure, "Rome has read much more into the text than can be found here."[12]

D. A. Carson writes summarizing the thrust of the Matthew 16 passage as follows: "The name *Peter* means 'Rock', and Jesus played on this meaning to designate Peter as the foundation of the new people of God. His leadership would involve the authority of the steward, whose *keys* symbolized his responsibility to regulate the affairs of the household. Peter would exercise his leadership by his authority to declare what is and is not permissible in the *kingdom of heaven* (to *bind* and to *loose* have this meaning in rabbinic writings). The story of the early years of the church in Acts shows how Peter fulfilled this role. But the same authority was shared with the other disciples in 18:18 (where *you* is plural; here it is singular). He was thus a representative leader rather than an overlord."[13]

In brief, no matter whether Peter is the "rock" to which Christ referred or not, the Roman concept of the papacy cannot be legitimately derived from it. What is more, the evidence is very strongly in favor of the verse not referring to Peter as the "rock" on which the church is built. Thus, the primary verse of the foundational doctrine of the Roman Church is found not to support the Roman claim. This places their whole case in serious jeopardy.

John 21:15–17

This text is used by Roman Catholics to prove that "Christ installed Peter (and his successors) as the supreme pastor over the whole flock." For Ludwig Ott writes, "The task of teaching Christian truth and of protecting it from error is part of the function of the supreme pastor. But he could not fulfill this task if, in exercise of his supreme teaching office, he himself were subject to error."[14] In response, several observations are relevant.

First, in both the immediate and more remote contexts it is not authority but pastoral care that is in view. Noted New Testament commentator Leon Morris made the point well when he noted, "This passage

12. Geisler, *The Church and Last Things*, 77.
13. D. A. Carson, *New Bible Commentary: 21st Century Edition*. 4th ed. (Downers Grove, IL: InterVarsity, 1994); available from Logos Bible Software ED 3.0.
14. Ott, *Fundamentals of Catholic Dogma*, ibid., 287–88.

must be taken in conjunction with Peter's threefold denial of his Lord. Just as he had a short time ago [John 18:25–27] in the presence of the enemy denied all connection with the Lord, so now in the presence of his friends he affirms three times over that he loves his Lord." So, "There can be little doubt but that the whole scene is meant to show us Peter as completely restored to his position of leadership. He has three times denied his Lord. Now he has three times affirmed his love for Him, and three times he has been commissioned to care for the flock. This must have had the effect on the others of a demonstration that, whatever had been the mistakes of the past, Jesus was restoring Peter to a place of trust."[15]

Second, the context of the passage demonstrates Jesus' restoration of Simon to properly administer pastoral care to the flock. But nowhere does this text suggest that this leadership role involved a charism of infallibility. One does not need to be infallible to tend the flock of Christ. In point of fact, "feeding is a God-given pastoral function that even non-apostles had in the New Testament."[16]

Third, what is more, Peter did not demonstrate an exemplary infallibility in faith and practice, even in the New Testament times when the apostle Paul had to rebuke him for his fallible practice (Gal. 2:11ff.) contrary to the gospel. So serious was what Peter exhibited by his life that Paul called it "hypocrisy" and a denial of the straightforward "truth of the gospel." This was not an ordinary inconsistency that any mortal person, including a pope, might fall into. In short, Peter's denial was a *de facto* denial of the gospel. This is seriously inconsistent with the Roman claim that he is the primary teacher of faith and practice in the church.

Finally, the fact that Jesus singled out Peter does not show his infallibility but his fallibility. After all, he was the one who denied Christ three times and needed to be restored by a threefold affirmation. If anything, the passage implies Peter's primacy in evil for he alone, not the other apostles, denied his Lord outright on three occasions. If Peter was going to be used as a leader in the future, he needed to be restored. Thus, the focus here is on Peter because he alone had committed these serious sins.

Luke 22:31–32

The third major verse used for direct support of the Roman dogma of Peter's infallibility is Luke 22. It is argued that, since Christ prayed for

---

15. Leon Morris, *The Gospel According to John*, New International Commentary on the New Testament (Grand Rapids, MI: Eerdmans, 1995), 767.
16. Geisler, *The Church and Last Things*, 80.

Peter alone that his faith would not fail, this indicates that he alone had infallibility as teacher over all other apostles, while none of them had infallibility as an individual. However, such an interpretation is scarcely found in this scant reference.

First, careful examination of this text and its parallel passage in Mark's Gospel reveals that it is not a unique reference to Peter's powers but to the other apostles' as well.[17] Mark's Gospel provides additional information not found in Luke. Peter said to Jesus, "Even though all may fall away, yet I will not" (Mark 14:29 NASB). Mark follows with Jesus' prediction of Peter's denial. Mathison provides a clear explanation of these series of circumstances that unfold in Mark: "All of the Apostles are told they will stumble. Peter alone informs His Lord that He is wrong. Peter claims that even if everyone else falls away, he will not. It is more likely, then, that the reason Jesus singled Peter out for a special prayer was because of Peter's special arrogance in this situation. Peter dramatically overestimates his own faith despite Jesus' warning. . . . Therefore Jesus, because of His love for Peter, prays especially for him."[18] So, this text shows nothing about Peter's infallibility.

Second, Catholic theologian Hans Küng, whom the Catholic Church censored for his pointed critiques of the papacy, wrote that the Catholic proof-texts in no way support the doctrine of the papacy. Küng writes, "In Luke 22:32 (and in Matthew 16:18 and John 21:15). . . . In short, Catholic commentators have to read back into the text their peculiar interpretation in order to yield their papal conclusions."

Third, if Peter was the prime teacher among the apostles, why does the apostle Paul play a much greater role in the New Testament, both in spreading the gospel and in writing inspired Scripture? While Peter wrote only two short epistles, Paul wrote nearly half of the New Testament (13 of 27 books) and maybe more, if he wrote Hebrews. Further, Peter was not the primary agent for the spread of the gospel. Little is heard of him after the first several chapters of Acts. Instead, it is the apostle Paul who is attempting to fulfill Jesus' command to take Christ's message to the end of the earth (cf. Col. 1:23).

Fourth, to be sure, Peter did have a significant leadership role in the early church (which no Protestant can deny); but, again, this is not the same thing as affirming that Peter had an infallible office of authority in the New Testament church or that his successors have the same.

17. Mathison, *Shape of Sola Scriptura*, 192.
18. Ibid., 192–93.

Other than the possible historic use of the "keys" for Jews (Acts 2) and Gentiles (Acts 10), Peter was not given any unique authority that was not later assigned to the rest of the apostles—all were given the *same* authority to bind and loose (see Matt. 18:18 cf. John 20:21–23). He was one of the "eminent apostles" (plural, 2 Cor. 12:11, NASB), but not the "chief apostle."[19]

Fifth, in spite of the Catholic claim that Peter was positionally superior to Paul, Paul under the guidance of the Holy Spirit revealed the contrary, namely, that no other apostle was superior to him—including Peter! For the apostle Paul says, "For in no way was I inferior to the most eminent [super] apostles ... " (2 Cor. 12:11 AT).[20] When reading the epistles of Paul, eg., Galatians, it is difficult to come away with the impression that any of the apostles were superior to Paul, since, as Paul himself says, he received his revelation independently of the other apostles. Instead the revelation that Paul had received came from the original source, namely, from the risen, glorified Christ (see Gal. 1:12). Paul, then, was on equal footing with Peter by virtue of his receiving revelation from Christ; thus they shared the same status. Indeed, as seen above, Paul used that revelation to rebuke Peter when Peter vacillated between his association with the Gentiles and his unbelieving Jewish kinsmen (Gal. 2:11ff.), thus engaging in a *de facto* denial of the gospel.[21]

Sixth, if Peter enjoyed the errorless primacy of the first pope, it is strange he and John were commissioned (or "sent") by the other apostles on a mission to Samaria, which suggests that Peter was not the superior apostle as Catholicism claims (see Acts 8:4–13). Indeed, if Peter was the God-ordained superior apostle, it would be strange that more attention is given to the ministry of Paul than to Peter's in Acts. Peter is the focus in chapters 1–12; Paul is the dominant figure in 13–28.[22]

Seventh, it is true that Peter addressed the church's first council in Jerusalem (see Acts 15); however, it is also true that Peter exercised no infallible authority over the others.[23] As the text demonstrates, the final decisions of the council were carried out by *all* of the apostles and the elders, as well as with the consent of the entire church (15:22)—thus at once demonstrating more of a collegial or conciliar model rather than a

19. Ibid., 78.
20. Ibid.
21. Ibid.
22. Ibid.
23. Some might take verse 7 as implying Peter's primacy; however, the *context* of the entire passage reveals that the decisions were carried out by all of the apostles and not by Peter alone; see Mathison, *Shape of Sola Scriptura*, 196–98.

"Petrine" Roman model. Moreover, some scholars have observed that it was *not* Peter who presided over the council, but it was James instead (15:13–21).[24]

Eighth, Peter never refers to himself as *the chief* pastor of the church, but only as a *"fellow* elder" (1 Pet. 5:1–2), which would be a strange admission for one who allegedly possesses unique infallibility.[25] In fact, in his epistle addressed to the dispersed Christians throughout the Roman Empire, he salutes them by addressing himself as *"an* apostle" (1:1). Since Peter was one of the church's "pillars" (*plural*) nowhere does Peter ever write that he was *"the* apostle," nor does he ever write that he was *"the* bishop of Rome."[26]

Again, most commentators recognize that Peter had a significant role (as the initial leader) in the early church, as the Book of Acts repeatedly demonstrates. Yet, the biblical data suggest that Peter did not possess any superiority greater than the other apostles; he was simply one of *many* pillars of the church.[27] It may be a *necessary* condition for Peter to have been the leader of the apostles to fit the papal description, but it is not a *sufficient* condition for primacy; that is, there are other ways Peter could have been the leader of the apostles without requiring him to be the first pope—he could have simply been the leader of the apostles

24. Ibid. Concerning Petrine and collegial models, at the First Vatican Council (1870) there were two schools of thought present, the majority party called the "ultramontanists" (for they sought authority "beyond the mountain," that is, the Alps), and the minority party (led by John Henry Newman) who held to a form of "conciliarism." Concerning the former, the minority group wished to see infallibility linked to all of the bishops and not to the pope alone. Out of the some seven hundred bishops present at Vatican I, one hundred of them opposed the doctrine of papal infallibility (Geisler and MacKenzie, *Roman Catholics and Evangelicals*, 460). In fact, Gregory the Great (pope from AD 590–604) reproached patriarch John the Faster of Constantinople for calling himself the universal bishop. In Gregory's mind, this universal claim of supreme authority in a bishop was a sure identification of the corruption of the church, or even the work of the Antichrist. Thus Gregory reacted in such a way to defend the rights of all bishops, and not simply because he sought the title for himself; see Harold O. J. Brown, *Protest of a Troubled Protestant* (New Rochelle: Arlington House, 1969), 122.

25. Stephen Ray attempts to counter this point by arguing that Peter was simply manifesting the humility he was exhorting his readers to practice. In addition, Ray asserts that Peter never denies the primacy bestowed upon him by Jesus. Ray attempts to use the analogy of a presidential address whereby the president refers to himself as a "fellow American" when addressing the nation, even though he holds the highest office in the nation (Ray, *Upon This Rock: St. Peter and the Primacy of Rome in Scripture and the Early Church* [San Francisco: Ignatius Press, 1999], 59, n 79). This analogy does not work since the power claimed for the presidency and the power claimed for the papacy are not the same—the Pope is said to possess a charism of *infallibility* as the vicar of Christ; the president is simply recognized as the national leader to whom neither infallibility nor absolute jurisdiction is ascribed. To answer Ray's second question, Peter never denies his primacy because he *never* had it to begin with (as the biblical evidence demonstrates). Ray's assertion simply begs the question.

26. Geisler, *The Church and Last Things*, 78.

27. Ibid., 78–79.

(nothing more, nothing less). As noted before, all the apostles were given the same authority to bind and loose, even though Peter was given this authority first (Matt. 18:18).

A Response to Other Verses Used to Support Papal Infallibility

As for the other verses offered by Rome in support of the infallibility of Peter (see above), all of them fail to support the claim of infallibility.

In Isaiah 22:22, the "key" refers to the stewardship of the house of David that would be in the hands of Eliakim. It has nothing to do with Peter or the New Testament church. Matthew 7:24 refers to a wise man building his house on the rock and has absolutely nothing to say about Peter being the rock for the church. Matthew 10:2 and Mark 3:16 list Peter's name first because he was *a* leader among the apostles. But it says nothing about his being *the* leader among them, to say nothing of his being the divinely authoritative leader.

In Matthew 17:1 Peter's active role among the three apostles reveals his leadership, as well as his impetuous nature, which also led Jesus to say to him: "Get behind me, Satan!" (Matt. 16:23). The fact that in Matthew 17:27 Peter did a miracle does not show his primacy, since the other apostles had the same power (Matt. 10:8; Heb. 2:3–4; 2 Cor. 12:12), as did even some laypersons (Acts 8:6). In Matthew 26:37 Peter came with Jesus to the garden, but so did James and John. This proves nothing of Rome's claims that uniquely pertain to Peter. The same is true when these same three witnessed the awakening of Jairus's daughter in Mark 5:37. Luke 5:3 tells us of the availability of Peter's boat from which Jesus could preach. It says nothing about Peter's infallibility.

John 10:16 says nothing about Peter but merely about Jesus' other (Gentile) sheep he will bring into the fold. Using John 11:49–52 as an analogy to show "the high priest possessed an official revelatory function" is a false analogy that proves too much. It proves that Israel had a divinely authoritative magisterium too—something both Rome and Jesus rejected (Matt. 5:31–32; 38–39; 43–44; 15:1–6). The use of Acts 1:12–16, 20–26; and 2:14 to show leadership in the early church is accepted by all, but it tells us nothing about Peter being the first pope. In Acts 15:7 Peter was the first to speak at the Jerusalem Council, but James was apparently the leader there, since he spoke last and summed up the whole matter (15:13–21) leading to the decision of all the "apostles and elders" present (15:22–29).

In 1 Corinthians 15:5 Peter is listed as the first of the apostles to see the resurrected Christ, but the Gospels tell us that the women saw Jesus before Peter. But Rome would not take that as proof of the infallibility of women over men. In Galatians 1:16–19 it was Peter whom Paul saw first because he was one of many "pillars" of the church (Gal. 2:9), not because he had primacy over the others, let alone infallibility. Indeed, Paul even had to rebuke Peter for his denial, in practice, of the gospel he taught (Gal. 2:11ff.). Revelation 1:18 and 3:7 do not speak of Peter directly but only that keys symbolize power and dominion, but all the apostles had this power (Matt. 18:18). It was not limited to Peter.

In summation, there is no direct evidence for Peter's infallibility in any of these texts. Further, some of Rome's positions are arguments from false analogy. Other verses show only Peter's leadership in the early church, not his infallibility. And some verses prove absolutely nothing. All in all, it is a pathetic attempt to give indirect justification for a doctrine that has no direct justification in the New Testament.

An Evaluation of the Historical Argument for the Infallibility of Peter

Roman Catholics also support their argument for infallibility by their appeal to the teachings of the early fathers. Protestants reject the use of this as an authoritative argument, since they believe that the Bible, not the Fathers, is the only authoritative source for faith and practice. So, we must first address the issue of the authority of the Fathers.

The Fathers Had No Authority as Individuals

The first thing to note is that the fathers held many contrary views on Christian doctrine and practice and, hence, they cannot all be right. So, any alleged divine authority that there may be in one father's writings would be canceled by the fact that the same authority would exist in an opposing father's view. In short, their alleged authority as individuals is self-canceling.

The Universal Consent of the Fathers

Roman Catholics attempt to circumvent the above argument by appealing to the so-called "universal consent of the Fathers." They claim that such universal agreement of the Fathers makes their view true. But there are at least three major problems with this view: definitional, logical, and historical.

First, the very principle of universal consent of the Fathers is problematic. The first problem is definitional. How do we know who qualifies as a "father" and by what standard do we judge? We cannot use orthodox Christian teaching as the standard for that presupposes that we already know from some other source what qualifies as "orthodox." So we would be using orthodoxy as a standard for testing orthodoxy, which is a vicious circle.

Second, the logical problem is that it is actually possible that all the Fathers were wrong on a given doctrinal point of universal agreement. After all, neither Catholic nor non-Catholic Christians believe their writings were divinely inspired and infallible. But if they are fallible, then it is logically possible that all of them could be wrong on a given point. So, even universal consent could be no more than consent to error.

The historical problem is that even given the criterion of universal consent, still many of the disputed areas do not have universal consent. In fact, depending on who qualifies as a "father," apart from most of the great essentials of the Christian faith, there is disagreement among the Fathers. So, while universal consent of the Fathers would appear to be a solid principle in theory, nevertheless, in practice there are few disputed areas in which it is useful. For example, Roman Catholics appeal to this principle of universal consent to support many of their dogmas when there is no such universal consent on the point. This is true, for example on the Immaculate Conception of Mary, which even the great Catholic theologian of all time Thomas Aquinas rejected.[28] The same is true of the bodily assumption of Mary, the veneration of the host, and the infallibility of the pope. So, for all practical purposes there is no practical purpose for the principle of universal consent.

Applied to the historical basis of Peter's primacy, there is no universal consent. Yet Rome insists that there must be for any of its dogmas. The First Vatican Council and numerous other Catholic decrees unequivocally insisted that one *must* interpret the Scriptures according to *the unanimous consent of the Fathers*. Trent proclaimed that the faithful should confess: "I shall never accept nor interpret it [the Bible] otherwise than in accordance with *the unanimous consent of the Fathers*."[29] Similarly, the First Vatican Council stated, "no one is permitted to interpret Sacred Scripture itself contrary . . . to the *unanimous agreement of*

---

28. Ibid., 78–79. Aquinas affirmed, "The sanctification of the blessed Virgin before her animation is unintelligible" (*Summa Theologica* 3a, 27, 4).
29. Denzinger, *The Sources of Catholic Dogma*, no. 995, p. 303.

the Fathers."[30] But even as Catholic authority Ludwig Ott admits, some of the Fathers themselves took "the rock on which the Lord built the Church as meaning the faith of Peter in the Divinity of Christ."[31] So, by Rome's own criterion, the primacy of Peter fails the test of qualifying for a Roman dogma!

One final point needs to be made. Even if one modifies the criterion to "many early Fathers" agree (which would be an inadequate criterion), we would still run into serious problems with Peter's infallibility for several reasons. First, there are not many early, undisputed references to Peter's infallibility. Only a few relatively early references exist, and most of them are disputable. Tertullian (c. 160–225) speaks of "the Church [which was] built upon him [Peter]" (*On Monogomy*, 8, p. 65 in Schaff, vol. 4, ANF). "But the reference is oblique and nondidactic with no explanation of what it meant. What Ott omits is informing us of a clear didactic passage where Tertullian affirms teaching contrary to the primacy of the Roman hierarchy. In addressing Matthew 16:19, he says clearly: "You therefore [wrongly] presume that the power of binding and loosing has derived to you, that is, to every Church akin to Peter, what sort of man are you, subverting and wholly changing the manifest intention of the Lord, conferring (as that intention did) this (gift) personally on Peter? 'On thee.' He says . . . and 'I will give to thee the keys,' not to the Church." He adds, "Accordingly, 'the Church,' it is true, will forgive sins: but (it will be) the Church of the Spirit, by means of a spiritual man; not the Church which consists of a number of bishops." [32] But this is directly contrary to what the Roman Church teaches about the gift given to Peter in Matthew 16.

Irenaeus of Lyons (c. AD *130–c. 200).* This supposed reference to the universal authority of the Catholic Church is both disputed and inadequate. First, "it is a matter of necessity that *every Church should agree* [Latin, *convenire*] *with this Church*, on account of its preeminent authority, that is, the faithful everywhere, inasmuch as the apostolic tradition has been preserved continuously by those faithful men who exist everywhere" (*Against Heresies* [hereafter, *Haer.*] 3.3.2, emphasis

---

30. Denzinger, *The Sources of Catholic Dogma*, no. 1788, p. 444, emphasis added. Ibid., 444, 1788, emphasis added. For another similar statement concerning the unanimous consent of the Fathers, see Pope Leo XIII's encyclical, "Providentissimus Deus," (November 1893) quoted in Denzinger, *The Sources of Catholic Dogma*, 1944, 489.

31. Ott, *Fundamentals*, 280.

32. Tertullian, *On Modesty*, 21, in Schaff, *Nicene and Post-Nicene Fathers*, 99–100.

added). But it can be argued that this spoke of Rome only reflectively of the whole church, not authoritatively over the whole church (see Appendix 1). As even a Roman Catholic noted, it could be translated as follows: "For to this Church, on account of more potent principality, it is necessary that every Church (that is, those who are on every side faithful) *resort*; in which Church ever, *by those who are on every side*, has been preserved that tradition which is from the apostles."[33]

St. Cyprian (c. AD 200–258). Cyprian could be called the first Catholic, though his view is more Eastern Catholic than Western (Roman) Catholic. He did hold to the primacy of Peter, yet with an important Eastern church twist. But he has nothing directly to say about Peter's infallibility. He spoke of "the foundation of the one Church which was based by Christ upon the rock [Peter]."[34] But he also held, "The Church is founded upon the bishops, and every act of the Church is controlled by these same rulers." He affirmed that none "have God as his Father, before he has the church for his Mother."[35] The way Cyprian reconciled these divergent thoughts was to point out that while the gift was given to Peter alone, nonetheless, all the other apostles participated in it in an undivided partnership (*Epistles* 74.16, p. 394). In short, Peter is first among equals.

But the fact that there is a primitive primacy teaching in Cyprian is not surprising. He was writing two hundred years after the time of the apostles. That was more than enough time for a false teaching to develop. Indeed, there were heresies like Docetism (1 John 4) and an incipient kind of Gnosticism (Col. 2) right in the New Testament. Even an incipient primacy practice is implicit in 3 John 3 in "Diotrephes who loves to have the preeminence among them." What Roman Catholic scholars must find—and is conspicuously absent—is not the primacy of Peter but his infallibility in the early Fathers.

By the time of the first pro-Christian Emperor Constantine (AD 325) the Roman hierarchical imprint had firmly implanted itself on the church, and it is understandable that there would be more Fathers cited on the side of Peter's primacy. These included Cyril of Jerusalem (c. AD 315–386), St. Augustine (d. 430), and even the Council of Ephesus (431), and Leo the Great (d. AD 461) who said, "'As that which Peter believed in Christ lives for ever, so also that which Christ instituted in Peter lives

---

33. Cited in Schaff, *Ante-Nicene Fathers* (Grand Rapids, MI: Eerdmans, 1885), 1.415.
34. Cyprian, *The Epistles of Cyprian*, 74.16.
35. Ibid., 26.1.

for ever' (Sermo 3, 2)"[36] and, "'Only Peter was chosen out of the whole world to be the Head of all called peoples, of all Apostles and of all the Fathers of the Church' (Sermo 4, 2)."[37] Yet here again, primacy is in view, not infallibility. One can be held to have unique authority, like a president, but without infallibility.

Even as late as Thomas Aquinas (d. 1274), this great Catholic theologian declared:

> We believe the prophets and apostles because the Lord has been their witness by performing miracles. . . . And *we believe the successors of the apostles and prophets only in so far as they tell us those things which the apostles and prophets have left in their writings.*[38]

But as is often noted, Rome was not built in a day and neither was the Roman Catholic Church. It developed gradually from New Testament churches with a plurality of bishops or elders (Phil. 1:1; Acts 14:23) in each church, to one bishop over elders in each church (by the second century), to one bishop over an area of churches, to one bishop over all the churches—which is the Roman teaching of Peter's primacy. Then primacy later—much later (in 1870)—was given infallibility. *It is a gigantic leap from the New Testament teaching about Peter's leadership among other apostles to the Roman Catholic view of his infallibility over all the church!*

An Evaluation of the Theological Evidence for the Infallibility of Peter

Roman Catholic scholars offer several theological arguments in favor of the primacy and infallibility of Peter. Most of them boil down to two categories. First, there is the need for an official interpreter of the teachings of Christ. The reasoning goes like this. The Bible is not self-interpreting. Therefore, there is a need for an interpreter. Further, to preserve the teachings of Christ from corruption, there must be a divinely authorized interpreter. Christ chose Peter to fit this role.

Response to the Argument for a Need for an Infallible Interpreter

Non-Catholics and Eastern Orthodox Catholics offer differing responses to this claim. The Eastern church believes that reliable (non-infallible) tradition is sufficient to accomplish this task. Protestants appeal to *sola Scriptura* (the Bible alone) and the doctrine of perspicuity (clearness)

---

36. Cited by Ott, *Fundamentals of Catholic Dogma*, 281.
37. Ibid.
38. Aquinas, *On Truth*, 14, 10 and 11, emphasis added.

as a solution. That is, the main message of the Bible alone is sufficient and has no need for an authoritative interpretation other than the Holy Spirit, who can enlighten the reader's mind to the central teachings of the Bible.

The following comments are sufficient to show the fallacy of the argument.

First, other religious traditions and governments have survived without an infallible interpreter. The Eastern Orthodox Church is a good example. Actually, they are older than the Roman Catholic Church since there was a church in the East before there was one in the West.

Also, Islam has survived well as a religion for nearly a millennium and a half without an infallible interpreter.

Second, an alleged infallible interpreter of the Roman Church did not prevent it from the largest and longest lasting split in Christendom—that between East and West, which occurred about AD 1054. What good, then, is an infallible interpreter of the faith, if he cannot save Christendom from the great schism?

Third, an infallible interpreter has not been able on a practical level to avoid the reality of the many anti-papal disputes. Often there were two or more popes, each excommunicating the other. Once, a church council had to be called to solve the matter. And contrary to the papal pronouncement at Vatican I (AD 1870), they fired both popes and set up a third one! The Council of Constance (AD 1413–1418) proclaimed the superiority of an ecumenical council over the pope, declaring (in *Haec Sancta*, "this alone") that "this council holds its power direct from Christ; everyone, no matter his rank of office, even if it be papal, is bound to obey it in whatever pertains to faith."[39] This is in direct conflict with the Vatican I Council, which affirmed that the pope, apart from the council, could infallibly define doctrine.

Fourth, on a practical level, an infallible pope has been of no definitive value on many occasions when there were competing popes (see Appendix 2). For there was no infallible way to tell who was the real pope. This leads to another problem.

Fifth, positing an infallible pope leads to a need for an infallible source to determine which popes were infallible. But there is none. And even if there were one, how would we know they were infallible? There is no infallible way to determine that. This leads to another problem.

39. "The Council of Constance" in *Documents of the Christian Church*, revised, eds., Henry Bettenson and Chris Maunder (Oxford: Oxford University Press, 1999), 149.

Sixth, there are no infallible lists of infallible popes. Considering the many antipopes, the lists differ considerably. Even if one list were considered official, it would not be inspired.

So, we are left with the practical dilemma of not being able to determine who indeed were these infallible popes. Of course, this leaves us in doubt of which official statements of the popes are binding on the faithful, since we do not even know infallibly which one was the infallible pope.

Seventh, what is more, even Roman Catholic scholars are not sure which statements of allegedly infallible popes are infallible statements. For only *ex cathedra* statements are infallible, and there is no infallible way to determine which statements are *ex cathedra*. No pope or ecumenical council has even ruled in principle and in practice which statements by previous popes are infallible.

Eighth, the alleged infallible Roman interpreters have made many fallible interpretations. Pope Honorius was charged with heresy. How is it that an infallible interpreter of faith and practice can be wrong on an essential doctrine of the faith? Peter himself, the alleged first pope, was wrong on a practical matter of the faith and had to be rebuked by another apostle. The inspired Scripture informs us that Peter and others he had led astray were not "straightforward about the truth of the gospel" (Gal. 2:14). If this is infallibility in practice, then Roman infallibility is a very fallible thing!

Further, the treatment of Galileo was a very fallible decision of an infallible church.

Response to the Argument for the Need to Avoid Proliferation of Sects and Cults

The second argument is that without an infallible interpreter, there will be a proliferation of sects, cults, and heresies—all laying claim to the truth of Christ. In order to avoid this, God set up a magisterium (in the apostles) for his visible church over which he placed Peter and his successors. In this way, the unity and perpetuity of the church of Christ can be preserved on earth. But this argument fails the test on practical and historical grounds.

First, there have been both major and minor splits with its alleged infallible interpreter in place. The two major splits are well known. The East-West split began in AD 1054. The Catholic-Protestant split began in AD 1517. In addition to these major splits—which infallibility did not prevent—there were numerous minor ones that Rome has had to deal with down through the years, from the Montanists to the Donatists to the Jansenists.[40]

Second, in order to avoid more splits Rome has tolerated both aberrant teaching and behavior within its ranks. In spite of the official teaching to the contrary, Rome has housed homosexuals, lesbians, abortionists, as well as practical idolatry, and many other doctrinal deviations. Neither has an infallible interpreter kept Rome from division in the religious orders, the influence of religious liberalism, negative higher criticism of the Bible, and Darwinian evolution. I personally had a Roman Catholic teacher at a Jesuit institution I attended who was an atheist. When I asked how he could be a Catholic and an atheist, he replied: "You do not have to believe in God to be a Catholic. You just have to keep the rules of the Church."

Third, as for the alleged proliferation of sects and cults without a Roman magisterium, it is important to note that evangelical Protestants who hold to the infallibility of Scripture and the historical-grammatical means of interpreting Scripture have retained essential orthodoxy without any kind of authoritative tradition or Roman magisterium. The truth is that an infallible Bible is sufficiently clear without an infallible interpretation to yield the essential orthodox doctrines of the Christian faith.

An Evangelical Response to Other Catholic Arguments for Papal Infallibility

As noted earlier (in chap. 4) Catholics offer many arguments in favor of infallibility. But, as we will see, none of these is infallible. Indeed, all are answerable.

Response to the Argument That the Effect Cannot Be Greater Than the Cause

It was argued by Catholic scholar Peter Kreeft that since (1) for every effect there is a cause and (2) the effect is never greater than its cause and the infallible Bible came into existence (was caused by) the church,

40. F. L. Cross, *The Oxford Dictionary of the Christian Church* (Oxford: Oxford University Press, 1978). The Montanists were a second-century apocalyptic group founded by Montanus in Phrygia. They were ascetic, stressed the role of the Holy Spirit, and made predictions about end-time events. Tertullian joined the group c. AD 206. They were condemned by Eastern Synods and, hesitantly, by Pope Zephyrinus. The Donatists were a late fourth- and early fifth-century North African group who refused to accept Caecilian, Bishop of Carthage, on the grounds that his consecrator, Felix of Aptunga, was a traitor. They were opposed by St. Augustine and persecuted by the Roman Catholic Church. The Jansenists were a French Catholic group (17th c.) who held strong "Calvinistic" beliefs and lived a rigorous life. Some of their teaching was condemned by the church. Blaise Pascal was associated with the group.

then it follows that the church must be infallible, too (since the effect is never greater than its cause).

But as a fellow Thomist, Kreeft knows the difference between an efficient cause (God) and an instrumental cause (the church). He also knows and believes that God inspired the infallible Bible through fallible authors. For God can use a crooked stick to make a straight line!

Therefore, it is not necessary to have an infallible church (instrumental cause), but only an infallible God (efficient cause) to produce the Bible.

Further, Kreeft's view presupposes the wrong view of the canon of Scripture.[41] The church did not "create" (or determine) the canon as such. The church merely *discovered* the canon of Scripture. The fact that the canon was ratified by the church does not mean that it was created by it, fundamentally.[42] That is, the church discovered which books bore the marks of divine inspiration and classified them as such. In fact, this is exactly what the First Vatican Council appears to say: "But the Church holds these books as sacred and canonical, not because, having been put together by human industry alone, they were then approved by its authority; nor because they contain revelation without error; but because, having written by the inspiration of the Holy Spirit, they have God as their author and, as such, they have been handed down to the Church itself."[43] Here is a case where official Catholic dogma appears to maintain the evangelical position concerning the reception and recognition of the canon of Scripture; and if true, then Kreeft's argument from causality (that the cause be equal to its effect, or greater) fails.[44] The chart below illustrates the proper and improper views of the canon of Scripture:[45]

Rome's View of Canon	The Biblical View of Canon
Church determines Canon	Church discovers Canon
Church is Mother of Canon	Church is Child of Canon
Church is Magistrate of Canon	Church is Minister of Canon
Church Regulates Canon	Church Recognizes Canon
Church is Judge of Canon	Church is Witness of Canon
Church is Master of Canon	Church is Servant of Canon

41. Peter Kreeft in utilizing the principle of causality presupposes what Vatican II says about the canon; namely, that the church determined the canon (Geisler and MacKenzie, *Roman Catholics and Evangelicals*, 192).
42. Yves Congar, *Tradition and Traditions* (New York: MacMillan, 1967), 419.
43. Denzinger, *The Sources of Catholic Dogma*, no. 1787, p. 444.
44. Geisler and MacKenzie, *Roman Catholics and Evangelicals*, 192.
45. Ibid.

This same response applies to the Catholic argument about the extent of the canon. It does not take an infallible church to discover which books belong in the Bible. God determined that by only inspiring a fixed number of books (66 in the Protestant canon). If he had inspired more, then there would be more. All the early "church" did was recognize the earmarks of divine revelation on these specific books. They did not determine the canon; they merely discovered it based on the supernatural earmarks God had placed upon these books.[46]

Response to the Argument Based on the Nature of Truth

Another of Rome's philosophical arguments is based on the nature of truth. That is, it is impossible to know truth unless it is known without error. Thus, it is argued that the only way Scripture can be known without error is through the church's infallible magisterium.

In response, several points need to be made. First of all, while it is true that one cannot know truth unless it is known without error, it is also true that one can know something *truly* without having to know it *fully* (or even "infallibly").

Second, just because humans can (and have) misread Scripture, doesn't mean that humans *always* err in their interpretation of Scripture. This is a clear denial of the perspicuity of Scripture (namely, that the main teachings are clear).

Third, if one employs the historical-grammatical approach, he or she is less liable to misinterpret the text than is someone looking at it through the eyes of a distorted "tradition" which has made major misinterpretations of Scripture such as the Immaculate Conception, the veneration of Mary, the bodily Assumption of Mary, worshiping the host, purgatory, transubstantiation, good works as a necessary condition for salvation—for which there is no real biblical support or universal consent of the Fathers. On all of these the "glasses" of the magisterium have obscured the plain truth of Scripture, rather than aid in it.

Fourth, "to claim that God's infallible unveiling in the Bible needs further infallible unveiling by God says that it was not unveiled properly to begin with. To be sure, there is a difference between objective disclosure (revelation) and subjective discovery (understanding)."[47]

---

46. See Norman L. Geisler and William Nix, *A General Introduction to the Bible* (Chicago: Moody, 1986), chaps. 12–13.

47. Geisler and MacKenzie, *Roman Catholics and Evangelicals*, 214. What is more, Catholic theology "maintains that unbelievers can and should understand the truth of *natural law* apart from the Roman Magisterium." If this is what people *ought* to do, why, then, should God's special revelation be any different? (Geisler, *The Church and Last Things*, 86).

Fifth, as already demonstrated, councils can and have erred in the past. Indeed, they have made contradictory "infallibility" pronouncements on the very topic of infallibility. For instance, the twentieth ecumenical council of Rome (Vatican I in 1870) declared the infallibility of the pope alone, without the consent of the church. Yet the sixteenth ecumenical Council of Constance (AD 1413–1418) declared that the Church has authority over the pope. Indeed, it used its superior authority to end the Great Schism of three simultaneous popes!

Response to the Argument Based on the Self-defeating Nature of Denials of Infallibility

Catholic apologists insist that evangelicals engage in self-defeating statements in their attempt to deny the need of an infallible magisterium. They claim the statement "There is no infallible authority for the church" is self-defeating because they are elevating a certain "authority" or "tradition" of their own by asserting that "no authority is needed" to interpret the Bible. For when an individual is doing just that, he is providing an authority by which Scripture is interpreted, namely, one's own understanding.

In response, first of all, there is confusion here between the determination and discovery. The authority to determine the meaning of Scripture is the author's, and God is the ultimate author through the human writer. The reader of Scripture has no authority to determine its meaning; only the author does, for it is he who is the efficient cause of it. Therefore the reader has no legitimate authority over the meaning of Scripture.[48]

Second, the reader is under the authority of Scripture as meant (determined) by God, as he attempts to discover (not determine) what it means. He is not an authority over the meaning of the text. God alone is that. The reader is reading under the authority of the text. Hence, its meaning is not determined by the reader. This is a postmodern fallacy.

Third, when one correctly discovers what God has determined in Scripture he no more needs to be infallible than does a person who correctly understands a speeding law (or most other laws). That ordinary non-infallible understanding of God's revelation is sufficient is evident in God's holding even unsaved people responsible for understanding and not obeying it (Rom. 2:12–15). Indeed, they are held "without excuse" because God has revealed it to them (Rom. 1:20). If the Catholic

---

48. See Norman L. Geisler, *Systematic Theology*, vol. 1: *Introduction and Bible* (Bloomington, MN: Bethany, 2002), chaps. 6 and 10.

argument were correct, one would have to posit an infallible magisterium in every unsaved person for him or her to have an adequate and culpable understanding of general revelation and the natural law. The truth is that in both general and special revelation from God one can have an adequate and sufficient understanding without having an infallible understanding. Indeed, all other major sections of Christendom have come to the same basic understanding on the essential doctrines of the faith they all hold in common.[49] If all these essentials of the faith—including the Trinity, virgin birth, deity of Christ, his atoning death, bodily resurrection, bodily ascension, and second coming—can be known by non-Catholics without an infallible magisterium, then it is proof positive that an infallible magisterium is not needed to come to a sufficient and saving knowledge of the common essentials of the Christian faith.

It is agreed that self-defeating statements are false. However, it is also false that there is an infallible authority for the church—and that Rome is that authority. As noted earlier, Rome has not demonstrated that she alone holds claim to that authority. For she has been wrong on many occasions. She has held contradictory views, which cannot both be infallibly true, and there is historical evidence for equal or greater antiquity of the Eastern church. Rome is not the oldest jurisdiction within Christendom (Eastern Orthodoxy is), therefore she cannot claim to be "the authority" of the Christian church. Where was the authority prior to the advent of the church in Rome and Peter's arrival there? And if Rome is the true church, then what about the churches of the East? Are they not part of the true body of Christ?

A Response to the Catholic Argument against Sola Scriptura

The primary theological argument used by Catholic apologists today to demonstrate the supposed need of an infallible magisterium is the negation of the Protestant principle of *sola Scriptura*. Catholics believe that evangelicals are deadlocked into a chaotic enterprise because of the adherence to the "Scripture only" principle.[50] But there are two main

49. These are all expressed in the creeds of the first five centuries of the church. For an enumeration of them see Norman L. Geisler and Ron Rhodes, *Conviction without Compromise* (Eugene, OR: Harvest House, 2007), part 1.
50. Catholics often misrepresent the evangelical position by insisting that *sola Scriptura* means that the Bible is the "only" authority for faith and doctrine. Evangelicals deny this and insist instead that it is the *final* authority rather than the "only" authority. Evangelicals appeal also to the laws of logic, commentaries, creeds, confessions, and the like to help formulate or articulate doctrines.

problems with this argument. First, it is logically flawed. More precisely, it is a false disjunction because there are other alternatives. Second, even granting the disjunction, their arguments against *sola Scriptura* fail, amounting to non sequiturs.

First, the false disjunction will be discussed. The logic of their argument can be put in this form: either the Protestant view of *sola Scriptura* is true or else the Roman Catholic view of an infallible magisterium is true. But this is clearly false both logically and historically. Historically, there are several other alternatives to an infallible pope. Eastern Orthodoxy and Anglicanism are two major cases in point. Both have survived in their official doctrinal orthodox forms without an infallible magisterium. Furthermore, logically, (1) the Bible alone, and (2) the Bible as interpreted with the help of a non-infallible source are not logical contradictions.

As long as one understands it to mean that (1) the Bible alone is the infallible basis for all doctrine and morals, and (2) we can be helped in our interpretation of the infallible Bible by means of some non-infallible (but reliable) sources: the creeds, tradition, or just good old common-sense rules of interpretation.

Second, the Catholic arguments against the Protestant principle of *sola Scriptura* do not follow. This will be shown by a point-by-point response.

Sola Scriptura *Leads to Denominational Splintering.* This is an ironic statement, since there are many sects (and differing opinions) even within the Catholic Church.[51] In fact, the first major split of the Christian church occurred in AD 1054, five hundred years prior to the Reformation. Thus the Roman Church is actually the first "Protestant" group, since she first protested against the Eastern church and sought to sever all formal ties with it. In fact, there exists more unity among those who hold to a proper view of *sola Scriptura* than among most Catholics. Indeed, all the essential Christian doctrines expressed in the Creeds of the first five centuries—which are held in common by all major sections of Christendom—are derived without an infallible magisterium by all the non-Catholic groups.

51. In fact, on October 1, 2005 renowned contemporary Catholic apologists, Robert Sungenis and Gerry Matatics (former evangelicals), debated the nature of the Mass, the central act of worship in Rome. What is more, Matatics (and a small group of Catholics known as "traditionalists") holds to a peculiar doctrine of the papacy, namely, *sedevacantism*, which holds that the "real" office of the papacy has been "vacant" since the time of the death of Pope Pius XII in 1958 (or in some cases, the death of Pope John XXIII), thus maintaining that the Catholicism of today is really apostate.

Sola Scriptura *Is Meaningless*. Catholics maintain that *sola Scriptura* is meaningless because it cannot even be stated without a defining authority of the Church. This is simply false. There is distinction between Rome's authority and that of the early church in general, as expressed in the early creeds. Furthermore, one can formulate "a true doctrine without giving any authority to any church of tradition," as seen above.

Sola Scriptura *Violates the Principle of Causality*. As shown earlier, it is not true that the Church *determined* the canon; rather she merely *discovered* the canon. It is fallacious to argue that because the church preceded the New Testament canon, she is therefore its cause. There existed a body of Scripture prior to the advent of the church, namely, the Old Testament. Likewise, Israel in no way determined the canon of the old writings, but like the church simply discovered it.

Sola Scriptura *Is Unbiblical Since It Is Not Mentioned in Scripture*. First, "a doctrine can be stated in the Bible that is based on the Bible alone." The Catholic Church, on the other hand, holds to a form of *sola ecclesia* (the "church alone" principle). By the same logic, one could claim this was self-defeating. For example, the Papal dogma is by the church and about the church. Second, the Bible does teach *sola Scriptura* in numerous places: Matthew 5:17–18; 15:1–5; Luke 24:27; 2 Timothy 3:16–17, etc. Of course, since the canon was a growing collection, then in practice no one statement, not even the last statement in the Bible, can refer to the whole Bible since the whole Bible was not finished by that time. But that does not negate *sola Scriptura*. It would be like trying to claim that the 1789 statement that every legitimate law in the U.S. must be constitutional could not also apply to every legitimate law added since that time to the present. For in principle every legitimate law in the U.S. is contained in the statement made in 1789 that all legitimate laws must be constitutional. Thus, Catholic apologists have designed a false conundrum which rightly construed does not eliminate *sola Scriptura*.

Sola Scriptura *Is Unworkable*. Catholics hold that "at no time in the history of the Church has this doctrine ever brought about a unity in the Church." First, this is false because the undivided church for the first four hundred years did achieve this unity based on this principle. Conversely, the doctrine of infallibility has not achieved unity; in fact, the doctrine of infallibility has caused chaos even among Catholics. Second, evangelicals who use the proper historical-grammatical method of interpretation achieve [unity] better than the Catholic hierarchy does.

Third, Eastern Orthodox and orthodox Anglicans have achieved essential orthodoxy by the legitimate non-infallible use of tradition.

Sola Scriptura *Is Illogical.* Catholic apologists say that Scripture does not teach *sola Scriptura*, hence it is self-defeating. However, the Bible does in fact teach it (see above). Further, a teaching can be biblical even if it is taught implicitly, as are the doctrines of the Trinity and the sovereignty of God.

Sola Scriptura *Does Not Define the Limits of the Canon.* That is, there is no inspired table of contents in the Bible. Therefore, there must be an infallible external source to define the canon." But this does not follow because it at best only shows there is a *role* for the church, not that it must be an infallible role. Fallible sources can make true statements. People do it all the time. Since all of—and only—the books of the canon have the earmarks of divine inspiration and since these earmarks are clear, one does not have to be infallible to recognize them. Just as Jesus could be recognized as divine by his nature and actions, even so the Bible can be recognized as divine by fallible men by the same means. Of course, as with the disciples, it is not "flesh and blood" (Matt. 16:7) but God who enlightens fallible men to this truth.

Sola Scriptura *Is Not Clear.* Catholics argue that since the Bible alone does not clearly present the essential truths of the Christian faith, an infallible magisterium is needed. However, there was no such magisterium for the first four hundred years of the church. Yet they were able to formulate and express in creeds the great fundamentals of the faith. Further, evangelicals who use the common historical-grammatical approach find essential agreement on the basic doctrines without a Catholic-like infallible teaching hierarchy. Thus, this Catholic objection fails.

Sola Scriptura *Was Not the Practice of the NT Church.* It is argued that the NT Church did not have all of Scripture, since it was not all written. However, "the growing size of the canon does not affect the doctrine that only the canon is infallible and binding. New revelation became binding when it was written and became part of the canon (cf. Dan. 9:2; 2 Pet. 3:15–16). The new revelation came with its own signs of divine authenticity. It did not take an infallible teacher to recognize them any more than it did for a lost Nicodemus to know that Christ was sent from God when he said, "Rabbi, we know that You are a teacher come from God, for no one can do these signs [miracles] that You do unless God is with him" (John 3:2 NKJV).

Sola Scriptura *Resulted from Extrabiblical Sources.* Catholics argue that many extrabiblical sources gave rise to the emergence of the belief that the Bible alone is sufficient for faith and practice, without an infallible teaching authority. There was, for example, the political desire for freedom from Rome; the cultural factor of the printing press; the intellectual rise of nominalism, and the social rise of individualism. Without these, the Protestant Reformation, with its teaching of *sola Scriptura*, would not have emerged. However, on examination this objection fails for many reasons. First, the early church believed and practiced *sola Scriptura* without all these factors. Second, as shown above, even if the early church used some form of apostolic tradition as an aid to understanding Scripture, there is no evidence that it was vested in an infallible teaching authority known as the Roman Catholic Church (see chap. 3). Third, the "tradition" used to understand the Bible was not infallible but historical (see Appendix 3). It was, in fact, only an apostolic tradition, meaning a demonstration that the later teachings of the church Fathers were historically traceable to that of the apostles and prophets of Christ who composed the New Testament. Finally, the Reformation was not a new creation out of these alleged later factors. Rather, it was a providential restoration to a large degree of the original position of the early church that arose in response to Rome's rejection of the biblical and early church view. Of course, God providentially utilized social factors such as the rise of the printing press and the throwing off of the shackles of medieval authoritarianism to aid in his restoration of the primitive truth of Christianity.

Sola Scriptura *Results in Mistranslation Errors.* Catholics argue that errors in translation of the Bible have arisen from the Protestant Reformation doctrine of the Bible alone. By neglecting an authoritative guide in forming and interpreting the Bible, Protestants have allegedly fallen into many errors. However, this argument overlooks several important factors. First, the presence of an infallible guide did not solve the problem, as Pope Sixtus's translation of the Vulgate demonstrates, since it contained literally thousands of errors. Further, even Jerome's prized Catholic version of the Vulgate, long considered the official translation of the Roman Church, mistranslated "repent" as "do penance," thus supporting the false view that works are a necessary condition of salvation.[52]

Further, this great Catholic scholar did not believe in the Roman Catholic canon since he rejected the apocryphal books Rome added to the Bible with an infallible pronouncement at the Council of Trent (in AD 1546).[53] Finally, while there are a few cultic mistranslations of the Bible (like the Jehovah's Witnesses' *New World Translation*), there are

52. See Geisler and MacKenzie, *Roman Catholics and Evangelicals*, chap. 12.
53. See Geisler and Nix, *General Introduction to the Bible*, chap. 15.

no major translations produced by Protestant scholars that deny any of the major essential doctrines of the Christian faith held in common by all major sections of Christianity from the first few centuries of the Christian church. Yet all of these many fine Protestant translations have been produced without an infallible ecclesiastic guide.[54]

Sola Scriptura *Needs an Interpretive Framework.* Rome states, the "Bible does not stand alone; it needs an interpretation." But, "only an infallible church provides this." The response to this is twofold. First, the Bible, like any normal human communication, needs no interpretive framework superimposed on it. All it needs is good exegesis, that is, reading the meaning out of it that the author put into it. It does not need eisegesis, that is, reading meaning into it from any outside source. In other words, the Bible simply needs historical-grammatical exegesis, not ecclesiastical eisegesis.

Further, as noted repeatedly, even if outside sources are used as an aid in understanding (such as understanding words and cultural setting), these need not be infallible to be helpful. Using such sources is a daily and common practice by both laypersons and scholars. It is sufficient for everyday life. It is used to understand road signs, news reports, and books. Housewives, courts, and judges employ it. There is nothing special, uncommon, or infallible about it. Yet it is sufficient for life and death matters. It provides an adequate and sufficient means for discovering truth without either claiming to be or being infallible. Even Roman Catholic laypersons and scholars use it all the time in their life and profession. Why then is an infallible guide (other than the Holy Spirit) needed when approaching Scripture? The fact is that there is no such need. Indeed, historically, we can compare the results of this *sola Scriptura* method with the results of the early Fathers, and the results are the same on all the basic doctrines of the Christian Church.[55] This should be no surprise because the commonsense, everyday (historical-grammatical) method is the same one used by the early Fathers when they derived the essential doctrines of the faith from Holy Scripture.[56]

Belief in sola Scriptura *Leads to a Misunderstanding of Scripture.* Catholics argue that "the belief in [the] Bible alone leads to a distortion of

54. Ibid.
55. Ibid.
56. This is not to say that no early father ever deviated from this method or employed other methods than this literal method on the Bible. Some, like Origen, did, but all the orthodox Fathers did not when deriving the essentials of the Faith, though some of them did on other matters. And when they deviated in nonessential doctrines, it was because they inconsistently deviated from the historical-grammatical method of interpretation.

historical facts since it does not use tradition to guide it." In response, several lines of evidence contradict this conclusion. First of all, it should be pointed out that "this is an assumption disguised as an argument." Second, exactly the opposite is true of Rome. For it is the use of traditions (many of them late ones) that misled Rome to posit the unbiblical doctrines of the bodily assumption of Mary, the veneration of Mary, prayers to her, transubstantiation, works necessary for salvation, and the infallibility of the pope. Third, "*sola Scriptura* need not reject early traditions. Indeed, they support it."[57] For history (the good sense of tradition) shows that the early Fathers of the first few centuries did not deviate from Scripture on these essential doctrines of the faith, as their famous creeds and confessions show.

Sola Scriptura *Misunderstands the Church Fathers.* Catholics further argue that the "Church Fathers affirmed the unique authority of Scripture but not its interpretation apart from tradition." This, they believe, supports the Roman Catholic view. However, it does not for several good reasons. First, the Roman view demands the primacy and infallibility of Peter and his successors, but the earliest Fathers do not substantiate this (see chap. 3). Second, this criticism of *sola Scriptura* begs the question for it assumes that Rome's interpretation of the Fathers is correct when, as we have shown, it is not. Third, "even if tradition is needed, it does not support the Catholic view." For the Eastern church, Anglicans, Lutherans, and even others have a legitimate role for tradition. It is used to support and express biblical truth but not to supplement or negate it. To repeat, as even the great Catholic scholar Thomas Aquinas said, "We believe the prophets and apostles because the Lord has been their witness by performing miracles. . . . And we believe the successors of the apostles and prophets only in so far as they tell us those things which the apostles and prophets have left in their writings." Finally, as noted above, the "Bible can be interpreted correctly apart from an authoritative tradition," as noted earlier in this chapter.[58]

Sola Scriptura *Leads to Hermeneutical Anarchy.* According to Catholic writers, "Hundreds of denominations that profess it do not even agree on fundamental teachings." The only alternative to this, they believe, is to accept an infallible interpreter of Scripture. However, this is clearly overstated. First, even if an external interpretive structure were needed, it would not have to be infallible, nor would it have to be Rome. Second,

---

"there are other influences, such as modernism, naturalism, rationalism, paganism, popularism, individualism," that have led to this apparent hermeneutical anarchy. *Sola Scriptura* should not be blamed for what they have done. Indeed, if we had properly heeded *sola Scriptura* via the historical-grammatical method, these external influences would not have distorted the central message of Scripture. Third, "[again,] those with the proper means of interpretation [i.e., the historical-grammatical approach] have wide agreement on essential doctrines."[59] There is no real demonstrated need for an infallible authoritarian structure. Nor is there any substantial biblical or historical evidence that Rome is that alleged structure (see chaps. 2 and 3).

Sola Scriptura *Is Not Taught by Any Church Council or Fathers*. This claim of Rome is both misleading and false. First, it is misleading since the early Creeds presuppose and imply the Scriptures as their basis. It is implied in the Apostles' Creed by its reference to biblical truths and even using biblical terms, such as God being Creator of "heaven and earth"; Jesus being "crucified" under "Pontius Pilate" and rising on "the third day," and coming again to judge "the living and the dead." The Nicene Creed (AD 325) likewise speaks in biblical language of Christ as the only "begotten" Son of God; creation of "heaven and earth"; the "virgin Mary"; and Jesus coming to judge "the living and the dead."

Second, the early creeds even explicitly refer to Scripture as their source. They speak of Scripture as that which was "spoken through the prophets." The Chalcedonian Creed (AD 451) affirms the earlier creed with its biblical phrases. It also explicitly describes Scripture as what "the prophets of old testified" and containing what "the Lord Jesus Christ himself taught."

Third, something does not have to be explicitly taught in Scripture to be true. Even other essential teachings of the faith were not explicitly taught in the technical sense of this term. The doctrine of the Trinity is a case in point. All the essential components of the Trinity are taught in Scripture. For example, (1) There is one God; (2) There are three persons who are called God: the Father, the Son, and the Holy Spirit. Now the Trinity is a necessary and logical conclusion from these clearly taught biblical premises, but the formal doctrine of the Trinity as such is not explicitly taught in Scripture. Likewise, *sola Scriptura* need not be explicitly taught in the creeds to be true. Fourth, it is false to claim that no early Fathers taught *sola Scriptura*. As we have demonstrated

59. Geisler and MacKenzie, *Roman Catholics and Evangelicals*.

elsewhere (in Appendix 4), the early Fathers did believe in *sola Scriptura* in the formal sense. Indeed, even the Roman Catholic Church acknowledges that special divine revelation ceased with the New Testament. That is, the infallible canon is closed. They claim only that there is an infallible interpreter of that canon, namely, the bishop of Rome. But this is the point in dispute for which no definitive arguments have yet been presented. Indeed, the chain of argument has been found weak or broken at every major link (see chaps. 2–5).

Finally, the church councils never taught another great doctrine of the faith held by all major sections of Christendom—the divine inspiration of Scripture. For "Church Councils never taught the inspiration of the Bible either. But they everywhere assume it."[60]

Sola Scriptura *Results in the Undermining of Pastoral Authority and Discipline.* This argument, like others, does not follow from the premises. There has always been a discipline problem in the church. But it is a giant and unjustifiable leap from this to the necessity of an infallible pope. First of all, there were serious pastoral problems in the New Testament church, even when authoritative apostles were on hand. True, a big problem was solved at Jerusalem (in Acts 15). But the decision was made by "the apostles and elders" (15:23), not by Peter as the first pope. James seemed to be in charge, since he summed up the conference leading to the final decision by the group as a whole (see vv. 15:13ff.). Second, another serious problem arose, but this time it was the first Roman pope himself who was the problem and had to be rebuked by another apostle because he had led others astray by not being "straightforward about the truth of the gospel" (Gal. 2:14 NASB). Ironically, it was the Roman Catholic pope being rebuked by another apostle, not Peter as pope rebuking another. Third, even with its claim of an infallible pope, Rome is guilty of the very thing it is claiming about Protestants. Orthodox Protestants, all of whom hold to all the essentials of the faith, were not in charge when Rome's allegedly infallible pope could not stop the greatest schism in the history of the church, that between the Eastern and Western churches (AD 1054). Indeed, it was the Roman insistence on its primacy that was at the base of this divide. So, rather than unite the church, Rome was largely responsible for dividing it. Likewise, it was Rome's infallible and unerring magisterium on faith and morals that was unable to discipline its own members from errant doctrine and morals that led to the need for a reformation. So, the blame should

60. Aquinas, *On Truth*, 14, 10 AD 11.

not be on Protestants, who tried to reform and restore the church to its early, more pure status.

Rather, it was Rome who deviated in doctrine and practice from the early, more pure form of Christianity that prompted the need for a reformation.

Summary and Conclusions

As we have shown, neither the biblical nor the theological arguments for infallibility are sound. The evidence is to the contrary. Rome's argument fails historically, factually, and logically, leaving the doctrine of infallibility in rational limbo. There are no good reasons to support it, and if one decides to believe it, then it is largely a matter of faith (see chap. 8).

Indeed, not only does the doctrine of papal infallibility lack sufficient evidence, but there is strong evidence against it both biblically and theologically. Biblically, the best case one can justifiably muster is for Peter's early leadership among the apostles but not his primacy over the apostles and the whole church. Theologically, the doctrine is fraught with serious problems, as even some Catholic writers (like Kühn) admit. We need only mention the facts that: (1) some popes taught heretical doctrines; (2) one Pope published an "inspired" Bible with hundreds of errors in it; (3) two ecumenical councils contradict each other, one (AD 1413–1418) affirming the authority of the Council over the pope and the other (1870) affirming the authority of the pope over the council; (4) other popes have made serious errors such as condemning Galileo for his heliocentric beliefs; 5) at other times there were multiple popes at the same time, leaving the fallible elect to try to determine who their infallible leader really was; 6) then too there were no infallible lists of what the infallible statements of the pope were. Hence, for all practical purposes having an infallible pope is no advantage over not having one. Or to put it another way, (7) by the time one adds up the non-infallible list of qualifications of what constitutes infallible statements, the doctrine of infallibility proves to be just as fallible as non-infallible statements made by opposing groups in Christendom.

In short, infallibility in its straightforward, unqualified form sounds like a wonderful thing. But in its qualified form it "dies a death by a thousand qualifications." In theory it looks sturdy, but in practice it is a weak and wobbly chair in which Peter's successor sits. It looks on the surface as if the doctrine is built on a solid rock. But after careful analysis and critique, the fallibility of infallibility becomes clear.

CHAPTER 6

THE ROMAN ARGUMENT
FOR APOSTOLIC SUCCESSION

here are many links in the Catholic argument for the apostolic
succession of the present bishop of Rome, including those for his
primacy and infallibility discussed in previous chapters. First, it
must be shown that Jesus and his apostles set up an episcopal primacy
in the New Testament (chap. 2). Second, it must be demonstrated that
Peter was chosen to serve as the first bishop in that system (chap. 3).
Third, it must be proven that the primacy of Peter involved his infallibility when teaching on doctrine and morals (chap. 5). Finally, it must
be shown that by apostolic succession the present bishop of Rome
rightfully inherits the chair of Saint Peter set up by Christ.

But even if one could demonstrate that Jesus established a chair to
be filled by his vicar, and that he appointed Peter to occupy that chair,
and that whoever speaks from that chair does so infallibly, there is
still another very important missing link in the argument. It must be
proven that Jesus established apostolic succession—by which through
a historic chain the current bishop of Rome (pope) rightfully occupies
Peter's chair.

There are two important steps in the doctrine of apostolic succession.
First, it must be demonstrated that Jesus set up and the apostles practiced this apostolic succession. Second, it must be shown that there is
an unbroken apostolic chain from Peter to the current pope. As anyone

familiar with the issue knows, these are by no means self-evident truths. In fact, as we will discover, there are serious challenges on both points.

The Alleged Basis for Apostolic Succession

The Roman Catholic biblical claims for apostolic succession can be divided into three basic arguments. First, Jesus established it and the apostles practiced it. Second, the preservation of Christian truth demands it. Third, history confirms it.

The Alleged Biblical Basis for Apostolic Succession

We have already discussed—and found wanting—the alleged biblical basis for the primacy and infallibility of Peter (chaps. 4–6). But the texts used to support those doctrines do not as such support apostolic succession. For even if Jesus had given primacy to Peter, that in itself would not prove he intended that Peter would have the power to pass this on to someone else. Given this, even the alleged textual basis for apostolic succession is scant. Consider the following:

Matthew 28:20

Catholic authority Ludwig Ott argued, "The promise of His aid given to the Apostles 'even to the consummation of the world' (Matt. 28:20) presupposes that the apostolic office is perpetuated in the successors of the Apostles."[1]

Response: In context nothing is said here about the transfer of apostolic powers. It speaks only of Christ's promised presence to the end of the age as the fulfillment of his great commission to "make disciples of all nations." This is something that is promised to all disciplers, not just bishops and popes.

Acts 14:23

Luke wrote of the apostle Paul and his associate, "When they had appointed elders in every church . . . they committed them to the Lord in whom they had believed." This is taken by some to indicate the transfer of apostolic power and succession.

Response: First of all, the text does not say they ordained other apostles to oversee a group of churches. This appointment was only for a local church. Second, they ordained elders (plural), not a single bishop over the elders or over other churches. Finally, the apostles also "laid hands on" a group of deacons (in Acts 6:6), but this was clearly not a transfer

1. Ludwig Ott, *Fundamentals of Catholic Dogma* (Rockford, IL: Tan, 1960), 278.

of apostolic authority to them. It was simply endowing them with gifts for their ministry. Indeed, one of the deacons (Philip) on whom they laid hands had the gift of both evangelism and healing (Acts 8:6), but his converts did not receive the Holy Spirit through him. Philip had to call for the apostles to perform this act directly (Acts 8:15–18). So, "laying on of the apostles' hands" did not grant Philip any powers of apostolic succession.

Timothy and Titus

Catholics also argue that "the Apostles, following the will of Christ, handed over their powers to others, for example, Saint Paul to Timothy and Titus, cf. 2 Timothy 4:2–5, Titus 2:1 (teaching power); 1 Timothy 5:19–21, Titus 2:15 (pastoral power); 1 Timothy 5:22, Titus 1:5 (sacredotal power). In the position of the two disciples of the Apostles, the monarchial episcopate, into which apostolic office finally evolves, appears clearly for the first time."[2]

Response: Nothing here speaks of apostolic succession, but of pastoral care, which was the duty of all elders (1 Pet. 5:1–4; Acts 20:17, 28) of which there was a plurality in every New Testament church (Acts 14:23; Phil. 1:1; Titus 1:5). As for the alleged "sacredotal power" of a monarchial bishop, the text cited says no such thing. Instead, it refers to a plurality of "elders" appointed in every city (Titus 1:5). Again, in Philippians 1:1 the reference is to a plurality of bishops (= elders) in a local church, not one bishop over a local church or group of churches. Acts 14:23 says clearly that the apostles "appointed elders [plural] in every church."

Revelation 2–3

Ott insists that "The 'angels' of the seven communities in Asia Minor (Apc. 2–3) are, according to the traditional interpretation, which, however, has been contradicted, monarchic bishops."[3]

Response: Even Ott admits that this interpretation is disputed. The word *angel* simply means "messenger" sent by John the apostle. That they were not authoritarian bishops but apostolic delegates is indicated by several things. First, the word "bishop" is not used of these messengers. Since the word was a common New Testament word (Phil. 1:1; 1 Tim. 3:1; Titus 1:7) and since it stood for a person of authority in the local church, surely it would have been used had John been referring to an

2. Ibid.
3. Ibid.

individual with authority in the local church, like a bishop. Second, if it had been a person responsible for the oversight in that church, then surely he would have been condemned for allowing the sins listed to go on in that church. Third, there would have been no need for John the apostle to write these condemnations. The local bishop could have handled them. And if a higher authority was needed, why not appeal to whoever occupied Peter's chair at the time? Fourth, apostles used delegates to administer their authority in churches needing it, as Paul used Titus in Crete, saying, "For this reason I left you in Crete, that you should set in order the things that are lacking" (Titus 1:5 NKJV). Fifth, if the "messengers" had been part of that local church, then surely they too would have been called upon to repent (2:5), but they were not. Sixth, the word *bishop* (or its synonym *elder*) is never used in the singular as an overseer of a single church or group of churches. Paul wrote to "the bishops and deacons" (Phil. 1:1). They appointed "elders" (Acts 14:23) in every city in which they established a church. Paul called the "elders of the church" at Ephesus together (Acts 20:17) and said God made "overseers" (i.e., bishops) of the flock. Indeed, Peter himself acknowledged "the elders" as "overseers" of their church (1 Pet. 5:1, 2). The elders or bishops were explicitly told that they were undershepherds, not overlords of the flock (1 Pet. 5:3) and that Christ as the invisible "Chief Shepherd" ruled the church (1 Pet. 5:4).

The Alleged Historical Basis for Apostolic Succession

According to Ott, there is early and continual evidence for apostolic succession. He sees this in a number of passages, beginning with Clement of Rome.

Clement of Rome (AD 95–97)

"The disciple of the Apostles, St. Clement of Rome, narrates concerning the perpetuation of the hierarchical powers by the Apostles: In countries and towns they preached and appointed their neophytes after they have proved these in spirit, as bishops and deacons of the future faithful: (*Cor.* 42, 4)." Clement adds, "Our Apostles through the Lord Jesus Christ, knew that disputes would arise about the episcopal office. For this reason, as they received exact knowledge of this in advance, they appointed the above named, and subsequently gave directions that when these should fall asleep, other tried men should take over their duties (*Cor.* 44, 1–2)."

Response: There is no evidence in Clement for the Roman position. Clement of Rome is one of the earliest nonbiblical writers. He instructed "the Church of God which sojourneth in Corinth" to be "submitting yourselves to your rulers [plural] and rendering to the older men among you the honour which is their due" (1). He speaks of the apostles Peter and Paul as "most righteous pillars [plural] of the Church" (5). Believers are not urged to submit to the authority of Rome but to "conform to the glorious and venerable rule which hath been handed down to us" from the apostles (7) and to "do that which is written" in the Scripture (13; cf. 23). He did not hold to the primacy of Peter and warned against leaders exalting themselves over others, declaring, "For Christ is with them that are lowly of mind, not with them that exalt themselves over the flock" (16). Rather, "Let us reverence our rulers; let us honour our elders" (21), clearly indicating a plurality of elders in the church of "Smyrna" to whom he is writing (1). Clement speaks of "the Apostles" who "appointed . . . bishops and deacons" (42) in the church. He rebuked those who got rid of their sound and godly bishops, saying, "These men [plural] we consider to be unjustly thrust out from their ministration" (44). Clement speaks of the Corinthian church's "sedition against its presbyters [elders]" (47). They were told, rather, to "submit yourselves unto the presbyters" [plural] (57). So, Clement, one of the earliest and best testimonies on this topic, is far from supporting the Roman Catholic view of even the primacy of Peter, let alone his infallibility or apostolic succession.

Ignatius of Antioch (d. AD 115)

Ott contends, "Ignatius of Antioch attests that at the head of the Asia Minor communities, also in the farthest countries (Eph. 3, 2), there stands in each a single (monarchic) bishop, in whose hands the whole religious and disciplinarian conduct of the community lies. Nobody is supposed to do anything which concerns the Church without the bishop. Only that Eucharist is regarded as valid and legal that is consummated under the Bishop or by one authorized by him. There, where Jesus is, the Catholic Church is. . . . He that honours the Bishop is honoured by God; he that does anything without consulting the Bishop serves the devil" (Smyrna. 8, 1–2; 9:1).

Response: In response, several things are important to remember. First, there are questions about both the date and authenticity of Ignatius's epistles.[4] No dogma should be based on a disputed text. Second, even

4. Ibid.

on the assumption they are early second-century and without interpolations, at best, it merely manifests an early form of a minimal episcopal
form of church government in which each church has a bishop in addition to elders and deacons. Third, there is nothing here about either
the infallibility of Peter or his successors. Other than an early example
of a congregation having a lead elder (or bishop) among a plurality rule,
there is no indication of a single ruling bishop of a local church, let
alone a universal church. Indeed, he speaks of God who is "the Bishop
of all" (3). He adds, "Neither do ye anything without the bishop and
the presbyters" (7), showing a plurality and co-ordinate leadership. He
also speaks of a group of "churches" (12) as independent entities that
have their own elders and bishop (pastor) and of his being a "member"
of a local church (13). Ignatius disavowed apostolic status, saying, "I do
not enjoin you, as Peter and Paul did." He gave equal status to Peter
and Paul[5] (Smyrneans, 3), saying, God is the shepherd of the church at
Smyrna" and "Jesus alone" is its bishop (9).

Justin Martyr (ca. AD 100–165)
According to Ott, Justin is called the bishop, "the overseer of the brethren, "the one who celebrates the liturgy" (Apol. 1.65, 67).

Response: It is a serious stretch to find apostolic succession in this
meager phrase. Further, Justin is a whole century after the time of the
apostles, during the same period that other serious doctrinal and practical challenges emerged against the church. He was not a contemporary
to anyone who was contemporary with the apostles.

Irenaeus (ca. AD 130–200)
He said, "We can enumerate the bishops installed by the apostles and
their successors from their times down to our own" (Adv, *Haer.* III, 3, 1).
He gives the oldest known list of bishops of Rome from the apostles to
the twelfth successor (III 3, 1).

Response: As we have shown elsewhere (chap. 3 and Appendix 1),
Irenaeus does not support the Roman view on either the primacy of

5. Many have challenged the authenticity of these works. But Anglican scholars like Bishop
Usher and J. B. Lightfoot have strongly defended them. Nonetheless, a later date is not without
reasons. First, there is no manuscript evidence forcing belief in an early date. Second, there
are differing manuscript traditions, one of which is shorter, indicating changes that have been
made from the original. Third, the more highly developed form of authoritarian episcopal
governments fits better at a somewhat later date. Fourth, the repetitive references to a single
authoritative bishop found throughout these epistles seem a bit forced and contrived. Finally,
if an earlier date is assumed, it contradicts other books from this period just discussed.

Peter or apostolic succession. This is borne out by many facts. First, even the founding of the church at Rome was said to be by two apostles, Paul and Peter,[6] not by Peter alone. Second, he speaks often of "the apostolic tradition"[7] and "the blessed apostles" (plural) who "founded and built up the Church."[8] He wrote, "These [apostles] are the voices of the Church from which every Church had its origin." Third, he speaks of a plurality of elders in the local church, saying, *"Nor will any one of the rulers (Bishops) in the Churches, however highly gifted he may be in point of eloquence, teach doctrines different from these (for no one is greater than the Master)."*[9] In short, Christ is the invisible Head of all the visible churches, and Christ's teaching through the authority of his apostles is the basis for the unity of the one true church. Fourth, Christ, not Peter, is the head of the church. Irenaeus declared: "The Word of God [Christ] is supreme, so also in things visible and corporeal *He might possess the supremacy, and, taking to Himself the pre-eminence, as well as constituting Himself Head of the Church,* He might draw all things to Himself at the proper time."[10] Clearly, Christ has no vicar on earth; he himself heads his universal church. As even Peter himself said, elders are only undershepherds who lead the local congregations to follow the "Chief Shepherd" (1 Pet. 5:1–4). Fifth, the only sense in which the apostles are still present in the church is not through apostolic successors but through apostolic doctrine. He refers to apostolic unity in all the churches based on "the doctrine of the apostles" (Acts 2:42). Sixth, his reference to "that tradition derived from the apostles . . . by means of the succession of the bishops" was a supplemental and apologetic argument used against heretics to show that history supported his claim to the correct interpretation of apostolic teaching. Seventh, Irenaeus said, "It is a matter of necessity that *every Church should agree* [Latin, *convenire*] *with this Church*, on account of its preeminent authority, that is, the faithful everywhere, inasmuch as the apostolic tradition has been preserved continuously by those faithful men *who exist everywhere."*[11]

But noted expert on the early fathers, J. N. D. Kelly, explained that to take this in an authoritarian Roman Catholic sense is wrong for many

6. J. B. Lightfoot and J. R. Harmer, eds., *The Apostolic Fathers* (Grand Rapids, MI: Baker, 1988), 151.
7. Irenaeus, "Against Heresies," in *Ante-Nicene Fathers*, ed. Alexander Roberts and James Donaldson (Grand Rapids, MI: Eerdmans, 1989), 1.414.
8. Ibid., 1.416.
9. Ibid., emphasis added.
10. Ibid., emphases added.
11. Ibid., 3.443, emphasis added.

reasons: (1) The weakness of the final clause strikes them as "intolerable."[12] Second, "the normal meaning of *convenire* is 'resort to,' 'foregather at,' and *necesse est* does not easily bear the sense of 'ought.'"[13] Indeed, the editor of the *Apostolic Fathers* volume in *The Ante-Nicene Fathers*, A. Cleveland Coxe, cites one candid Roman Catholic scholar who translates it as follows: "For to this Church, on account of more potent principality, it is necessary that every Church (that is, those who are on every side faithful) *resort*; in which Church ever, *by those who are on every side*, has been preserved that tradition which is from the apostles."[14] Coxe adds, "Here it is obvious that the faith was kept at Rome, by *those who resort there* from all quarters. She was a mirror of the Catholic World, owing her orthodoxy to them; not the Sun, dispensing her own light to others, but the glass bringing their rays into focus."[15] This is in direct contrast to the proclamation of Pope Pius IX (see below) who "informed his Bishops, at the late Council (in 1870), that they were not called to bear their testimony, but to hear his infallible decree."[16] In short, Rome, as the capital of the empire, had attracted people there from all over so that its influence was *reflective* of the whole church but not *authoritative* over it.[17] In short, there is no good reason to believe that Irenaeus held that there was an authoritative line of bishops established by Christ beginning with Peter and followed by all his apostolic successors.

Tertullian (AD 160–222)

According to Ott, "Tertullian, like Irenaeus, bases the truth of the Catholic teaching on the apostolic succession of the Bishops (De praesc. 32)."[18]

Response: Besides the dispute about the authenticity of this text, this list does not correspond to that of Irenaeus. The list attributed by Ott to Tertullian is Linus, Cletus, and Anacletus. Whereas, the list given by Irenaeus (*Haer.* 3.2) is Linus, Anacletus, and Clement. Further, the alleged text by Tertullian says, "Of whom the first whom Peter bade to take his place and sit upon this chair in mightiest Rome where he himself sat, was Linus" (Book 3, 360 in Schaff, 156). Yet the Irenaeus text said "the blessed Apostles, then, having founded and built up the Church, committed into the hands of Linus, the office of the episcopate." Further, as

---

12. Ibid., 1.415–16, emphasis added.
13. Ibid.
14. Ibid.
15. Cleveland Cox, "Apostolic Fathers," in *Ante-Nicene Fathers*, 1.415.
16. Ibid.
17. Ibid., 461.
18. Ibid.

shown elsewhere, Irenaeus did not believe in the sole universal authority of a bishop in Rome over all churches (see Appendix 1). He believed Rome, as capital city ("mightiest Rome"), was reflective of the universal church but not authoritative over it (see also chap. 3).

The Arguments against Apostolic Succession

The arguments against the Roman doctrine of apostolic succession are both biblical and historical. First, let's look at the biblical arguments.

Biblical Arguments against the Primacy of Peter

The Roman Catholic arguments for apostolic succession are based, first of all, on the primacy of Peter. For if Peter did not have apostolic primacy, as Rome argues that he had, then there is no way he could pass it on to anyone. You simply cannot give what you do not have to give. This being the case, the first link in the argument for apostolic succession is broken. For as we have shown earlier (in chap. 3) both the biblical and theological arguments for the primacy of Peter fail. The most that can be shown biblically is that Peter had early and temporary apostolic leadership among the apostles. But there are no texts to support an apostolic primacy over the other apostles.

Indeed, to the contrary there is strong evidence from the New Testament that Peter did not have any primacy after the early part of Acts and his using the "keys" to open the historic door to the Jews (Acts 2) and Gentiles (Acts 10). This is indicated by the following facts: (1) Peter was only part of the foundation along with the other apostles (Eph. 2:20); (2) the same power to bind given to Peter was also given to the other apostles (Matt. 18:18); (3) Peter was sent out by others in his local church (Acts 8:14); (4) he was held to account by the local church (Acts 11:1–18); (5) he was rebuked for his error by another apostle (Gal. 2:11–14); (6) Peter never passed any apostolic authority to others. Instead, the apostles appointed elders in each local church (Acts 14:23); (7) Peter did not head up the first interchurch meeting in Jerusalem (Acts 15); James did since he summed up the issue and the decision (Acts 15:13–21); (8) after the first chapters in Acts, Peter virtually vanishes from the scene and Paul is the dominant apostle; (9) Paul, under inspiration of the Holy Spirit, declared that he was not inferior to any other apostles for, he said, "they added nothing to me" (Gal. 2:6). He added elsewhere, "In no way was I inferior to these super-apostles . . . " (2 Cor. 12:11);[19] 10) Peter considered himself merely to be a "fellow elder" (1 Pet. 5:1), not a uniquely authoritative bishop over them.

The second link in the chain for apostolic succession is also broken. For there is no evidence in the New Testament after the birth of the church and its foundation in the apostles (Eph. 2:20) that apostles could or did pass on their apostolic office to others. Indeed, there is strong evidence to the contrary. Here are the facts as recorded in the New Testament.

First, before the church was born by the baptism of the Holy Spirit (Acts 1:5; cf. 1 Cor. 12:13), Judas, one of the twelve apostles, had defected and died. After prayer and in fulfillment of Scripture (Acts 1:20, 24), he was replaced by a vote of the brethren by Matthias (Acts 1:16) who was thereafter numbered with the other eleven (Acts 1:26).

Second, once the twelfth apostle was in place, no new apostles were added to the unique group of twelve. They were unique because they are the foundation of the church (Eph. 2:20), and their names are inscribed, one each, on the foundations of the Holy City in Revelation (21:14). They were also unique in their "doctrine," which was the foundation of the church (Acts 2:42). They were also unique in their authoritarian role of discipline in the early church (Acts 5:5, 10). Further, they were unique in their ability to speak supernaturally in a foreign language unknown to them on Pentecost (Acts 2) and to pass this gift on to others (Acts 8, 10). Later, an apostle, though not of the twelve, also passed the gift of tongues on to the Ephesians (Acts 19).

Third, the twelve apostles were also unique because to be in their group one had to (1) have been with Jesus from the beginning (cf. John 15:27; Heb. 2:3), and (2) be an eyewitness of the resurrection (Acts 1:22). The apostle Paul was not one of the Twelve even though he was an eyewitness of the resurrected Christ (1 Cor. 9:1; 15:7). For Paul refers to "the twelve" apostles as "all the apostles" in 1 Corinthians 15:5, 7. Indeed, if Paul wrote Hebrews, as many believe, he puts himself in another category ("us") from "those who heard" him (Christ) (Heb. 2:3). He also had his message confirmed by the twelve apostles, as he said, "to make sure I was not running or had not run in vain" (Gal. 2:2). So, the Twelve were a unique category of apostles who were considered the "foundation" of the church and were given special gifts to prove that, including healing incurable diseases, raising the dead (Matt. 10:8), speaking in a foreign language known to the listener but not to the speaker

19. Ludwig Ott, in ibid.

(Acts 2:5), bringing supernatural judgment on believers who lied to God (Acts 5:4, 10), and performing instantly successful exorcisms on those demon possessed (Acts 16:16–18).

Fourth, the apostles had the ability to give spiritual gifts to others to aid in their ministry. They laid hands on select deacons (in Acts 6:6), one of whom was Philip who had both the gift of evangelism (Acts 8:4–6) and healing (Acts 8:6–7). Paul reminded Timothy of the spiritual gift he had given him (2 Tim. 1:6). But in no case did the apostles give anyone the gift of apostle to enable him to replace one of the final group of twelve who had been established just before Pentecost. Indeed, when the apostle James died (Acts 12:2) he was not replaced by another apostle to fill his shoes. James, being there on Pentecost when the church was founded, was one of the apostles whose name will be on the Holy City of the New Jerusalem (Rev. 22:12).

Fifth, there were others who were some "apostles" in another sense of the term than part of "the twelve." Paul was called to be an "apostle" (Gal. 1). Indeed, he had seen the resurrected Christ (in Acts 9) as he reminded the Corinthians (1 Cor. 9:1; 15:8). He even had special miraculous "signs of an apostle" (2 Cor. 12:12), but he was not one of the unique group of twelve who were there from the beginning of Jesus' ministry (Acts 1:22), there from the foundation of the church at Pentecost (Acts 1:5; 2:1ff.), and whose names will be there in the Holy City (Rev. 22:12). Barnabas was called an apostle too (Acts 14:14), but he was this by association with an apostle. Others like Timothy and Titus served as apostolic delegates (Titus 1:5). But all these fell short of the qualifications to be one of the Twelve (Acts 1:22).

Sixth, when Jesus commissioned Peter for a special mission to use the "keys" to open the door of the gospel to both Jews (Acts 2) and Gentiles (Acts 10), Jesus said, "I give *you* [not 'your successors'] the keys of the kingdom" (Matt. 16:19). The "keys" Peter used to open these doors were singular, one-time events [cf. Acts 11:15; 15:14; Heb. 2:3–4], with no New Testament indication that divine, apostolic (let alone infallible) authority was given to the apostles' successors. Jesus never said, "I give *you* [not your successor] the keys . . . " (Matt. 16:19). If the Roman view were correct, he should have said, "I give to you and your successors the keys."

Seventh, when the apostles did pass anything on to their successors it was either their "apostles' doctrine" (Acts 2:42), a gift for ministry (Act 6:6; 2 Tim. 1:6), or helping them to start a self-governing and self-propa-

gating church by appointing "elders" (Acts 14:23; Titus 1:5). It was not
to make new apostles to replace themselves at or before their deaths.

Further, these original, select individuals were given certain unmistakable "signs of an apostle" (2 Cor. 12:12 NKJV), including the ability
to raise the dead on command (Matt. 10:8), immediately heal diseases
that were naturally incurable (Matt. 10:8; John 9:1–7), speak messages
in languages they had never studied (Acts 2:1–8; cf. 10:44–46), and
give gifts to others so that they could assist in the apostolic mission of
founding the church.

Eighth, these unique miraculous powers given to the apostles ceased
during their lifetimes. Hebrews 2:3–4 refers to these gifts as already
past (by ca. AD 64–69) when Hebrews was written.[20] These apostolic
signs were of great importance in confirming the message of God to the
people of God. Without these unmistakable signs there would be no
sure way to determine whether God had communicated or not. These
were "signs" exclusively given to the apostles and passed on by them
to their first-century associates during the transitional period of the
church's existence. These sign gifts enabled the apostles to speak and
act with unmatched authority as those who established the foundation
of the church.

Ninth, it is clear from all of the above that the gift of an apostle was
a one-time, temporary gift, and this negates the Roman notion of apostolic succession.[21] The argument can be summarized as follows: (1) The
apostles in the special gifted and authoritative sense lived only in the
first century since they had to be an eyewitness of the resurrected Christ
(Acts 1:22). (2) They were only needed for the church's foundation
(Eph. 2:20) on which others could build later. (3) The special gifts of an
apostle (2 Cor. 12:12) ceased in the first century (Heb. 2:3–4).[22] (4) Jesus
gave these special apostolic powers only to the apostles to establish his
church (Matt. 16:18), not to their successors. That is to say, the twelve
apostles never appointed apostles to succeed them (Acts 12:2; 14:23).
(5) Not only the gifts of an apostle, but the very term *apostle* faded in
later New Testament usage (see 2 John 1; 3 John 1; Rev. 1:1). (6) A
confirmation that true apostles lived only in the New Testament is that
second-century impostors had to claim apostleship to gain acceptance

20. Ibid.
21. See Norman L. Geisler, *A Popular Survey of the New Testament* (Grand Rapids, MI: Baker, 2008), chap. 22.
22. Ibid., 92.

for their writings and forged writings in apostles' names such as *The Gospel of Peter* and *The Gospel of Thomas.*

Given all this, the bishop of Rome (or anyone else after the apostles) falls far short of being a true successor to Peter and the apostles.[23] Thus, *"the absence of these apostolic gifts proves the absence of apostolic authority;* what remains today is the apostolic *teachings* (in the New Testament) not the apostolic *office.* The authority of the apostolic *writings* replaced the authority of the apostolic *writers."*[24] How, then, can Rome claim apostolic authority for the bishop of Rome when his authority is unaccompanied by apostolic signs as the true New Testament apostles were?

Of course, the Catholic apologist may appeal to the so-called "miracle of the mass," namely, transubstantiation—where the conversion of the whole substance of the bread and wine is said to become the whole substance of the body and blood of Christ.[25] However, this miraculous claim of the mass is unverifiable. This so-called miracle, then, is not of the same nature as those miracles performed by the apostles, since their signs and wonders were empirically verifiable (i.e., via the senses)—which included the physical healing of the sick (touch), the bodily raising of the dead (sight), and the speaking of unlearned foreign languages (sound). But even after its consecration the wine still looks like wine, smells like wine, and tastes like wine! And to believe that it is really anything else is a sheer act of faith unsupported by any empirical evidence.[26]

Historical Arguments against Apostolic Succession

This may be addressed both negatively and positively. Negatively, there are no good arguments for the apostolic primacy of Peter, which is basic to his having any apostolic power to pass on to anyone (see chap. 3). Second, the arguments for the infallibility of Peter fail (see chap. 5), and this is the kind of apostolic authority Peter is supposed to have passed on to his successors. Third, as shown above, none of the Catholic argu-

23. This does not mean God has done no miracles since then but only that the special *gifts* of an apostle have ceased. The *fact* of miracles is possible as long as God exists, but the special *gift* of miracles existed only as long as God needed them.
24. Geisler, *Systematic Theology,* vol. 4: *The Church and Last Things* (Bloomington, MN: Bethany House, 2005), 80. Emphasis added. What is more, Peter wasn't infallible; and if he wasn't infallible, how then could he be the first pope, since, according to Rome, "infallibility" is of the *very nature* of the office of the papacy? If he wasn't the first pope, he certainly couldn't have had successors to continue a nonexistent office (Geisler, *A Popular Survey,* 920).
25. Ibid., 80, emphasis added.
26. While it is believed that the *substance* of the bread and wine changes into the body and blood of Jesus, the *accidens* remain the same; thus it still looks, smells, and tastes like bread and wine; E. A. Livingstone, *Oxford Concise Dictionary of the Christian Church* (Oxford: Oxford University Press, 2000), 586.

ments from early church history really prove apostolic succession. The best they show—and then nearly a century later—is that a minimal form of episcopal church government was emerging in the early second century. They prove neither Roman primacy for Peter nor any succession of these kinds of apostolic power.

Positively, the picture from the earliest Fathers is contrary to the Roman view (see chap. 2).

1) There was a plurality of elders (bishops) in each local church, not a single bishop over a church, nor a single bishop over the universal church.

2) When later the concept of a single bishop arose, it was of a bishop along with a plurality of elders in a local church.

3) Even when this practice arose, it was a far cry from the Roman view of Peter as primate over all elders (bishops) and churches. A review of the detailed analysis and citations from the primary sources (in chap. 3) reveals a picture of church government more like that of the New Testament with a plurality of elders (bishops) and deacons in each local church which had no visible head.

4) Rather, it was based in apostolic teaching as expressed in the New Testament and had only an invisible Head, Christ himself.

5) The apostles did leave their lasting mark on the early church, which continued in "the apostles' doctrine" (Acts 2:42) and by establishing self-governing, self-propagating, and independent churches that operated under the Lordship of Christ their Head and his Holy Spirit as their guide (John 14:26; 16:13).

6) If Peter enjoyed the primacy of the first pope it is strange he and John were commissioned (or "sent") by the other apostles on a mission to Samaria, which suggests that Peter was not the superior apostle as Catholic teaching claims (see Acts 8:4–13). Indeed, if Peter were the God-ordained superior apostle, it would be strange that more attention is given to Paul's ministry than to Peter's in Acts. Peter is the focus in chapters 1–12; Paul is the dominant figure in 13–28.

7) It is true that Peter addressed the church's first council in Jerusalem (see Acts 15); however, it is also true that Peter exercised no primacy over the others.[27] As the text demonstrates, the final decisions of the council were carried out by *all* of the apostles and the elders, as well as with the consent of the entire church (15:22)—thus at once demonstrating more of a collegial or conciliar model rather than a "Petrine" Roman

---

27. Geisler, *The Church and Last Things*, 80.

model. Moreover, some scholars have observed that it was *not* Peter who presided over the council, but James instead (15:13–21).[28]

8) Peter never refers to himself as *the chief* pastor of the church, but only as a *"fellow* elder" (1 Pet. 5:1–2)—which would be a strange admission for one who allegedly possesses primacy.[29] In fact, in his epistle addressed to the dispersed Christians throughout the Roman Empire, he salutes them by addressing himself as *"an* apostle" (1:1). Since Peter was one of the church's "pillars" (plural) nowhere does Peter ever write that he was *"the* apostle," nor does he ever write that he was *"the* bishop of Rome."[30]

9) If Peter was the first bishop of Rome, it is strange that he is listed only as a cofounder of the church there along with the apostle Paul by one of our earliest sources on the topic. Irenaeus (c. 130–200) who knew Polycarp, the disciple of the apostle John, affirmed "that tradition derived from the apostles, of the very great, the very ancient, and universally known Church founded and organized at Rome by the two most glorious apostles, Peter and Paul."[31] If Irenaeus had known and believed Peter had primacy over Paul, then surely he would have mentioned it here.

28. Some might take verse 7 as implying Peter's primacy; however, the *context* of the entire passage reveals that the decisions were carried out by all of the apostles and not by Peter alone; see A. Mathison, *The Shape of Sola Scriptura* (Moscow, ID: Canon Press, 2001), 196–98.

29. Ibid. Concerning Petrine and collegial models, at the First Vatican Council (1870) there were two schools of thought present, the majority party called the "ultramontanists" (for they sought authority "beyond the mountain," that is, the Alps), and the minority party (led by John Henry Newman) who held to a form of "conciliarism." Concerning the former, the minority group wished to see infallibility linked to all of the bishops and not to the pope alone. Out of the some seven hundred bishops present at Vatican I, one hundred of them opposed the doctrine of papal infallibility (Norman L. Geisler and Ralph E. MacKenzie, *Roman Catholics and Evangelicals: Agreements and Differences* [Grand Rapids, MI: Baker, 1995], 460). In fact, Gregory the Great (pope from AD 590–604) reproached Patriarch John the Faster of Constantinople for calling himself the universal bishop. In Gregory's mind, this universal claim of supreme authority in a bishop was a sure identification of the corruption of the church, or even the work of the Antichrist. Thus Gregory reacted in such a way to defend the rights of all bishops, and not simply because he sought the title for himself; see Harold O. J. Brown, *Protest of a Troubled Protestant* (New Rochelle: Arlington House, 1969), 122.

30. Stephen Ray attempts to counter this point by arguing that Peter was simply manifesting the humility he was exhorting his readers to practice. In addition, Ray asserts that Peter never denies the primacy bestowed upon him by Jesus. Ray attempts to use the analogy of a presidential address whereby the president refers to himself as a "fellow American" when addressing the nation, even though he holds the highest office in the nation (Stephen Ray, *Upon This Rock: St. Peter and the Primacy of Rome in Scripture and the Early Church* [San Francisco: Ignatius Press, 1999], 59, n. 79). This analogy does not work since the power claimed for the presidency and the power claimed for the papacy are not the same—the pope is said to possess a charism of *infallibility* as the vicar of Christ; the president is simply recognized as the national leader to whom neither infallibility nor absolute jurisdiction is ascribed. To answer Ray's second question, Peter never denies his primacy because he *never* had it to begin with (as the biblical evidence demonstrates)—Ray's assertion simply begs the question.

31. In *Against Heresies* book 3.

Irenaeus repeatedly speaks of "the apostolic tradition"[32] and "the blessed apostles" who "founded and built up the Church,"[33] "the doctrine of the apostles,"[34] and "the tradition from the apostles."[35] He wrote: "these [apostles] are the voices of the Church from which every Church had its origin . . . these are the voices of the apostles; these are the voices of the disciples of the Lord, the truly perfect, who after the assumption of the Lord, were perfected by the Spirit."[36] For "He [God] sent forth His own apostles in the spirit of truth, and not in that of error, He did the very same also in the case of the prophets."[37] No primacy is given to Peter by Irenaeus.

Most commentators recognize that Peter had a significant role (as the initial leader) in the early church, as the book of Acts records (in chaps. 1–12). Yet, the biblical data suggests that Peter did not have any superiority over the other apostles; he was simply one of *many* pillars of the church.[38] It may be a *necessary* condition for Peter to have been the leader of the apostles to fit the papal description, but it is not a *sufficient* condition for primacy; that is, there are other ways Peter could have been the leader of the apostles without requiring him to be the first pope—he could have simply been the leader of the twelve apostles (nothing more, nothing less). As noted before, all the apostles were given the same authority to bind and loose (Matt. 18:18), even though Peter was given this authority first (Matt. 16:19).

32. Ibid., 3.3.2.
33. Ibid., 3.3.3.
34. Ibid., 3.12.4.
35. Ibid., 3.5.1.
36. Ibid., 3.12.4.
37. Ibid., 4.35.2.
38. Geisler, *The Church and Last Things*, 78.

CHAPTER 7

IS ROME THE TRUE CHURCH?

e began our study to find out whether Roman Catholicism is the true church of Christ on earth, as it claims to be. We finish it with the negative conclusion of our findings on the topic.

A Summary of the Case against Papal Infallibility

In addition to the lack of good arguments *for* papal infallibility (see chap. 5), there are many arguments *against* it. Some of them are implied in the above discussion. Others are added here. Together they make a formidable case against papal infallibility. Since both Catholic and non-Catholic orthodox Christians believe that the Bible is the only written and complete deposit of divine revelation, one might expect to find a solid biblical basis for such a crucial doctrine as this. But as we have seen earlier (chaps. 2–6), no such basis exists. Hence, the doctrine of papal infallibility is not biblical.

The Biblical Argument against Peter's Primacy

Given that the doctrine of Peter's *primacy* is a prerequisite for his infallibility, the whole question of his infallibility collapses with the failure to show that Peter even had primacy among the other apostles in the New Testament (chap. 3). We discovered that in spite of Peter's early leadership in the church and use of "the keys" to open the door of the gospel to Jews (Acts 2) and Gentiles (Acts 10), nowhere does the New

Testament affirm that Peter has any special abiding divinely authoritative role not given to the rest of the apostles. In the books of Acts, after the first few chapters, he is not even the central apostolic figure. James, our Lord's brother, appeared to be in charge of the council held in Jerusalem (Acts 15). Paul is the dominant figure from Acts 13 to 28, where Peter is scarcely mentioned. In his epistles Peter speaks of Christ as "the chief cornerstone" of the church (1 Pet. 2:6). He introduces himself as just "an apostle of Jesus Christ," not the chief among the apostles (1 Pet. 1:1). Indeed, he speaks of himself as a "fellow elder" (1 Pet. 5:1), all of whom should "shepherd the flock" (1 Pet. 5:2), not being "lords over" them (5:3), and all of whom were subject, not to him, but to "the Chief Shepherd" (Christ) whose coming they awaited (1 Pet. 5:4). In his second epistle Peter speaks only of the authority of the "apostles" (plural) (2 Pet. 3:2), not of any unique authority of his own. Indeed, he speaks with deference of the unique revelation given to Paul the apostle, which Peter, though he found it hard to understand, accepted as inspired "Scripture" (2 Pet. 3:15–16). But just how this allegedly infallible interpreter of God's revelation could not himself understand it fully is not compatible with the Roman Catholic view of Peter's primacy.

So, the New Testament view of Peter is a far cry from the Roman Catholic description of the unique primacy and power that Christ is alleged to have given Peter as head of the visible church on earth. Other than his temporary apostolic and leadership role as one of the early "pillars" of the faith (Gal. 2:9) and his collegiate role with the other apostles as part of the "foundation" of the church (Eph. 2:20), one looks in vain to the inspired New Testament for anything like Rome's claims for Peter.

Nor do the earliest Christians following the apostles affirm the primacy of Peter (see chaps. 2 and 3). In short, no real support is found in the New Testament church for the primacy and authority of Peter as the visible head of the church on earth. Nor is there any such evidence in the earliest Fathers of the church. As with other doctrinal deviations, one has to look outside the Bible to find the source of this unbiblical teaching.

The Biblical Argument against Peter's Infallibility

Not only is the biblical evidence for Peter's primacy (and thereby infallibility) lacking, but there is biblical evidence for Peter's *fallibility* in the very area in which he is alleged to be infallible.

Few New Testament followers of Christ are more fallible than Peter. He had to be rebuked by Jesus for wanting to detour him from the cross, with Jesus saying to him, "Get behind Me, Satan! You are an offense to Me, for you are not mindful of the things of God, but the things of men" (Matt. 16:23 NKJV). He denied the Lord three times (Matt. 26:75), and needed special restoration by Jesus (John 21). And both of these happened after he was allegedly given infallibility by Jesus (in Matt. 16:16–18). Salmon recognized this inconsistency and wrote: "If Peter were the foundation of the Church in any other sense than I have explained, it would have shaken immediately afterwards when our Lord said unto him: 'Get thee behind me, Satan,' and tottered to its base when he denied his Lord. *Immediately after Peter had earned commendation by his acknowledgment of Jesus as the Messiah, the doctrine of a crucified Messiah was proposed to him and he rejected it.*" So if "the Apostles had believed that the words 'On this rock I will build my Church' constituted Peter their infallible guide, the very first time they followed his guidance they would have been led to miserable error."[1]

Of course, Roman Catholics attempt to circumvent this conclusion by distinguishing between the fallibility of the man and the infallibility of his teaching on doctrine and morals. But this will not suffice for at least two reasons. First, Peter is addressing doctrinal and practical matters of the church. Second, making repeated qualifications for infallible statements both limits its scope to rare occasions and renders it useless for the continual needs of the church.

The case in Galatians is even more difficult to explain away as being a non-infallible example of Peter's leadership. Here Peter (an allegedly infallible apostle) was rebuked by Paul (a fallible apostle) for Peter's deviation from the gospel. He speaks of rebuking Peter because he was not "straightforward about the truth of the gospel" (Gal. 2:14 NASB). It is difficult to see how this does not come under his role as the alleged infallible teacher of faith and practice. This was not an ordinary inconsistency that any mortal person, including a pope, might fall into. It struck to the heart of the Christian message. In short, Peter denied the heart of the gospel. This is seriously inconsistent with the Roman claim that he is the primary teacher of faith and practice in the church.

1. George Salmon, *The Infallibility of the Church* (repr., Grand Rapids, MI: Baker, 1959), 343, emphasis added.

The Historical Argument against Infallibility

The infallibility of the current bishop of Rome depends on crucial historical links in the chain that are missing. As we showed earlier (chap. 3),
there is no real evidence in the New Testament for even the primacy of
Peter, let alone his infallibility. So, the first and most crucial link is totally
missing. This leaves the rest of the chain hanging in mid-air. Further, the
next main link is not supported by the documents, for the immediate
contemporaries and successors of the apostles do not support the Roman
view of the primacy and infallibility of Peter (chap. 2). Finally, the first
historical evidence for the primacy of Peter comes a hundred years after
the time of Christ—a time when many heresies were in full bloom. So,
it is no surprise that doctrinal deviations would occur in this area as
well. And even when the claim for Peter's primacy does later occur, it
is not accompanied with any explicit claims for his infallibility. Indeed,
this doctrine was not officially defined by the church until more than
1,800 years after the time of Christ!

The Argument from Conflicting Popes

As indicated elsewhere (in Appendix 2), there were numerous antipopes.
This means that in practice there was no visible and clearly distinguishable infallible leader of the church. So, the theoretical claim that only
one of these popes was infallible is of no practical value, since there
were in actuality two of them. In one case there were three popes (see
Council of Constance, 1413–1418)!

For example, in Avignon, France, the pope and the antipope both
claimed a charism of primacy and infallibility.[2] J. N. D. Kelly identifies
some thirty-nine antipopes in his *Oxford Dictionary of Popes*, some dat-
ing as early as the third century.[3]

The biggest problem with the existence of the antipopes is obvious:
there being two allegedly *infallible* yet *opposing* popes at the same time.
One can rightly ask which pope was the true one (if in fact there was
one), and by what infallible means could this be determined? This is
perhaps the historic "Achilles' heel" to the entire doctrine of the infallibility of the bishop of Rome. So, *there exists no infallible list of infallible
popes to determine which one was the true pope.* To propose that only one

2. Ibid., 217. Further, the Renaissance papacy (1470–1530), which included the tenures of
some antipopes, served to spark the Reformation. These six popes were Sixtus VI, Innocent
the VIII, Alexander V, Julius II, Leo X, Clement VII; see Barbara Tuchman, *The March of Folly*
(New York: Ballantine, 1984).
3. J. N. D. Kelly, *The Oxford Dictionary of Popes* (New York: Oxford University Press, 1989),
1–4. See Appendix at the end of this work.

of the popes was the true pope, as Catholic apologists dö, is at best a theoretical solution, not an actual one.[4]

The problem finally climaxed in Avignon, France, where three popes appeared simultaneously.[5] Avignon had been acquired as the new residence of the papacy, and it was from there that the bishop of Rome had ruled for a time. However, Pope Gregory XI "often declared his conviction that the proper seat for the pope was Rome. Only there could he exercise authority over the papal state."[6] Historian William J. La Due explains the developments at Avignon and the problems that climaxed there:

> Gregory XI ended the Avignon papacy, returning to Rome in 1377. However, within six months after his death in 1378, there were two popes—one in Rome and the other in Avignon. This arrangement resulted in deep divisions in every nation, with some dioceses and religious institutions pledging their allegiance to Rome, while others were sworn to Avignon. To solve this pathetic situation, cardinals from both camps met at Pisa in 1409, creating a third papal line, which only further exacerbated the state of things. It was the Council of Constance (1414–18)—a masterpiece of moderate conciliarism—that finally brought the scandalous and extremely corrosive Great Western Schism to an end. Popes Martin V (1417) and Eugene IV (1431–47) managed to thwart the moderate conciliarists and returned the papacy to its monarchical moorings. The last half of the fifteenth century witnessed the rise of the Renaissance popes, who proceeded to shrink the office down to the size and shape of a regional duchy, whose lord and ruler manifested less and less interest in the wider concerns of the Christian world.[7]

It was this predicament at Avignon that moved the Catholic Church to intervene. The Council of Constance (1413–1418) was convened by Pope John XXIII (who was later condemned as an antipope by Rome) to end the "Great Papal Schism." There was at once the need to appeal to an authority *greater* than that of the pope's in order to determine the ecclesiastical decision to install the "real" pope. So much for the claim that papal authority brings unity that non-Catholic sectors of

4. Norman L. Geisler and Ralph E. MacKenzie, *Roman Catholics and Evangelicals: Agreements and Differences* (Grand Rapids, MI: Baker, 1995), 217.
5. Church historians note that antipopes were present as early as the third century (i.e., Hippolytus), even before the problem at Avignon climaxed (see Appendix 2).
6. Kelly, *The Oxford Dictionary of Popes*, 225. For a full treatment dealing with the papacy at Avignon, see G. Mollat, *The Popes at Avignon: 1305–1378* (New York: Torchbooks, 1965).
7. William J. La Due, *The Chair of Saint Peter: A History of the Papacy* (Marky Knoll: Orbis Books, 1999), 182.

Christendom cannot have. Also, so much for the later Catholic infallible claim at Vatican I that the pope alone has authority over an ecumenical church council.

The Argument from Heretical Popes

Not only were there many opposing popes, there were also heretical popes. According to the doctrine of infallibility, the pope is infallible when he is exercising his teaching role on doctrine and morals. But according to history, Rome was *not* always right on doctrinal and ethical matters. Pelikan provides many examples of when the papacy was wrong:

> There are two celebrated cases in the first six centuries of church history when Roman bishops seem to have been on the wrong side in a theological debate. Both of them have occasioned much controversy since the promulgation of papal infallibility at the Vatican Council in 1870. The first concerns the Roman bishops Zephyrinus (d. 217) and Callistus I (d. 222). According to the theologian Hippolytus (d. ca. 235), both these men were guilty of the "modalistic" heresy. They did not distinguish between the "persons" of the Father and the Son, but made the Son a mere mode of manifestation of the Father. Roman Catholic theologians and historians have accused Hippolytus of slander and have defended the bishops. . . . In the second case Roman Catholic theologians have even greater cause of embarrassment. The sixth ecumenical council of the church, meeting at Constantinople in 680–681, solemnly condemned Pope Honorius for heresy in the doctrine of the person of Christ.[8]

Pelikan notes that "although [the] sources on Zephyrinus and Callistus are not reliable enough to substantiate a final judgment either way [supporting or condemning these two], the evidence regarding Honorius' teachings, and especially regarding the council's actions, is very incriminating."[9] And even if it were the case that Honorius is the only example of when a pope erred, it would suffice to collapse the whole notion of infallibility, since no chain can be stronger than its weakest link. This is not only a historical problem, but it is a very serious theological problem as well. Thus it is proper to ask, "If the papal

8. Jaroslav Pelikan, *The Riddle of Roman Catholicism* (New York: Abingdon, 1959), 40.
9. Ibid. Kelly points out that when Honorius received correction from the patriarch of Constantinople, Sergius I, concerning his modalistic paradigm of the Trinity, Honorius revised his position too hastily to the end that he proposed a different heresy, namely, monothelitism—the idea that Jesus (as the divine/human Son of God) had only one will (*Oxford Dictionary of Popes*, 70–71).

teaching office cannot mislead on doctrine and ethics, why then was a pope's teaching heretical?"[10]

It does not suffice to counter by claiming that the pope was *not* infallible on this occasion. For this only undermines his infallibility on other occasions. The truth is that there are no infallible lists of infallible statements, and "without an infallible list, the Catholic Church cannot provide infallible guidance on the doctrine and morals. If the pope can be fallible on one doctrine, why can't he be fallible on another?"[11] It is not sufficient to respond by pointing to so-called guidelines for infallible statements for several reasons. First, there are no infallible guidelines. Second, like the "unanimous" consent of the Fathers' interpretation of Scripture, there is no universal agreement on these criteria. Finally, there is no universal agreement as to how these or any criteria apply to every case.[12]

Attempts by Catholic scholars to avoid admitting the fallibility of allegedly infallible popes have been creative but futile. Catholic authority Ludwig Ott admits that Pope Leo II "confirmed his anathematisation" of Honorius, yet Ott attempts to undermine this by stating that it was "not for the reason given by the Council [of Constantinople (681)]. [Nor did Leo II] reproach him with heresy, but with negligence in the suppression of the error."[13] Ott further says that Honorius "*unwittingly* favored the Monothelite error."[14] But how can one know for sure whether the pope has not "unwittingly" set forth other dogmas that are heretical, since there is no objective way of verifying when he has or has not spoken infallibly? And as for the question of Leo's anathematization, there are several problems with Ott's assertion.[15]

First, this still raises the question of how Honorius could still be an infallible guide, i.e., on faith and morals, when he taught heresies, especially those dealing with the nature of Christ. And the claim that he was not speaking infallibly on this occasion is convenient but inadequate, since it only tends to undermine the authority of the far more numer-

10. Norman L. Geisler, *Systematic Theology*, vol. 4: *The Church and Last Things* (Bloomington, MN: Bethany, 2002), 84.
11. Ibid., 85.
12. Ibid., 85, n. 45.
13. Ott, *Fundamentals*, 150.
14. Ibid.
15. The following responses to Ott are borrowed from Geisler, *The Church and Last Things*, 85.

ous occasions when the pope is allegedly speaking with authority but not with infallibility.[16]

Second, "it does not explain why the Sixth General Council condemned Honorius as a heretic."[17] There is no question that Honorius was condemned for some heresy. Honorius's anathematization only makes sense in light of the monothelite heresy he espoused and the Council's affirmation of Christ's dual wills in conjunction with his two natures.

Third, "disclaiming papal infallibility in this and like situations makes supposedly infallible pronouncements extremely rare; for example, by this standard, a pope has spoken *ex cathedra* only one time in the last hundred years (on the bodily assumption of Mary). 'Infallibility' exercised this rarely has almost no practical value on almost all occasions. With the pope nearly always having fallible speech, Catholics are bound to accept his authority on faith and morals when he may be (and sometimes has been) wrong. The infallible guidance the papacy is supposed to provide is negligible at best, and, by the Church's admission, on the overwhelming number of occasions there is no supposed infallible guidance at all."[18]

In view of Honorius's condemnation, there is strong reason to believe that he taught heresy. Besides Pope Leo II's anathematization of Honorius, Küng reminds his readers that the Trullan synod of 692 and the seventh and eighth ecumenical councils (and other subsequent popes) repeated Leo's anathematization.[19] Further, Pope Sixtus in 1590 stated the following in the preface of his authorized edition of the Vulgate: "By the fulness of apostolic power, we decree and declare that this edition, approved by the authority delivered to us by the Lord, is to be received and held as true, lawful, authentic, and unquestioned, in all public and private discussion, reading, preaching, and explanations."[20] Due to the numerous errors contained in Sixtus's version of the Vulgate, it had to be corrected and reissued within two short years of its release.[21] But "if ever an infallible pope laid claim to an infallible pronouncement, this is it."[22] It is hard to escape Sixtus's strong authoritative language recorded in his preface (see Appendix 5).

16. Ibid.
17. Ibid.
18. Ibid.
19. Hans Küng, *Infallibility? An Inquiry*, trans. Edward Quin (Garden City, NY: Doubleday, 1971), 114.
20. Cited in Kieth A. Mathison, *The Shape of Sola Scriptura* (Moscow, ID: Canon Press, 2001), 222.
21. Geisler, *The Church and Last Things*, 85.
22. Ibid.

Honorius and Sixtus are not the only popes who have erred.[23] Some five popes are recorded as either espousing heresy or teaching heresy—not to mention the inconsistent statements from one decree to another. For example, the Second Vatican Council is not consistent with Pope Boniface VIII's Bull, *Unam Sanctum*. For the Second Vatican Council declared that those *outside* the Catholic Church could be saved, i.e., Eastern Orthodox and Protestants ("separated brethren")—not the least of which Jews, Muslims, pagans, and sincere atheists could be saved, too.[24] On the other hand, Boniface stated in his Bull, "We declare, state, define and pronounce that it is altogether *necessary* to salvation for every human creature to be subject to the Roman Pontiff."[25] Yet, if Boniface's statement is correct, then the statement from Vatican II cannot be true, namely, that those outside Rome could be saved (and vice versa). "But if non-Roman Catholics, non-Christians, pagans, and atheists may attain to salvation, as Vatican II asserts, then it is *not* altogether *necessary* to salvation for *every* human creature to be subject to the Roman Pontiff. According to Vatican II, some who are not subject to the Roman Pontiff may be saved."[26]

The law of noncontradiction affirms that these two mutually exclusive ideas cannot both be true at the same time and in the same sense. It does not help to assert that Boniface was not speaking *ex cathedra*. All one has to ask is, according to what infallible criteria can one determine whether he spoke *ex cathedra* or not?

The Argument from the Condemnation of Galileo

The infamous Galileo pronouncement is another case in point when Rome was wrong. It presumed to speak authoritatively on matters pertaining to science when it condemned Galileo's discovery that challenged the outdated Ptolemaic geocentric universe.[27] "Galileo [1546–1642], using his telescope to view the heavens, adopted the Copernican view that the sun, not the earth, was the center of the solar system. This, of course, was opposed to the prevailing theological position of an earth-

23. Mathison lists Pope Zosimus, who reversed the official judgment of a previous pope (Innocent); Pope Vigilius, due to his acceptance of Nestorianism; Pope Honorius (see above), and Pope Sixtus V and Boniface VIII (see above as well); *Shape of Sola Scriptura*, 220–23.
24. See Austin Flannery, *Vatican Council II* (Boston: St. Paul's Books and Media, 1992), 738 ff.
25. Boniface VIII, "Unam Sanctam," in *Documents of the Christian Church*, rev. ed., ed. Henry Bettenson and Chris Maunder (Oxford: Oxford University Press, 1999), 127, emphasis added.
26. Mathison, *Shape of Sola Scriptura*, 221.
27. Geisler and MacKenzie, *Roman Catholics and Evangelicals*, 218.

centered system held by the Roman Catholic Church."[28] In 1616, the Copernican theory was condemned by Rome, and Galileo was summoned by the Inquisition (shortly thereafter in 1632) where he was tried and punished for heresy.[29] Rome may once again conveniently say that no *ex cathedra* was given in Galileo's case, but the charges leveled at him came with papal authority. To this day Rome struggles to regain respect in the scientific community for this very fallible "infallible" pronouncement. Here again, the Galileo case seriously undermines the church's claim to infallibility.[30]

The Argument from Contradictory Decisions of Ecumenical Councils

After the embarrassment of three rival popes, the Council of Constance claimed in its celebrated and unanimous decree that everyone, *the pope included*, is subject to it in matters of faith.[31] In short, "the Council proclaimed the superiority of an ecumenical Council over the Pope."[32] For the council unequivocally declared: "[That the] General Council, representing the Catholic Church . . . has its authority immediately from Christ; and that all men, of every rank and condition, *including the Pope himself*, is bound to obey it in matters concerning the Faith."[33]

The problem is that the preceding statement is in direct contradiction with the decrees of Vatican I, which stated the exact opposite, namely, that "the Roman Pontiff [has authority of] himself, [and] *not from the consensus of the Church* . . ."[34] The council further declared that if anyone deviated from this position, he or she would be anathema."[35]

The Catholic response to this has been disastrous for the doctrine of infallibility. So-called progressive Catholics have in effect denied the infallibility of Vatican I, claiming that the pope is infallible only as he speaks in collegiality with the other bishops in "one voice." Cardinal John Henry Newman echoed the progressive sentiment almost a century before the drafting of Vatican II. For he said, "It is to the Pope *in*

28. Ibid.
29. Ibid.
30. Ibid., 219–20.
31. Salmon, *Infallibility of the Church*, 321, emphasis in original.
32. Norman L. Geisler, "The Historical Development of Roman Catholicism" in *Christian Apologetics Journal* 4.1 (2005): 42.
33. "The Council of Constance" in Bettenson and Maunder, 149, emphasis added.
34. Henry Denzinger, *The Sources of Catholic Dogma*, trans. Roy J. Deferrari (London: Herder, 1957), 457.
35. "The Vatican Council (1869–70)" as cited in *The Church Teaches: Documents of the Church in English Translation*, ed. John F. Clarkson, S. J., et al. (Rockford, IL: Tan, 1973), 210.

Ecumenical Council that we look [for the seat of infallibility]."[36] Newman held that Christian dogmas evolve over time, albeit in continuity with the original revelation in Scripture.[37]

Leslie Dewart, a progressive Catholic theologian, explains the developmental (or "evolutionary") nature of dogmas, which denies the nature of absolute truth. He wrote: "The Christian faith, thus, appears able to develop not only as a subjective and individual disposition. Its *truth can also develop*. Christian dogmas can undergo true development; they can, and in the normal course of events ought to, transform themselves culturally as their concepts undergo cultural evolution. This process can be properly called a *transformation*, because it is precisely the form that changes. It can be properly called an *evolution*, because the emergent form cannot be reduced to the act of the potentiality of the original form."

It is double-talk for him to state that "the cultural transformation of the Christian faith and the development of its truth do not imply either the discovery of a new, different truth which it did not previously possess, or betrayal of the truth that it previously possessed."[38] The law of noncontradiction dictates that logically opposite positions cannot both be true. If one is true, then the other is false. But both claim to be infallibly true statements. This case alone refutes the Roman doctrine of infallibility. Dewart adds, "Infallibility, thus, can hardly mean that the teaching of the magisterium is always as adequate as it could be—it only means that it is not less adequate than it absolutely must be if the Christian faith is to survive."[39] Yet this assertion does not correspond with Vatican I's explanation that the charism of infallibility is a gift that

---

36. John Henry Newman, *Apologia Pro Vita Sua* (New York: Penguin, 1994), 228, emphasis added.

37. Norman L. Geisler, "Newman, John Henry," in *Baker's Encyclopedia of Christian Apologetics* (Grand Rapids, MI: Baker, 1999), 538. For a detailed treatment of Newman's view, consult his work entitled *An Essay on the Development of Christian Doctrine* (South Bend, IN: University of Notre Dame Press, 1989).

38. Leslie Dewart, *The Future of Belief* (New York: Herder, 1967), 118 (emphasis added). Dewart's process view of truth reflects Alfred N. Whitehead's process view of reality, which is logically inconsistent. Truth by definition is that which *corresponds to its object or referent*, or that which *is*. One of the primary characteristics of the nature of truth is that it is *unchanging*. Truth is also non-contradictory, absolute, and sometimes discovered. Truth as such cannot undergo any kind of "evolution," as Dewart claims, i.e., in reference to its "form"; its form must remain the same for everyone at all times and in all places. So, if Peter's infallibility was bestowed upon him by Christ in the first century, then it would have been true for all persons living in the first century, as it would also still be true for those living in subsequent times. Logically, Peter's infallibility could have been *discovered* at a later time other than the first century, but it would have been, nonetheless, true for all peoples everywhere the moment he was endowed with the gift.

39. Ibid., 128.

is "never failing." It is little wonder that traditional Catholics reject this way of thinking, since it is a rejection of absolute truth. They are left with an absolute contradiction.

Jesuit writer, Luis M. Bermejo, makes another futile attempt to explain this contradiction. Concerning the First Vatican Council and the Council of Constance he writes,

> Now the unavoidable and troublesome question arises, namely, whether Constance can be reconciled with Vatican I, or, more precisely, whether *Pastor Aeternus* and *Haec Sancta* can stand side by side. The least one can say is that, as a consequence of the profound ecclesiological transformation brought on by the Reformation, the mentality in the theological world as regards authority in the Church was poles apart from that which had prevailed at the time of Constance. The Fathers at Constance certainly never imagined that four and a half centuries later, another general council of the Catholic Church would officially sanction the very principles Constance was trying to oppose. For it would have been as impossible for the Fathers at Constance with their strong conciliarist mentality to write *Pastor Aeternus* as it would have been unthinkable for the 1870 bishops to enact *Haec Sancta*—two different ecclesiological worlds which, at first blush, seem to have very little in common. For the strongly papalist, centralizing tendencies prevailing at Vatican I do not mix with the conciliarist mentality of Constance. . . . It seems to me plainly impossible to reconcile *Haec Sancta* and *Pastor Aeternus* on this point.[40]

Given this admission, it is futile for Bermejo to contend that an effort should be made, as far as possible, "to avoid an open historical confrontation between two successive councils of the same Church, [since] both of them [are] endowed with equal authority."[41] Bermejo, however, offers a worthy but Catholic fatal solution: "One should carefully confront both councils with the supreme criterion of Scripture and that of the early apostolic tradition."[42] But this is a Protestant solution that puts Scripture over the ecumenical councils as the only truly infallible basis for truth in doctrine and morals.

The Epistemic Argument against Infallibility

Another problem with the *ex cathedra* statements is that the supposed need for an infallible magisterium is an insufficient basis for rising above

40. Luis M. Bermejo, *Infallibility on Trial: Church, Conciliarity, and Communion* (Westminster, MD: Christian Classics, 1992), 285–87.
41. Ibid., 286.
42. Ibid., 289.

the level of probable knowledge.[43] Since there is no infallible evidence to substantiate the church's infallibility, this supposition is at best an inductive argument based on probability rather than certainty. In other words, they have no infallible evidence to support their infallible conclusion. Since the argument has historical links that are based on only probable evidence, the claim to infallibility has no infallible basis.

Like any other historical argument, it is at best only a reliable argument based on degrees of probability. One can never be sure the Roman Church is infallible. Hence, on an epistemic basis the doctrine of infallibility is in no better position than that of non-Catholic Christians who claim to have the only reliable evidence for their infallible basis for faith, the Word of God.

Since Catholic scholars admit that no chain of reasoning is any better than its weakest link, and since the epistemic basis is only probabilistic, then it follows that there is no infallible basis for believing in infallibility. And if the basis is not infallible, then it is fallible. And if fallible, then it might not be true. Hence, the Catholic infallibilist is in no better position epistemologically than the Protestant who offers only good and reliable evidence for his belief in an infallible Bible.

The Argument from the Lack of Infallible Lists of Infallible Statements

The doctrine of papal infallibility is no better than the list of infallible pronouncements. But there are no infallible lists of infallible pronouncements. Hence, no Roman Catholic has infallible assurance of what the infallible statements are that he should believe and practice. Hence, the doctrine of papal infallibility does not accomplish its goal in providing unerring principles for the life of the faithful.

Even if one were to agree with the commonly stated criteria for determining an infallible pronouncement (see chap. 1),[44] there are still problems that undermine the doctrine. First, the criteria are not infallible. Second, there is no infallible way to apply them to specific situations. Third, there is no infallible list of pronouncements that result from applying them. Finally, even universally recognized infallible

43. Geisler and MacKenzie, *Roman Catholics and Evangelicals*, 216.
44. The pope is said to be infallible only when: (1) speaking in fulfillment of his office as supreme pastor and teacher of all Christians; (2) speaking in virtue of his supreme apostolic authority, i.e., as successor of Peter; (3) determining a doctrine of faith and morals (i.e., a doctrine expressing divine revelation); (4) imposing a doctrine to be held definitively by all [see Dulles, "Infallibility," 79–80]; (5) he is the real pope (as opposed to rival popes); and (6) his decision is ratified by an ecumenical council (Geisler and Mackenzie, *Roman Catholics and Evangelicals*, 216–17).

178 IS ROME THE TRUE CHURCH?

statements (like those of ecumenical councils) are flatly contradictory (as shown above).

The Argument from Death by Qualification

In actual practice, the attempt to keep infallibility alive by qualifying it is in effect killing it both in principle and in practice. In principle, if a papal pronouncement is only infallible when all the stated criteria are applied[45] then infallible statements are very rare—about one a century for the last two centuries. For all practical purposes, the church's sel-dom-made *ex cathedra* statements provide no ongoing practical value for the life of the church. Day by day in the intervening century there is no infallible guide in Peter's chair, for everything the church says be-tween these rare infallible statements is fallible. For example, there is a gap of almost one hundred years between the last two alleged infallible papal pronouncements, both promoting an unbiblical teaching,[46] the iImmaculate conception of Mary (1854) and the bodily assumption of Mary (1950).

If, on the other hand, one admits more than these, then surely there are numerous occasions when popes have made fallible decisions on doctrinal and practical matters (as has been shown above). So, either the doctrine suffers "death by qualification" or else it suffers death by application, as is evident in the cases of Sixtus and Galileo.

Logical Extension Argument against Infallibility

Catholic apologists sometimes argue for infallibility in the following way:[47]

1) The gospel is known.
2) The gospel cannot be known without an infallible chain of authority.
   a. No chain is stronger than its weakest link.
   b. To be an infallible chain, every link must be infallible.
3) Hence, every link in the chain bringing the gospel to us must be infallible.
   a. It must be infallibly revealed.
   b. It must be infallibly transmitted.
   c. It must be infallibly interpreted.

45. Ibid.
46. Ibid., chap. 15.
47. Geisler and MacKenzie, *Roman Catholics and Evengelicals.*

4) The Roman Catholic Church [i.e., the pope] is both transmitter and interpreter of the gospel.

5) Therefore, the Roman Catholic Church [i.e., the pope] must be the infallible authority by which we know the gospel.

There are two problems with this argument. First, not all the premises are infallibly true. Indeed, some are false. For example, premise (2) is false. God revealed the Bible to prophets who were not infallible since not even Rome contends for the infallibility of every Bible author but only of the bishop of Rome. Also, premise (3) is false for God can draw a straight line with a crooked stick. God does not need an infallible channel to produce an infallible effect. The instrumental or secondary cause need not be infallible; only the efficient cause does. The same logic applies to premise (4). So, the argument is a logical non sequitur.

The second problem is a *reductio ad absurdum*. By the same logic, there must be not only an infallible transmitter and an infallible interpreter, but there also must be infallible understanding and infallible memories. For, as acknowledged, no argument is stronger than its weakest link. Hence, the faithful must have an infallible understanding and memory of the infallible message in order to obey it. But clearly Roman Catholics do not believe this. Hence, by the same token it is not necessary to have an infallible interpreter of the message. Or, if it is, then it could be the Holy Spirit, not the Holy Roman Catholic Church.

Hear the Conclusion of the Whole Matter

Is Rome the true church with an infallible magisterium headed by the bishop of Rome? Clearly, the evidence is to the contrary. There is no good basis for even the primacy of Peter, let alone his infallibility or Rome's exclusivity. Hence, the claim to be the true church on earth whose head sits in Peter's chair in Rome given to him and his successors by Christ is simply without foundation, as a survey of the evidence presented (in chaps. 3, 5, and 6) demonstrates.

What then does the claim to be the true church with an infallible interpretation of the teachings of Christ and his apostles show? Several things.

Rome Is Not the True Church

So, whatever else Rome may be, it is not the true Church of Christ on earth. Their claim is a gigantic over-claim. Not only is Rome not a bastion of all Christian truth, it is the repository for numerous, serious doctrinal and practical errors.[48]

These include: (1) worshiping the consecrated host; (2) venerating Mary; (3) praying to Mary; (4) the bodily assumption of Mary; (5) the immaculate conception and sinlessness of Mary; (6) venerating images; (7) purgatory; (8) praying for the dead; (9) adding the apocryphal books to Bible; (10) making works a necessary condition for receiving eternal life; (11) the sale of indulgences; (12) the treasury of merit, and (13) the infallibility of the pope.

These are serious doctrinal errors against which Protestants have rightly stated their view by contrast as belief in (1) salvation by grace *alone*, (2) received by faith *alone*, (3) made possible by the work of Christ *alone*, and (4) based on the Bible *alone,* and (5) all for the glory of God *alone.*

Is Rome a False Church?

This must be answered in parts and with qualifications. First, the Roman Catholic Church makes some major false claims: for example, that Rome is the true church of Christ on earth and it has an infallible interpretation of God's revelation. But Rome is not the true church of Christ on earth (see chaps. 1–7a), and it does not have an infallible interpretation of God's revelation. These false claims are serious.

Second, Rome teaches major false doctrines (thirteen of which are listed above), and these doctrines have deceived and misled millions of its followers. They range from idolatry (in worshiping the consecrated host) to making works a condition for receiving eternal life.

But is the Roman Catholic Church a false church? If Rome is judged by the standard of the fourteen (or sixteen)[49] salvation essentials embodied in the creeds of the first five centuries, the answer is no. In this case, Rome is *a* true church with significant error. If judged by the standards of the Protestant Reformation, however, the answer is yes. In this case, Rome is a false church with significant truth.

Some evangelicals argue that Rome is a false church because it makes works a necessary condition for obtaining salvation (eternal life). Other

---

48. See Geisler and MacKenzie, *Roman Catholics and Evangelicals,* part 2.

49. Of course, there is a difference on which books belong in the infallible "Bible," but the exact content of the Bible has never been a matter on which any creed or council of the church ruled in the first five centuries that constitutes the basis for orthodoxy in the sense in which we are using it. See Norman L. Geisler and Ron Rhodes, *Conviction without Compromise: Standing Strong in the Core Beliefs of the Christian Faith* (Eugene, OR: Harvest House, 2007), part 1 of which has a chapter on each of the 14 salvation essentials.

evangelicals argue that Rome is not a false church because it teaches that grace is absolutely necessary for salvation, that even the good works deemed necessary for salvation are prompted by God's grace, and that Christ's work on the cross is totally sufficient for saving sinners from guilt and eternal condemnation.

Evangelicals agree, however, that Rome is guilty of denying in practice what it affirms in theory. For example, it affirms that only God should be worshiped, but it approves of the veneration of Mary, which is often indistinguishable from worship.[50] Rome affirms the necessity of grace for salvation, but it has built up a system and institution of salvation around it that requires one to work *for* grace, thus making works necessary for salvation. Rome affirms that Christ's sacrifice alone paid the penalty for our sins, but denies that this covers the temporal consequences of one's sins, for which one must pay in purgatory. Rome affirms that Christ alone is the Mediator between God and man, yet it allots to Mary the role of Mediatrix in dispensing this salvation. Therefore, Rome has "practical heresy," if not both practical and doctrinal heresy.

What Is the True Church?

If Rome is not the true church, then where can it be found? Our answer is in two parts:

First, it can be found in the spiritual body of Christ which consists of every true believer who has been baptized into the body of Christ by the Holy Spirit (1 Cor. 12:13; cf. Eph. 1:22–23; 4:4), no matter his denominational affiliation. As C. S. Lewis said, denominations are like rooms in a large mansion, and mere Christianity "is more like a hall out of which doors open into several rooms. If I can bring anyone into that hall I shall have done what I attempted." But "when you have reached your own room [denomination], be kind to those who have chosen different doors."[51] We are all in the house, and that is what matters.

Second, the true church of Christ is found on earth in any church that confesses the fourteen (or sixteen) salvation essentials.[52] This includes churches in every major section of Christendom, including Roman Catholicism, Eastern Orthodoxy, Anglicans, and all major sections of Prot-

50. See Geisler and MacKenzie, *Roman Catholics and Evangelicals*, chap. 15.
51. C. S. Lewis, *Mere Christianity* (New York: HarperCollins, 2001), *xvi*.
52. We are aware that sacramental churches consider the use of the sacraments (at least communion and baptism) as essential to the definition of a true church. While this may be true, our focus here is only on the *doctrinal* essentials of orthodoxy, not the *liturgical* ones. Again, no general creed or council of the first five centuries ruled on this question. In this sense, the question is outside of the norm for orthodoxy.

estantism (Lutheran, Presbyterian, Methodist) and Anabaptist, Baptist, Free Church, and independent.

A false church is one that denies one or more of the fourteen (sixteen) essentials of the Christian faith. Since some deny more than others, they are deeper into falsehood than others.

Who Is the Head of Christ's Visible Church on Earth?

While both Roman Catholics and non-Catholics agree that Christ is the Head of the invisible church, the spiritual body of Christ, they disagree on the head of the visible church on earth. Rome insists that there must be a visible head, and that the Roman pope is it. But we have already shown that this claim is without foundation (chaps. 1–6).

How, then, does the visible church operate without a visible head? Non-Roman Catholics differ on the answer. We offer a twofold response. First, Christ is the invisible Head of the visible church in general and of each visible church in particular.

Second, the question confuses true unity with other things. Professor Merrill Tenney summarized the differences succinctly: "*Unanimity* means absolute concord of opinion within a given group of people. *Uniformity* is complete similarity of organization or of ritual. *Union* implies political affiliation without necessarily including individual agreement. *Unity* requires oneness of inner heart and essential purpose, through the possession of a common interest or a common life."[53]

Now when Jesus prayed for the unity of his church ("that they may be one," John 17:21), clearly he was not praying for complete unanimity or uniformity, and even the Roman Catholic Church does not have that. Nor was he praying for union, otherwise his prayer has been unanswered for at least a thousand years now since the major schism between Rome and Eastern Orthodoxy. Rather, Jesus was praying for "*unity* [which] requires oneness of inner heart and essential purpose, through the possession of a common interest or a common life."[54] And true believers in every denomination have this, for they possess both doctrinal unity on all the essential doctrines, and they have love for one another (John 13:35). Certainly, this is better than an organizational union, which may lack the essential spiritual and doctrinal cohesiveness of a true church.

53. Merrill Tenney, *John: The Gospel of Belief* (Grand Rapids, MI: Eerdmans, 1975), 248.
54. Ibid.

In the wisdom of God, he knew that "power corrupts and absolute power corrupts absolutely." Hence, he did not establish any one fallen, depraved human being to head up his visible church on earth. Instead, he set up a checks-and-balances system of a plurality of local churches, each under a plurality of elders with no central, early head. So, the apostles, instead of passing on apostolic powers and a head of the apostles (Peter), established independent churches with their own plurality of leaders (elders) who "continued steadfastly in the apostles' doctrine" (Acts 2:42 NKJV). This teaching was inscripturated in the New Testament, and its essential doctrines were later codified in the Apostles' Creed, which contains all the fourteen essential doctrines, and reaffirmed by the Nicene and Chalcedonian creeds. Hence, the collective body of all churches that confess this (Roman Catholic or whatever) are Christ's visible church on earth over which he is still its invisible Head and in which he rules in accordance with his infallible Word.

That there was no visible head of Christ's church on earth in the New Testament is clear from the following:

1) Christ never gave primacy to any one apostle on earth (see chap. 3).

2) Christ never gave infallibility to any one or group of apostles (see chap. 5).

3) Christ never established the succession of this apostolic power (see chap. 6).

4) The New Testament—our only inspired record of what happened— never reveals the operation of a visible head of the church on earth:

   a. The only general gathering on an important issue was in Jerusalem (Acts 15), and it was a group decision of "apostles and elders" (Acts 15:23) in which James, not Peter, was the leader (Acts 15:13ff.).

   b. Paul brought his teaching to a plurality of apostles (Gal. 2:9) lest he had "run in vain" (Gal. 2:2).

   c. He even speaks of rebuking Peter because he was not "straightforward about the truth of the gospel" (Gal. 2:14 NKJV).

   d. The apostles established independent churches with a plurality of elders in them (Acts 14:23).

   e. When the apostle James died he was not replaced with another apostle (Acts 12:2).

f. Late in the first century when John wrote Revelation to seven
    independent churches, there is no indication of a visible head
    of the church on earth (let alone in Rome). Rather, it is the
    invisible Christ who walks among his churches and judges
    them (Rev. 1:10–20). Elsewhere, the ascended Christ is the
    "head over all things to the church which is His body" (Eph.
    1:22–23 NKJV).

Summary

We have seen that the Roman Catholic claim to be the true church is
false. The biblical, theological, and historical arguments against it are
strong. Indeed, on either standard of orthodoxy Rome falls short, and
on the Reformation standard of orthodoxy Roman Catholicism is a false
church with significant truth in it. So at a minimum it has practical heresy, and at a maximum it has both doctrinal and practical heresy. The
apostle Paul charged Peter, whom Rome claims as their first pope, with
practical heresy, declaring that Peter was "not straightforward about the
truth of the gospel" (Gal. 2:14). Not that Peter had denied the gospel in
principle, but that he was not living the gospel in practice. Most Roman
followers of Peter do no better.

In brief, even if Rome is judged not to be a cult, it is in many respects,
nonetheless, cultic in its practices. While it does not deny any of the
major creedal universal orthodox doctrines, nonetheless it falls short
of the biblical and Reformational standards of salvation by grace alone
through faith alone grounded in the work of Christ alone and based in
the Bible alone. Thus there are essential truths inside the Roman Catholic
Church, but the essential claims (about the pope and salvation) are not
essentially true. They are indeed false claims.

This is not to say that the Roman Church has no true believers in
it, nor that it has no essentially true beliefs. It has both. It is only to say
that not only is its central claim to infallibility false, but so is its plan
of salvation.

Nor is this to say that there is no continuity between Rome and the
original church of the New Testament. It has a historical lineage to
Pentecost. But like present-day America, there are significant changes
from what the founders believed. Yes, Americans have the same history
and Constitution, but this document has been seriously amended and
reinterpreted by those in authority. The same is true of Rome. It has
the same original doctrinal constitution as expressed in the Apostles',

Nicean, and Chalcedonian creeds. But who can deny that there have been serious amendments and reinterpretations?

Current Roman Catholicism in general is a combination of four factors: (1) a basic Christian doctrinal core, (2) a Roman hierarchical structure (borrowed from the dying Roman Empire), (3) a Jewish ritualistic form (borrowed from the Old Testament), and (4) significant pagan content and practices. Depending on the time and place, one or more of these factors may dominate. Thus, depending on the critic's focus, one may get widely divergent conclusions about Roman Catholicism ranging from Christian to cult. The truth is that Rome is many things to many people. To borrow the title of Jaroslav Pelikan's excellent tome, this is "the riddle of Roman Catholicism."

CHAPTER 8

WHY SOME PROTESTANTS CONVERT TO ROME

If there are no good biblical, philosophical, or historical arguments for the infallibility of the Roman pope, then why do some intelligent people convert to Catholicism? The simple answer is that their decision is not prompted primarily by rational considerations, but is made on other grounds. There have always been converts going both ways between Roman Catholics and Protestants. Thousands of Catholics have converted to evangelicalism. The primary reason for the conversion of Catholics is that they did not find a personal relationship with Christ in the Catholic Church. To many, it professed a form of godliness but denied the power thereof (2 Tim. 3:5). At the same time, in recent years a number of evangelical intellectuals have decided that "Rome is home." Strangely, however, their primary motivation has not been intellectual arguments. But before we look at what the real reasons were, it is instructive to consider why so many Catholics have converted to evangelicalism.

Why Catholics Become Evangelicals

In some of the megacongregations near Los Angeles, the number of ex-Catholics exceeds fifty percent. A leading figure at Vatican II, and one of the four moderators at the Council, Léon Joseph Cardinal Suenens addressed this issue in *A New Pentecost?*[1] Suenens quotes French bishop G. Huyghe who comments that Vatican II was held to inspire Catholics to be evangelists. But this presupposed that they themselves were believers. "In fact, this was true only of a few."[2] For conversion, a personal encounter must occur: "A Christian is a changed person, a convert; he has turned away from himself, so as to adhere to Jesus of Nazareth. . . . He has found in Jesus the Savior and Lord of all mankind."[3]

In his book, *Hungry for God*,[4] charismatic Catholic lay leader Ralph Martin interviews Maria Von Trapp, of *Sound of Music* fame. He discusses with her the reasons why many Catholics lack a personal commitment to Christ in their lives. Von Trapp states that many in the Catholic Church are "over sacramentalized" and "under-evangelized." Indeed, "we may even go to daily communion all our lives and yet never have confronted the great issue of whether [Jesus] is my Savior and Lord."[5]

Father Avery Dulles, S. J., who is arguably the leading theologian in the American Catholic Church, addresses this issue in the volume *John Paul and the New Evangelization*.[6] Dulles states many Catholics, although baptized, "were never effectively evangelized." These people "have never made a living personal commitment to Christ and the gospel." Further, "evangelicals can help Catholics to focus on the central Christian message, to achieve a deep personal relationship with Christ."[7]

Why Some Evangelicals Become Catholics
This being the case, the question is why some evangelicals are becoming Catholic. Admittedly, it is a much smaller migration, but it is a significant one since some noted evangelical leaders have been among them.

Well-known apologist Peter Kreeft converted to Roman Catholicism some thirty years ago. Kreeft was exposed to the typical Calvinist anti-Catholicism, which holds that Catholics believe "another gospel."

1. Leon Joseph Cardinal Suenens, *A New Pentecost?* (Ann Arbor: Servant Books, 1975).
2. Ibid., 120.
3. Ibid., 115. For material on Suenens, see: D. D. Bundy, "Suenens, Léon Joseph," in Stanley M. Burgess and Gary B. McGee, eds., *Dictionary of Pentecostal and Charismatic Movements* (Grand Rapids, MI: Zondervan, 1996), 834–35.
4. Ralph Martin, *Hungry for God* (Garden City: Doubleday, 1974).
5. Ibid., 68. Another book by Ralph Martin, *A Crisis of Truth* (Ann Arbor: Servant Books, 1982) analyzes how this problem exists in the Catholic Church in Latin America. Martin salutes the evangelistic efforts of Protestant evangelicals and charismatic Catholics in the area.
6. This volume, edited by Ralph Martin and Peter Williamson (San Francisco: Ignatius Press, 1995), has a number of Catholic leaders and scholars who address the problem of insufficient evangelism among nominal Catholics primarily in Third World countries. A few evangelicals, including Charles Colson and Vinson Synan, make contributions as well.
7. Ibid., 30, 35 (Father Dulles is now Cardinal Dulles).

While taking a class in church history, Kreeft claims to have discovered such Catholic dogmas as the Real Presence in the Eucharist, prayers to and for the departed saints, devotion to Mary, and apostolic succession. He writes that Calvin and Luther's "denial of free will made human choice a sham game of predestined dice."[8] One of the last doctrines to be resolved by Kreeft was justification by faith. His reading in Anselm and Thomas Aquinas led him to believe that in spite of Catholic failure to properly catechize their members, God saves us, we do not save ourselves. He joined the Roman Catholic Church in 1960.[9] Another well-known ex-evangelical, Thomas Howard, left Gordon College near Boston, where he taught. Howard is brother to Elisabeth Elliot, who is a highly respected leader and speaker in evangelical circles. He wrote a "coming-out" book, *Evangelical Is Not Enough*,[10] which details his spiritual journey to Catholicism. Howard concluded that the Catholic Church has a richer tradition and a more meaningful liturgy than the evangelical church home of his youth. And he acknowledges that Luther and Calvin, as well as other Reformation Catholic leaders such as Cardinal Contarini and Johannes von Staupitz,[11] had legitimate concerns about the state of the Catholic Church of their day. However, Howard asks the question, "Do I draw my skirts about me and stand fastidiously apart from the only church we have?"[12] He was received into the Roman Catholic Church in 1985.

The Reasons Given for Converting to Roman Catholicism

Many reasons have been offered for why some evangelicals have converted to Catholicism. Our conclusion about such conversions is connected with the above chapters, which showed that no such biblical,

8. Peter Kreeft, "Hauled Aboard the Ark," in *Spiritual Journeys Toward the Fullness of Faith*, ed. Robert Baram (Boston: St. Paul Books & Media, 1988, rev.), 174.
9. Peter Kreeft is a professor of philosophy at Boston College and is a prolific author. Among his efforts is the *Handbook of Christian Apologetics* coauthored with Ron Tacelli, S. J. This work is used as a text in some evangelical institutions. Kreeft interacts and speaks at conferences with evangelicals.
10. Thomas Howard, *Evangelical Is Not Enough* (San Francisco: Ignatius Press, 1984). Howard has written a number of books including *Christ the Tiger*, which he wrote prior to becoming Roman Catholic.
11. Contarini was a lay theologian who was made a cardinal by Paul III in 1535. He represented the pope at the Conference of Ratisbon (1541). This was an ill-fated attempt to find common ground on the doctrine of justification between Protestants and Catholics. Von Staupitz was vicar-general of the order of the Augustinian Hermits in Wittenberg and Luther's father confessor.
12. Thomas Howard, "From Evangelicalism to Rome," in *Spiritual Journeys*, ed. Robert Baram, 162.

philosophical, and historical arguments exist to support the Catholic claim to be the true church with an infallible teacher in the Bishop of Rome (chap. 7). This being the case, we must look elsewhere for the real grounds of these conversions. When we do so, several things emerge.

The Appeal of Antiquity

Since many evangelicals identify their roots in the sixteenth-century Protestant Reformation, Catholic apologists have been apt at pointing out that Roman Catholicism existed long before that. Indeed, a respected Baptist theologian, Timothy George, confirms that evangelicals often have an incomplete understanding about the history of the church. In his church history class, he told his students, "My job is to inform you that there were Christians between your grandmother and Jesus."[13]

Response: Jaroslav Pelikan addressed this issue in *The Riddle of Roman Catholicism*. He writes about the evolution of Roman Catholicism in chapters including, "How Christianity Became Catholic" and "How Catholicism Became Roman."[14] In brief, antiquity is not a sufficient test for authenticity. Age does not determine truth. Neither does continuity determine true catholicity.

Just because the current Roman Catholic Church can trace its heritage to the Ancient Catholic Church, which in turn has a connection with the early New Testament church, does not mean it is faithful to its apostolic founders. There is a direct continuity between the pluralistic, liberal Harvard University today and the original evangelical institution started by the Puritans, but who would argue that they have been faithful to their founders' beliefs? Likewise, there is a direct continuity between our current government and the founding fathers who signed the Declaration of Independence, but all knowledgeable persons know that we no longer make belief in a Creator, His creation, and God-given moral absolutes the basis of our government and schools as they did.

Likewise, there is a great gulf between the New Testament church to which Catholics trace their heritage and the current church of Rome that has added eleven apocryphal books to the Old Testament, instituted

13. Timothy George is founding dean of the Beeson Divinity School at Samford University and an executive editor of *Christianity Today*. He has worked with "Evangelicals and Catholics Together" to bring attention to what C. S. Lewis termed "Mere Christianity."
14. Jaroslav Pelikan, *The Riddle of Roman Catholicism* (New York: Abingdon, 1959). Pelikan was Lutheran and taught for many years at Yale University. He has since become Eastern Orthodox.

prayers for the dead, offers veneration and prayers to Mary, worships the consecrated host, uses images in worship (cf. Ex. 20:4), installed an infallible pope, and claims to be the only true institution of God on earth whose patrons must perform good works as a condition for receiving eternal life!

Further, even on the antiquity test, Roman Catholicism is not the oldest jurisdiction in Christendom—Eastern Orthodoxy is. "It is an undeniable fact of history that Christianity was Eastern before it was Western. The Church was born in the East. For there was a church in Jerusalem (Acts 2) before there was one in Rome. It was an Eastern Christian, Ananias from Damascus, Syria, who baptized the apostle Paul (Acts 9:1–19). Further, "Antioch, Alexandria and Jerusalem were more important than Rome during the early years of church history. . . ."[15] A number of evangelicals who were looking for a more liturgical, older tradition with which to unite chose Orthodoxy over Roman Catholicism.[16] Besides this, there are ancient errors as well as recent truths. To assume that old is gold is to forget that new can be true. For truth can be rediscovered as well as lost.

The Appeal of Tradition

Much of current evangelicalism lacks a sense of history. For example, Thomas Howard states that as an evangelical he was unaware of great Christian leaders prior to the Wesleys, Calvin, and Luther. "Before them there was a blank until I came to the apostles."[17]

In a volume that contains testimonies of eleven people who have converted to Catholicism, Alex Jones wrote a chapter titled "Return to Apostolic Tradition" concerning oral tradition as understood in the Catholic Church.[18] He notes: "Not only is oral tradition on an equal par with Scripture, it contains *all* that the apostles handed on to their successors. . . ."[19]

15. Norman Geisler and Ralph MacKenzie, *Roman Catholics and Evangelicals: Agreements and Differences* (Grand Rapids, MI: Baker, 1995), Appendix A, "Churches of the East," 433.
16. Among this group would be Peter Gillquist and Jon Braun who were leaders in Campus Crusade for Christ and Frank Schaeffer, son of the late Reformed leader Francis Schaeffer. Gillquist's journey is detailed in *Becoming Orthodox* (Brentwood: Wolgemoth and Hyatt Publishers, 1990). Schaeffer's is in *Dancing Alone* (Brookline: Holy Cross Orthodox Press, 1991). A good treatment of Eastern Orthodoxy is Timothy Ware, *The Orthodox Church*, rev. (New York: Penguin Books, 1983).
17. Howard, *Evangelical*, 42.
18. Rosalind Moss, ed., *Home at Last* (San Diego: Catholic Answers, 2000), 37–50.
19. Ibid., 47, emphasis in original.

Response: We have addressed both the arguments from apostolic succession (see chap. 6) and tradition (see Appendix 3) and found them wanting for several reasons. First, there are good and bad traditions. Second, oral tradition is easily corrupted, as Jesus indicated by his condemnation of the Jewish traditions that had grown up around the Old Testament, saying, "Why do you also transgress the commandment of God because of your tradition?" (Matt. 15:3 NKJV). Further, tradition, even early tradition, can be corrupted. John tells of a mistaken oral tradition birthed in apostolic times that he would not die before Jesus came (John 21:20–23).

What is more, the Council of Trent demanded "universal consent of the Fathers" as a test for Christian dogma. However, most of the dogma added by Rome (just listed above) does not meet this test.

Further, tradition can be helpful, but it is not always a reliable, let alone infallible, test for truth. Certainly, the infallible Catholic decree at Trent has no grounds when it proclaims that "the traditions themselves . . . [have] been dictated either by Christ's own word of mouth, or by the Holy Spirit."[20] The venerable Catholic scholar had it right when he said, "We believe the prophets and apostles because the Lord has been their witness by performing miracles. . . . And we believe the successors of the apostles and prophets only in so far as they tell us those things the apostles and prophets have left in their writings."[21] What is ironic about this Catholic scholar is that he was very Protestant in his doctrine of Scripture.

Finally, Catholic scholars sometimes argue by analogy for an authoritative interpretation of the New Testament by Rome such as the Jews had of the Old Testament by Jewish leaders (see chap. 4). But this analogy is fatal to Rome's claims. For Jesus himself condemned the oral interpretation of the Old Testament by the Jewish leaders of his day, saying, "Thus you have made the commandments of God of no effect by your traditions" (Matt. 15:6). Indeed, Jesus said repeatedly in the Sermon on the Mount, "You have heard that it was said of old . . . but I say unto you . . . ." In so doing he used the imperishable "Law and Prophets" (v. 17) and what they had "written" (Matt. 4:4, 7, 10) to condemn the Jewish oral tradition which had "made the commandment of God of no effect by your tradition" (Matt. 15:6 NKJV). This is precisely what Rome has done to original Christianity (see chap. 7).

20. Roy Denzinger, *The Sources of Catholic Dogma* (St. Louis, MO: Herder, 1957), 244 (from Session 4 of Trent, 1546).
21. Thomas Aquinas, *On Truth*, XIV, 10, AD 11.

The Appeal of Beauty

As have those in other more aesthetically pleasing ecclesiastical liturgies, some converts to Rome have confused lace and grace. Since much of evangelicalism is aesthetically impoverished, it is not difficult to see why Catholicism appeals to them. Even the noted unbelieving psychologist William James wrote that "The strength of these aesthetic sentiments makes it rigorously impossible, it seems to me, that Protestantism, however superior in spiritual profundity it may be to Catholicism, should at the present day succeed in making many converts from the more venerable ecclesiasticism."[22]

Included in this appeal is the contention that evangelical venues also lack "liturgy." Most evangelical converts to Catholicism state that they find the many liturgical practices in their new ecclesiastical home more beautiful and meaningful. One such convert wrote: "I was like a man who all his life had been told that he must build a house but has never been given a hammer and a saw. Now, in the Divine Office, the rosary, the stations of the cross, and Eucharistic adoration, I had discovered a whole treasure-trove of tools."[23]

Response: While the aesthetic feeling one derives from a cathedral experience is understandably pleasing, nonetheless, by the same logic one might argue for the truth of Buddhism or Hinduism. In short, the beauty of Catholicism overpowers the truth of Protestantism for converts to Catholicism. Indeed, an aesthetic experience is not the same as a religious experience, the former being a sense of the sublime and the latter a sense of the Supreme. But many people confuse the two. As an Episcopalian friend of mine once said, "The problem with us Episcopalians is that we confuse lace and grace." The same is true for many Catholics.

Further, while beauty enhances a worship experience, it is not essential to it—at least not in its common, exterior sense of appeal. One can truly worship God in spirit and in truth (John 4:24) in a mud hut in the jungle and feel the cold chill of formalism in Westminster Abbey in London. The fact is that there is no direct correlation between beauty and truth. One can have a beautiful portrayal of error or an ugly presentation of truth.

What is more, if one is interested primarily in a "bells and smells" worship experience, Eastern Orthodoxy trumps—or at least equals—Roman

22. William James, *Varieties of Religious Experience* (New York: A Mentor Book, 1958), 350.
23. Thomas Ricks, "From That Old Time Religion to the Ancient Faith" in Rosalind Moss, *Home at Last*, 80.

Catholicism. Legend has it that in the late tenth century, Prince Vladimir of Kiev, who had been raised a pagan, desired to adopt a religion in order to stabilize his kingdom. To this end, he sent out envoys to examine the major religions (Eastern Orthodoxy, Roman Catholicism, and Islam) and advise him as to which would be best for his domain. When the emissaries returned to Kiev: "they recommended the faith of the Greek Catholics, for they reported that when they attended the divine liturgy in the cathedral of Hagia Sophia in Constantinople, 'we did not know if we were in heaven or on earth.'"[24]

There are unadorned Catholic churches in primitive sectors of the globe as there are ornate Baptist chapels in more civilized areas. Thus, a native African Catholic in the Congo might be more attracted to an ornate Protestant church in New York. The aesthetic appeal is no sure indicator of the true church. Using the analogy of many rooms [denominations] in a large house [the church] C. S. Lewis wisely observed, "Above all you must be asking which door is the true one; not which pleases you best by its paint and paneling. *In plain language, the question should never be: 'Do I like that kind of service?' but 'Are these doctrines true: Is holiness here?'"*[25]

The Appeal of Family Ties

Family influence is a strong factor for some in their conversions to Catholicism. I know of a number of evangelicals whose families have been a powerful factor in this decision. One well-known evangelical recently cited this reason for his re-conversion. In a radio interview on "Stand to Reason," Frank Beckwith cited the verse of Scripture from the Ten Commandments in support: "Honor your father and your mother" (Ex. 20:12). I have an evangelical friend whose dying Catholic father made him promise to return to Catholicism upon his father's death. While one should respect one's parents, one has no obligation to violate their convictions at their request—even their dying request.

24. Ronald Roberson, C. S. P., *The Eastern Christian Churches: A Brief Survey*, 5th ed. (Rome: Edizioni "Orientalia Christiana," 1995), 54. Vladimir was converted to Christianity and baptized around AD 988. I had a similar experience several years ago while on a teaching mission in Ukraine. Knowing my interest in Eastern Orthodoxy, my Ukrainian Baptist students offered to take me to view a liturgical ceremony at the Cathedral in Odessa. The occasion was the celebration of the "Circumcision of Jesus." Amid great pomp and circumstance, the metropolitan (primate comparable to an archbishop in the Roman Church) arrived, and the ensuing ceremony was spectacular. I also later traveled to Kiev and visited St. Vladimir's Cathedral, which is very impressive.
25. C. S. Lewis, *Mere Christianity* (New York: HarperCollins, 2001), *xvi*, emphasis added.

Response: While family influence on conversion to Catholicism is understandable, it is not justifiable as a ground for converting or reconverting to Catholicism. By the same logic a Christian could return to Buddhism, Hinduism, or a cult as a result of family prodding. Family ties are strong, but they are no sure test of truth. Indeed, Jesus had strong words for those who put father and mother before him, saying, "Whoever loves father or mother more than me is not worthy of me" (Matt. 10:37).

The Appeal of Intellectual Tradition

I [Norm] once asked a noted Catholic apologist why some evangelical intellectuals converted to Rome. I thought he would say that the smarter one gets the more likely he is to became a Catholic. Instead, he said that Catholicism has an older, deeper intellectual tradition than does evangelicalism. There are for example few Baptist Augustines and Methodist Aquinases. If one is going to advance in his intellectual understanding of Christianity, he is going to run into some great Catholic scholars, both ancient and modern.

Response: True as this may be, the fact of the matter is that there is no correlation between scholarship and truth. One can be an uneducated Christian and an educated non-Christian. Likewise, there are peasant Catholics and scholarly Protestants. There is no correspondence between truth and intellectual depth. One can be shallow in the truth or deep into error. Just as no Catholic would allow intellectual forms of Buddhism to take precedence over an uneducated Catholicism, even so an intellectually superior form of Catholicism does not give it an advantage over an uninformed form of Protestantism.

The Appeal to Certainty

It has been said that for many of those (i.e., evangelicals) who convert to Catholicism, "the road to Rome is the path to certainty."[26] Thus it appears that Rome not only provides uniformity through an unbreakable tradition, but offers a concrete solution to the perennial problems of schism and hermeneutical anarchy (as seen in evangelicalism): an infallible magisterium, which provides Scripture its official and infallible interpretation.

Response: It is true that within evangelicalism there are numerous denominations and differing interpretations on certain doctrinal issues;

26. Pelikan, *The Riddle of Roman Catholicism*, 206.

however, this is also true of Rome. Yes, there are conflicting opinions on crucial doctrines (and even different sects) within the Catholic Church. The existence of the many orders attests to this, e.g., Franciscans and Dominicans, as does the liberalism present within Rome. What is more, there exists a Catholic sect called the Old Catholic Church, which separated itself from Rome shortly after Pius IX proclaimed the dogma of papal infallibility at Vatican I (led by German priest and theologian Johann Joseph Ignaz von Döllinger [1799–1890]). Döllinger's group held to a conciliar view of infallibility rather than a Roman papal view.

Further, there have been recent intramural debates among Catholic apologists on *crucial* Catholic dogma. For example, noted Catholic apologists Robert Sungenis and Gerry Matatics—ironically former evangelicals—have debated the nature of two crucial Catholic dogmas: the mass and the papacy. The former deals with the *"Novus Ordo"* of the mass, which is the central act of worship in Rome. The debate centers on whether the mass should be carried out in the vernacular of the people or in the traditional Latin, thus questioning its proper order and validity. The latter is concerned with the *"Sedevacantism"* scandal, namely, whether the current pope (and those in succession after Vatican II) is truly St. Peter's successor.

Ironically, these are nonnegotiable dogmas for Rome, and thus tear at the very fabric of her theological integrity. This is not true of evangelicalism, all of which holds to the same *essential* doctrines—and that without the help of an infallible magisterium. An infallible interpreter is not needed for an accurate interpretation of Scripture; a good one suffices. An accurate interpretation can be achieved by utilizing a sound hermeneutic, i.e., the historical-grammatical approach. The wealth of biblical scholarship that Protestantism has produced (which even Catholics utilize) attests to this.

Uniformity is not a test for truth, for it is found within many of the modern cults too, which Rome would not consider "separated brethren" as she does her evangelical counterpart. Spiritual unity of the church is what Christ called for in his high priestly prayer in John 17, not the uniformity of an earthly organization. Catholics would do well to dismiss this charge of schism against evangelicals. In short, as H. Wayne House put it, "The Roman Catholic security blanket is thin cover for the Christian seeking *certainty* in doctrine. True doctrinal security is in the words of the prophets of the Hebrew Scriptures and the apostles of the Greek Scriptures."[27]

27. H. Wayne House, "Returning to Rome," *Christian Research Journal* 30.6 (2007): 26.

Conclusion

Upon examination, most converts to Catholicism—even intellectuals—did not do so primarily on biblical or rational grounds. They were prompted to convert to Catholicism because it was an older, deeper, richer, more beautiful tradition. Or, because of the ties of family or friends. However, none of these are good tests of truth. For one can have a deeper, richer, older, and more beautiful belief that is false. And he can embrace a more shallow, impoverished, younger, and less beautiful form of truth. As appealing as any one or more of these attributes may be, they are not indicators of authenticity. Truth demands evidence, not aesthetic appeal or antiquity. And error can come in beautiful, colorful, and intellectual forms. As the Bible says, "For Satan himself transforms himself into an angel of light" (2 Cor. 11:14 NKJV).

In the final analysis, the issue is not antiquity, intellectual profundity, beauty, or uniformity and identity; it is truth. And truth is confirmed by good evidence and sound arguments. Ultimately, the real issue concerning an evangelical converting to Roman Catholicism is truth. And, as we have shown above (chaps. 3–6), evidence is lacking for the Roman claim to be the true church. Indeed, its claim to infallibility and exclusivity are demonstrably false. It is in fact a system of serious errors.[28] Rome makes claims for herself "as the seat of infallible authority," makes "demands for allegiance . . . points to her priesthood as the one by which men are saved," and "asserts that no congregation is valid except as a tributary of herself. . . ."[29] But no one organization has a franchise on the essential truths of Christianity. True unity is spiritual, not organizational; genuinely converted Catholics and evangelicals have more in common than either born-again Catholics with nominal Catholics, or evangelicals with liberal Protestants (chap. 7).

C. S. Lewis: A Case Study

When attempting to address the issue of Protestants becoming Roman Catholic, the case of C. S. Lewis is very illuminating. Lewis, one of the leading Christian apologists and thinkers of the twentieth century, became a Protestant at his conversion and remained so throughout his life. This was true in spite of his close friendships with such committed Catholics as J. R. R. Tolkien and Christopher Derrick.[30] Lewis was also

---

28. Geisler and MacKenzie, *Roman Catholics and Evangelicals*, part 2, 157–355.
29. S. M. Hutchens, "C. S. Lewis and Mother Kirk," *Books & Culture* (Nov./Dec. 2004): 33.
30. This very issue is addressed by Christopher Derrick in *C. S. Lewis and the Church of Rome* (San Francisco: Ignatius Press, 1981). It should be pointed out that as much as Lewis

aware of the writing of G. K. Chesterton, who was a Roman Catholic apologist and literary giant in his own right.

A contemporary Roman Catholic literary biographer, Joseph Pearce, has written a book that deals with C. S. Lewis and his relationship with Catholicism.[31] Pearce is a great admirer of Lewis and addresses a topic that for Catholics is a great puzzlement: why didn't Lewis ever make the journey to Rome? In an article reviewing Joseph Pearce's book on Lewis, S. M. Hutchens writes: "Pearce's answer, reduced to its essentials, is that Lewis had a blind spot created by a bigoted Ulster Protestant upbringing; despite his exposure to Catholic teaching and the best of Catholics among his friends, he was never able to overcome this prejudice, even on his deathbed."[32] Pearce writes that Tolkien, who had a major role in Lewis' conversion, visited Lewis during his final illness, accompanied by his son Father John Tolkien. Tolkien had often expressed "disappointment that Lewis had never converted to Catholicism . . . and believed that Lewis' soul could be endangered should he fail to do so before his death. . . ."[33] Therefore, Tolkien, having his priest son at Lewis's bedside, was hoping for a deathbed conversion.

Finally, what are we to make of Lewis's resistance to the end of becoming Roman Catholic? As has been stated, he had many friends from the Roman communion and could be fairly described as "Catholic friendly."[34] Hutchens (quoted above) states that "Lewis may not necessarily have

---

is honored for presenting aspects of the Christian faith that are accepted by all Christians, evangelicals take exception to some of his views which are not a part of "mere Christianity." These would include a rejection of the inerrancy of the Scriptures and a belief that one might belong to Christ without explicitly acknowledging him. Also, in several of his books, including *The Great Divorce*, Lewis indicates his belief in the Catholic dogma of purgatory. A good treatment of C. S. Lewis and his strengths and weaknesses may be found in: Steven P. Mueller, "An Assessment of C. S. Lewis: Beyond Mere Christianity," *Christian Research Journal*, vol. 27 (No.4, 2004): 12–21.

31. Joseph Pearce, *C. S. Lewis and the Catholic Church* (San Francisco: Ignatius Press, 2003). Pearce is a highly acclaimed author whose works include treatments of G. K. Chesterton, J. R. R. Tolkien, Hilaire Belloc, and Oscar Wilde.

32. S. M. Hutchens, "C. S. Lewis and Mother Kirk," 30. It should be noted that another member of the Tolkien/Lewis group that met at the Bird and Baby Pub regularly, resisted the journey to Rome. Charles Williams was an Anglican poet and theological writer, who—while believing in the councils and creeds of the early church—never took the trip to Rome or Constantinople.

33. Pearce, *C. S. Lewis*, 148. This indicates a triumphalism, which was held by even informed Catholics prior to Vatican II and the introduction of non-Catholics being called "separated brethren."

34. Lewis's interaction with Catholics extended worldwide. An example would include a little-known correspondence which led to a close friendship between C. S. Lewis and Don Giovanni Clabria, a Roman Catholic priest in Verona, Italy. Cf. Martin Moynihan, *The Latin Letters of C. S. Lewis* (South Bend, IN: St. Augustine's Press, 1987).

denied the form of the Roman Catholic Church as a proper reflection that [sic] of the true church, but he would have resisted with full vigor the Roman claim that it, in its very self as a papal institution, is to be wholly *identified* with the true church. . . . "[35] Further, "Lewis was well aware that to convert to the Church of Rome, he would be required to confess it as the One, Holy, Catholic and Apostolic Church—and he made it clear in a number of places, particularly in his well-known account of the house with its various rooms in *Mere Christianity*, that he believed no such thing."[36] I would suggest that C. S. Lewis's view against joining the Roman Church was not because of his "bigoted Ulster Protestant upbringing." It was rather quite similar to that of many current evangelicals (such as I) who, while "Catholic friendly," make the distinction between "spiritual unity" and "ecclesiological uniformity."

My own experience is a case in point. My father and the vast majority of all my relatives are Roman Catholic. I attended two Catholic universities and studied under top Jesuit philosophers and theologians. My PhD in philosophy is from Loyola University in Chicago. I am a follower of the great Catholic thinker Thomas Aquinas. Yet despite my exposure to Catholic thinking at its highest level and long family ties, I have never had the slightest inclination to become a Roman Catholic. Why? Because I have examined its claims biblically, philosophically, and historically and find them seriously wanting. In short, I see no basis for its central claim to be the true church or to its outlandish claim to infallibility.

And when I examine the real grounds upon which others convert to Catholicism, I am not impressed. By the same logic of one looking for an older, deeper, richer, more intellectual, more beautiful tradition or rejoining the family tradition, one could easily justify becoming a Buddhist, Hindu, Muslim, pagan, or better, an Eastern Orthodox.

The fact is that truth is not determined by age, intellectual depth, family ties, or beauty. It is determined by facts and good reason. And after over a half-century of careful and extensive thought on the topic, I see no reason to make Rome home or to leave the historic biblical faith once for all committed to the saints. Any evangelical who is contemplating "swimming up the Tiber" to Rome in order to become "Catholic" would do well just to remain evangelical if he or she desires to become "catholic" in the most basic sense of the word.

35. S. M. Hutchens, "C. S. Lewis," 32, emphasis in original.
36. Ibid., 33.

IRENAEUS ON THE ALLEGED AUTHORITY OF THE CHURCH

A good deal of controversy revolves around a disputed text in *Against Heresies*, Book 3. Irenaeus referred to "that tradition derived from the apostles, of the very great, the very ancient, and universally known Church founded and organized at Rome by the two most glorious apostles, Peter and Paul; as also by pointing out the faith preached to men, which comes down to our times by means of the succession of the bishops." For "it is a matter of necessity that *every Church should agree* [Lat. *convenire*] *with this Church*, on account of its preeminent authority, that is, the faithful everywhere, inasmuch as the apostolic tradition has been preserved continuously by those faithful men who exist everywhere."[1]

The Roman Interpretation of Irenaeus

Noted authority on the early Fathers J. N. D. Kelly summarizes the dispute in these words: "If *convenire* here means "agree with" and *principalitas* refers to the Roman primacy (in whatever sense), the gist of the sentence may be taken to be that Christians of every other church are required, in view of its special position of leadership, to fall in line

1. *Against Heresies* (hereafter, *Haer.*) 3.3.2, emphasis added.

with the Roman church, inasmuch as the authentic apostolic tradition is always preserved by the faithful who are everywhere."[2]

Reasons to Reject the Roman Interpretation
However, Kelly and many other scholars have found fault with this translation for two reasons. First, the weakness of the final clause has struck them as "intolerable."[3] Second, "the normal meaning of *convenire* is 'resort to,' 'foregather at,' and *necesse est* does not easily bear the sense of 'ought.'"[4] Indeed, the editor of *The Apostolic Fathers*, volume 1 of *The Ante-Nicene Fathers*, A. Cleveland Coxe, cites one candid Roman Catholic scholar who translates it as follows: "For to this Church, on account of more potent principality, it is necessary that every Church (that is, those who are on every side faithful) *resort*; in which Church ever, *by those who are on every side*, has been preserved that tradition which is from the apostles."[5] Coxe adds, "Here it is obvious that the faith was kept at Rome, by *those who resort there* from all quarters. She was a mirror of the Catholic World, owing her orthodoxy to them; not the Sun, dispensing her own light to others, but the glass bringing their rays into focus."[6]

Reasons for the Non-Catholic Reflective View
In view of the foregoing discussion, it is more reasonable to conclude that Irenaeus held the reflective view of Rome's position in the early church, as opposed to the authoritative view of the Roman Catholics. This is in direct contrast to the proclamation of Pope Pius IX who "informed his Bishops, at the late Council, that they were not called to bear their testimony, but to hear his infallible decree."[7] In short, what Irenaeus meant was that Rome is the center of orthodoxy since she, by virtue of being the capital of the empire, was the repository of all Catholic tradition—"all this has been turned upside down by modern Romanism."[8]

Kelly concurs, observing that many scholars "have judged it more plausible to take Irenaeus's point as being that the Roman church [of that day] supplies an ideal illustration for the reason that, in view of

2. J. N. D. Kelly, *Early Christian Doctrines*, rev. ed. (New York: Harper, 1960), 193.
3. Ibid.
4. Ibid.
5. Philip Schaff, *Ante-Nicene Fathers*, 1.415.
6. Ibid.
7. Ibid., 461.
8. Ibid.

its being placed in the imperial city, representatives of all the different churches necessarily (i.e., inevitably) flock to it, so that there is some guarantee that the faith taught there faithfully reflects the apostolic tradition."[9]

Further confirmation of this comes from the fact that the apostles did not appoint more apostles to replace them after Pentecost where they became the "foundation" of the church, Christ being the chief cornerstone (Eph. 2:20). Rather, they appointed "elders in every church" (Acts 14:23). Irenaeus himself speaks of "the disciples of the apostles" as "presbyters" (elders).[10] He wrote: "We refer them [heretics] to that tradition which originates from the apostles, and which is preserved by means of the successions of presbyters in the Churches."[11]

The most that can be said for Irenaeus is that he appeared to reflect a growing episcopal view of church government as opposed to that of the New Testament church a century earlier. For he seemed to believe that each church has a single bishop over it, speaking of Polycarp as "bishop of Smyrna"[12] and a line of bishops in Rome beginning with Linus.[13] However, he in no way endowed this local bishop with more general authority, to say nothing of universal authority. Indeed, the final authority for Irenaeus rested in the Bible (see Appendix 5). Nor did he see an infallible authority of a universal bishop— a doctrine that was not officially pronounced by Rome for another 1,700 years (in 1870).

What is more, this episcopal form of government, even in its more primitive form of a bishop leader of the elders in a local church, is not found in the New Testament. For the New Testament is clear that every local church had its own plurality of "bishops and deacons" (cf. Phil. 1:1 cf. Acts 14:23).[14] And it was they whose leadership was to be followed by their congregations (Heb. 13:7, 17, 24), not any ecclesiastical authority in Rome. Christ, the Chief Shepherd, was the invisible Head

9. Ibid., 193.
10. *Haer.*, 5.35.2.
11. Ibid., 3.2.2.
12. Ibid., 3.3.4.
13. Ibid., 3.3.3.
14. Indeed, *bishop* and *elder* were used interchangeably in the New Testament (cf. Titus 1:5, 7), the former being the term Greeks used for leaders and the latter that Hebrews used. The qualifications are the same for both; the duties are the same; there was a plurality of both in even small churches (cf. Acts 14:23; Phil. 1:1). Thus, Irenaeus, writing over a hundred years after the apostles, is reflecting an emerging episcopal form of government not found in the New Testament, nor practiced by the apostles.

of the visible church. He walked among them and rebuked them for not recognizing his Headship (cf. Rev. 1–3).[15]

Conclusion

Because of his proximity to the apostles, Irenaeus is a key figure in the early church. He knew Polycarp, the disciple of the apostle John. He lived only 100 years after the time of the apostles. Hence, he was in a vantage point to reflect the view of the church of his time. But even so, as we have seen, he did not reflect the Roman Catholic view. His view of church government is not that of a universal episcopalism, nor for him was the bishop of Rome endowed with any universal authority, to say nothing of infallible authority. For Irenaeus only the Scriptures had infallible authority (Appendix 5). There was no apostolic succession and no apostolic authority beyond the original apostolic circle, except insofar as historical linkage was able to verify the apostles' testimony to Christ and to Scripture (Appendix 3). As for the role of Rome as the capital of the empire, it was only reflective, not authoritative, as we have shown above.

While the non-Catholic interpretation of Irenaeus is preferable for the many reasons given above, the outcome of this issue is not definitive for the debate about the alleged primacy of Rome. For if the authoritative interpretation is correct, it simply shows an earlier statement of what later developed into what came to be known as Roman Catholicism. If so, this would not be surprising for a couple reasons. For one thing, the beginning of false doctrine, even on the primacy of the episcopacy, was nearly a century before this time. John the apostle spoke of it in his third epistle when he warned: "I wrote to the church, but Diotrephes, who loves to have the preeminence among them, does not receive us" (3 John 9 NKJV). Further, Irenaeus lived over a century after most apostles had died—the very time that even apocryphal Gospels were emerging. Indeed, he is writing some time after the apocryphal *Gospel of Thomas* (c. 140). So, there was plenty of time for false views to emerge, even among those who were otherwise orthodox. What is more, considering the attacks on Christianity at the time, there was strong motivation to develop an ecclesiology that would provide a united front against the divergent heretical groups emerging at the time, which is reflected in Irenaeus's emerging episcopal view of church government.

15. See Norman L. Geisler, *Systematic Theology*, vol. 4: *The Church and Last Things*, ch. 4.

In short, there is no good evidence that Irenaeus favored the Roman Catholic view of the primacy of Peter. And even if he favored the primacy of Rome as the center of Christianity, he does not support the later Roman Catholic pronouncements on the infallibility of the pope. His constant appeal was to the Scripture and to original "apostles" (plural) as the God-established authority. He did not single out Peter as superior to others. Peter, at best, was only a cofounder of the church at Rome along with Paul. He was in fact on the same level as Paul and the other "apostles" to whom Irenaeus repeatedly refers. Furthermore, Irenaeus's stress on the primacy of Scripture as the final written authority of the Christian faith demonstrates that all ecclesiastical authority is based on Scripture, not the reverse. Finally, his stress on the sufficiency of the Holy Spirit and the proper mode of interpretation as sufficient to understand the Scripture denies the later Roman Catholic view that the church, in an organizational authoritative sense, is necessary to interpret Scripture.

A CHRONOLOGICAL LIST OF POPES AND ANTIPOPES

A serious problem with the Roman Catholic doctrine of infallibility (see chap. 5) is that there were numerous times in the history of the church when it was not possible to identify with certainty who the pope was. Indeed, there were competing popes called "antipopes." At these times, there was for all practical purposes a visible authority to guide the faithful. Hence, the alleged value of an infallible leader was in fact nonexistent. Further, competing popes, often with the same alleged authority, anathematized each other, leaving Rome with a theological enigma. A list of the popes and antipopes will focus the problem.[1] The antipopes are highlighted in italics.

Dates	Pope/Antipope	Dates	Pope/Antipope
until c. 64	St. Peter	c. 154–c. 166	Anicetus
	Linus	c. 166–c. 175	Soter
	Anacletus	175–89	Eleutherius
fl. c. 96	Clement I	189–98	Victor I
	Evaristus	198–217	Zephyrinus
	Alexander I	217–22	Callistus I
c. 117–c. 127	Sixtus	*217–c. 235*	*Hippolytus*
c. 127–c. 137	Telesphorus	222–30	Urban I
c. 137–c. 140	Hyginus	230–5	Pontian
c. 140–c. 154	Pius I	235–6	Anterus

1. Adapted from F. L. Cross and E. A. Livingstone, *The Oxford Dictionary of the Christian Church*, 2nd ed. (Oxford: Oxford University Press, 1974), 1515–18. Antipopes listed in bold.

Dates	Pope/Antipope	Dates	Pope/Antipope
236–50	Fabian	604–6	Sabinianus
251–3	Cornelius	607	Boniface III
251–257	*Novatian*	608–15	Boniface IV
253–4	Lucius I	615–18	Deusdedit or
254–7	Stephen I		Adeodatus I
257–8	Sixtus II	619–25	Boniface V
259–68	Dionysius	625–38	Honorius I
269–74	Felix I	640–2	Severinus
275–83	Eutychianus	640–2	John IV
283–96	Caius	642–9	Theodore I
296–304	Marcellinus	649–55	Martin I
308–9	Marcellus I	654–7	Eugenius I
310	Eusebius	657–72	Vatalian
311–314	Miltiades	672–6	Adeodatus II
314–35	Sylvester I	676–8	Donus
336	Mark	678–81	Agatho
337–52	Julius I	682–3	Leo II
352–66	Liberius	684–5	Benedict II
355–65	*Felix II*	685–6	John V
366–84	Damasus I	686–7	Cono
366–7	*Ursinus*	*687*	*Theodore*
384–99	Siricius	*687*	*Paschal*
399–401	Anastasius I	687–701	Sergius I
402–17	Innocent I	701–5	John VI
417–18	Zosimus	705–7	John VII
418–22	Boniface I	708	Sisinnius
418–19	*Eulalius*	708–15	Constantine
422–32	Celestine I	715–31	Gregory II
432–40	Sixtus III	731–41	Gregory III
440–61	Leo I	741–52	Zacharias
461–8	Hilarus	752	Stephen II
468–83	Simplicius	752–7	Stephen II (III)
483–92	Felix III (II)	757–67	Paul I
492–6	Gelasius I	*767–9*	*Constantine*
496–8	Anastasius II	*768*	*Philip*
498–514	Symmachus	768–72	Stephen III (IV)
498, 501–5	*Laurentius*	772–95	Hadrian I
514–23	Hormisdas	795–816	Leo III
523–6	John I	816–17	Stephen V
526–30	Felix IV (III)	817–24	Paschal I
530–2	Boniface II	824–7	Eugenius II
530	*Dioscorus*	827	Valentine
533–5	John II	827–44	Gregory IV
535–6	Agapetus I	*844*	*John*
536–7	Silverius	844–7	Sergius II
537–55	Vigilius	847–55	Leo IV
556–61	Pelagius I	855–8	Benedict III
561–74	John III	*855*	*Anastasius*
575–9	Benedict I		*Bibliothecarius*
579–90	Pelagius II	858–67	Nicholas I
590–604	Gregory I	867–72	Hadrian II

Dates	Pope/Antipope	Dates	Pope/Antipope
872–82	John VIII	1048	Damasus II
882–4	Marinus I	1048–54	Leo IX
884–5	Hadrian III	1055–7	Victor II
885–91	Stephen VI	1057–8	Stephen X
891–6	Formosus	*1058–9*	*Benedict X*
896	Boniface VI	1059–61	Nicholas II
896–7	Stephen VII	1061–73	Alexander II
897	Romanus	*1061–72*	*Honorius II*
897	Theodore II	1073–85	Gregory VII
898–900	John IX	*1080, 1084–*	*Clement III*
900–3	Benedict IV	*1100*	
903	Leo V	1086–7	Victor III
903–4	*Christopher*	1088–99	Urban II
904–11	Sergius III	1099–1118	Paschal II
911–13	Anastasius III	*1100–2*	*Theodoric*
913–14	Lando	*1102*	*Albert*
914–28	John X	*1105–11*	*Sylvester IV*
928	Leo VI	1118–19	Gelasius II
928–31	Stephen VIII	*1118–21*	*Gregory VIII*
931–5	John XI	1119–24	Callistus II
936–9	Leo VII	1124–30	Honorius II
939–42	Stephen IX	*1124*	*Celestine II*
942–6	Marinus II	1130–43	Innocent II
946–55	Agapetus II	*1130–8*	*Anacletus II*
955–64	John XII	*1138*	*Victor IV*
963–5	Leo VIII	1143–4	Celestine II
964–6	Benedict V	1144–5	Lucius II
965–72	John XIII	1145–53	Eugenius III
973–4	Benedict VI	1153–4	Anastasius IV
974, 984–5	*Boniface VII*	1154–9	Hadrian IV
974–83	Benedict VII	1159–81	Alexander III
983–4	John XIV	*1159–64*	*Victor IV[2]*
985–96	John XV	*1164–8*	*Paschal III*
996–9	Gregory V	*1168–78*	*Callistus III*
997–8	*John XVI*	*1179–80*	*Innocent III*
999–1003	Sylvester II	1181–5	Lucius III
1003	John XVII	1185–7	Urban III
1004–9	John XVIII	1187	Gregory VIII
1009–12	Sergius IV	1187–91	Clement III
1012–24	Benedict VIII	1191–8	Celestine III
1012	*Gregory*	1198–1216	Innocent III
1024–32	John XIX	1216–27	Honorius III
1032–44	Benedict IX	1227–41	Gregory IX
1045	Sylvester III	1241	Celestine IV
1045	Benedict IX (for the second time)	1243–54	Innocent IV
1045–6	Gregory VI	1254–61	Alexander IV
1046–7	Clement II	1261–4	Urban IV
1047–8	Benedict IX (for the third time)	1265–8	Clement IV
		1271–6	Gregory X
		1276	Innocent V

2. No account was taken of the previous antipope, who had resisted for a very short time.

Dates	Pope/Antipope	Dates	Pope/Antipope
1276	Hadrian V	1555	Marcellus II
1276–7	John XXI[3]	1555–9	Paul IV
1277–80	Nicholas III	1559–65	Pius IV
1281–5	Martin IV	1566–72	Pius V
1285–7	Honorius IV	1572–85	Gregory XIII
1288–92	Nicholas IV	1585–90	Sixtus V
1294	Celestine V	1590	Urban VII
1294–1303	Boniface VIII	1590–1	Gregory XIV
1303–4	Benedict XI	1591	Innocent IX
1305–14	Clement V	1592–1605	Clement VIII
1316–34	John XXII	1605	Leo XI
1328–30	*Nicholas V*	1605–21	Paul V
1334–42	Benedict XII	1621–3	Gregory XV
1342–52	Clement VI	1623–44	Urban VIII
1352–62	Innocent VI	1644–55	Innocent X
1362–70	Urban V	1655–67	Alexander VII
1370–8	Gregory XI	1667–9	Clement IX
1378–89	Urban VI	1670–6	Clement X
1378–94	*Clement VII*	1676–89	Innocent XI
1389–1404	Boniface IX	1689–91	Alexander VIII
1394–1423	*Benedict XIII*	1691–1700	Innocent XII
1404–6	Innocent VII	1700–21	Clement XI
1406–15	Gregory XII	1721–4	Innocent XIII
1409–10	*Alexander V*	1724–30	Benedict XIII
1410–15	*John XXIII*	1730–40	Clement XII
1417–31	Martin V	1740–58	Benedict XIV
1423–9	*Clement VIII*	1758–69	Clement XIII
1425–30	*Benedict XIV*	1769–74	Clement XIV
1431–47	Eugenius IV	1775–99	Pius VI
1439–49	*Felix V*	1800–23	Pius VII
1447–55	Nicholas V	1823–9	Leo XII
1455–8	Callistus III	1829–30	Pius VIII
1458–64	Pius II	1831–46	Gregory XVI
1464–71	Paul II	1846–78	Pius XI
1471–84	Sixtus IV	1878–1903	Leo XIII
1484–92	Innocent VIII	1903–14	Pius X
1492–1503	Alexander VI	1914–22	Benedict XV
1503	Pius III	1922–39	Pius XI
1503–13	Julius II	1939–58	Pius XII
1513–21	Leo X	1958–63	John XXIII
1522–3	Hadrian VI	1963–78	Paul VI
1523–34	Clement VII	1978	John Paul I
1534–49	Paul III	1978–2005	John Paul II
1550–5	Julius III	2005–	Benedict XVI

3. No pope bearing the name of John XX ever existed.

THE RELATION OF TRADITION TO SCRIPTURE

Various Views on the Role of Tradition

The role and meaning of "tradition" is a hotly debated topic within Christendom. On one end of the spectrum is the traditional Roman Catholic view that tradition is a separate source of revelation in addition to Scripture, which it can use to make infallible proclamations. On the other end of the spectrum is the Anabaptist and independent view that sees little or no place for tradition. In descending order from the Roman Catholic view is that of the Greek Orthodox, who highly value tradition as the means by which Scripture is understood. The High Anglican view is very similar, and even the Lower Anglican church view accepts a significant role of apostolic tradition in understanding the Scriptures. Most Lutherans respect tradition, especially early tradition, but give it no divine authority in interpreting Scripture. Next in descending order of the value of Scripture is the Reformed tradition, which holds that creedal tradition, particularly of the first five centuries or so, has value, but no divine authority, in interpreting Scripture. Anabaptist and independent churches give no authority to tradition, even early tradition, placing sole authority in Scripture. Even so, most agree with the essential doctrines expressed in the early creeds, not because they have any authority but because they agree with the only divine authority—the divinely inspired Scriptures.

The various views on tradition parallel the view on *sola Scriptura*. Roman Catholics reject *sola Scriptura*[1] since they believe apostolic tradition is preserved in and infallibly expressed by the Roman magisterium.

Eastern Orthodoxy and High Church Anglicanism, while rejecting an infallible magisterium in Rome, affirm the necessity of apostolic tradition handed down by apostolic succession in interpreting the Scriptures. The Lutheran and Reformed churches, while respecting early Christian traditions expressed in the creeds and councils of the first five centuries, do not believe they have divine authority or are absolutely necessary in properly interpreting the essential doctrines of Scripture. They have ecumenical value as the doctrinal basis for the Christian church in general and confirmational value to Protestant teaching about Holy Scripture, but no authority over Scripture or its clear teaching on fundamental truths. Last, most Anabaptist and independent churches pay little if any regard to early tradition of creeds, seeking the guidance of the Holy Spirit alone in understanding Scripture, even though they agree with most, if not all, of what is in the Apostles' Creed.[2]

The Role of Tradition in the Early Church

One of the Fathers in the best position to know the role of tradition in the early church was Irenaeus (ca. 130–200). He knew Polycarp, the disciple of the apostle John. He was the first great father in the West and wrote a major work titled *Against Heresies*, which treats this very topic.

Irenaeus refers to "tradition" in a historical sense of the unbroken chain transmitting the apostolic understanding of the gospel, that it came from John the apostle to Polycarp to Irenaeus. Indeed, he spoke of Polycarp as one "not only instructed by apostles, and conversed with many who had seen Christ, but also, by the apostles in Asia appointed bishop of the Church in Smyrna, whom I also saw in my early youth."[3]

Irenaeus wrote: "But, again . . . we refer them [heretics] to that tradition which originates from the apostles, and which is preserved by means

1. Some Catholic scholars accept *sola Scriptura* in a material sense that there is no new source of divine revelation since the canon of Scripture was closed. But they reject it in the formal Reformation sense that Scripture is perspicuous (clear) in its main teaching and needs no interpretive framework (other than the normal historical-grammatical hermeneutic) to understand these essential teachings.
2. Many reject the later phrase about Christ's "descending into hell," which was not in the earlier version of the creed.
3. *Haer.*, 3.3.4.

of the successions of presbyters in the Churches."[4] Indeed, Irenaeus refers to the "presbyters" as "the disciples of the apostles."[5] For, "It is within the power of all, therefore, in every Church, who may wish to see the truth, to contemplate clearly the tradition of the apostles manifested throughout the whole world; and we are in a position to reckon up those who were by the apostles instituted bishops in the Churches, and to demonstrate the succession of these men to our own times."[6] Irenaeus added, "These things are borne witness to in writing by Papias, the hearer of John, and a companion of Polycarp [who was a disciple of the apostle John], in his fourth book."[7]

On the Primacy of Scripture

No one reading the apostolic and other early fathers can help but be struck by their extensive and authoritative use of Scripture. Only seven major Fathers from Justin Martyr to Eusebius cite 36,289 verses from the New Testament—every verse but eleven (most of which are from the one-chapter book 3 John). Irenaeus alone cites 1,819 verses.[8]

Further, the manner in which they are cited reveals the great respect shown to the Scriptures as the very written Word of God. As we have already seen, Irenaeus believed that the very words of Scripture were God-given, perfect, without error—the very ground and pillar of truth.

Other than a few scant references in early fathers to the oral words of apostles confirming what is in their written word, which alone is God-breathed (2 Tim. 3:16; cf. 2 Pet. 1:20–21; 3:15–16), the Bible is not only the primary source of divine authority cited—for Irenaeus it is the only source. Hence, it is not simply a matter of the primacy of Scripture but the exclusivity of Scripture as the sole written God-breathed authority from God. Indeed, Irenaeus criticizes heretics because "they gather their views from other sources than the Scriptures" (1.8.1). Likewise, he condemns them because they "adduce an unspeakable number of apocryphal and spurious writings" (1.22.1). In this sense, Irenaeus held to *sola Scriptura* (the Bible alone)—one of the great principles of the later Reformation. "Tradition" was merely the historical link back to the apostles and their writings wherein the true divine authority rested.

4. Ibid., 3.2.2.
5. Ibid., 5.35.2.
6. Ibid., 3.3.1.
7. Ibid., 5.333.4.
8. Charles Leach, *Our Bible: How We Got It* (Chicago: Moody, 1897), 35–36.

Tradition itself had no authority other than an instrumental authority (of being a reliable historical channel) by which one can connect with the true authority, which was apostolic Scripture.

On the Perspicuity of Scripture

As J. N. D. Kelly notes, "Provided the Bible was taken as a whole, its teaching was self-evident.[9] Only when heretics wrenched texts out of their proper context did the basic message seem confused. Of course, because the Bible is "spiritual in its entirety" it is not surprising that there are some obscurities.[10] Nonetheless, with proper exegesis and the aid of the Holy Spirit, the main message of the Bible is clear.

Irenaeus criticized those who "accuse these Scriptures, as if they were not correct, nor of authority, and assert that they are ambiguous, and that the truth cannot be extracted from them by those who are ignorant of tradition."[11] This shows clearly that he not only believed in the perspicuity (clarity) of Scripture but also the sufficiency of the literal hermeneutic, apart from tradition, to understand what the Scriptures are teaching.

Irenaeus recognized, of course, that as clear as the Scriptures are, there are depraved minds that will not accept them. He said, "I shall for the benefit of those at least who do not bring a depraved mind to bear upon them, devote a special book to the Scriptures referred to . . . and I shall plainly set forth from these divine Scriptures proofs to satisfy all the lovers of truth."[12]

On the Interpretation of Scripture

Following on the clarity of Scripture is the belief in a literal historical-grammatical hermeneutic which alone can yield this clear message. Irenaeus believed that proper interpretation yields a harmonious and unambiguous understanding of Scripture. He wrote: "A sound mind . . . will eagerly meditate upon those things which God has placed with the power of mankind . . . and will make advancement in them, rendering the knowledge of them easy to him by means of daily study."[13] He added, "these things are such as fall plainly under our observation, and are clearly and unambiguously in express terms set forth in the Sacred Scriptures."[14]

9. J. N. D. Kelly, *Early Christian Doctrines* (New York: Harper & Row, 1960), 38.
10. Ibid., 61.
11. *Haer.*, 3.2.1.
12. Ibid., 2.35.4.
13. Ibid., 2.27.10.
14. Ibid.

Irenaeus concludes: "Since, therefore, the entire Scriptures, the prophets, and the Gospels, can be clearly, unambiguously, and harmoniously understood by all, although all do not believe them . . . those persons will seem truly foolish who blind their eyes to such clear demonstrations."[15]

As for difficult passages, "the parables shall be harmonized with those passages which are perfectly clear."[16] Hence, there is a proper and improper way to read a text. And "if, then, one does not attend to the proper reading of the passage . . . there shall be not only incongruities, but also, when reading, he will utter blasphemy."[17] While Irenaeus did not hesitate to offer "proofs [of] the truths of Scripture," he was quick to point out that "proofs of the things which are contained in the Scriptures cannot be shown except from the Scriptures themselves."[18] That is, the Bible speaks best and most clearly for itself.

Referring to the New Jerusalem, Irenaeus speaks against the allegorical method of interpreting prophecy, saying, "Nothing is capable of being allegorized, but all things are steadfast, and true, and substantial, having been made by God for righteous men's enjoyment. For as it is God truly who raises up man, so also does man truly rise from the dead, and not allegorically, as I have shown repeatedly. . . . Then, when all things are made new, he shall truly dwell in the city of God."[19]

As for Irenaeus's affirmation that the true exposition of the Scriptures is to be found in the church alone, the context indicates he simply means that, as the repository of the true teaching that has come down from the apostles, the church alone, as opposed to heretics outside it, contains the true meaning of Scripture. This is clear from what he says in elaborating on this very point. For he wrote: "It behooves us to . . . adhere to those who, as I have already observed, do hold the doctrine of the apostles."[20] And, "it is also incumbent to hold in suspicion others who depart from the primitive succession."[21]

Likewise, Irenaeus attributes the correctness of his teaching to this close link to the apostles, saying, "I have heard from a certain presbyter, who had heard it from those who had seen the apostles, and from their disciples, the punishment declared in Scripture was sufficient for the

15. Ibid.
16. Ibid.
17. Ibid., 3.7.2.
18. Ibid., 3.12.9.
19. Ibid., 5.35.2.
20. Ibid.,4.26.4.
21. Ibid., 4.26.2.

ancients in regard to what they did without the Spirit's guidance."[22] Hence, "True knowledge is that which consists in *the doctrine of the apostles*, and the ancient constitution of the Church throughout all the world, and the distinctive manifestation of the body of Christ according to the succession of the bishops, *by which they have handed down* that Church which exists in every place, and *has come even unto us, being guarded and preserved, without a forging of Scripture*, by a *very complete system of doctrine*, and *neither receiving addition nor suffering curtailment* in the truths which she believes; and *it consists in reading the word of God without falsification, and a lawful and diligent exposition in harmony with the Scriptures*; and above all it consists in the pre-eminent gift of love."[23]

It is evident from the emphasized words in the foregoing quote that the correct interpretation of Scripture is found by: (1) reading a text in its proper context; (2) in harmony with other Scripture; (3) as the apostles meant it; (4) as it is expressed in the apostolic doctrines; and (5) which is known to us by historical links with the apostles.

Thus, the succession of elders in the church were to be followed not because of any special divine revelatory authority that rests in them but because known historical links to the apostles give validity to their claim to be offering a correct interpretation of what the apostles taught.

In defense of his orthodox interpretation of Scripture, Irenaeus appealed to several arguments.

First, he advocated using the correct means of interpretation of Scripture. This entails several factors: taking their words in their literal sense and in the context of the overall theme of Scripture.

Second, he believed the presence of the Holy Spirit in the church guides it to correct interpretation.[24] Indeed, the church is viewed as the home of the Holy Spirit, who through its Spirit-endowed men vouchsafed the truth of the gospel.[25]

Third, he referenced an unbroken chain of bishops going back to the apostles to verify it was the correct interpretation.[26]

22. Ibid., 4.27.1.
23. Ibid, 4.33.8, emphases added.
24. Ibid., 3.21.4.
25. Ibid., 4.26.2, 5.
26. Ibid., 3.2.2.

Finally, in connection with this latter argument was Irenaeus's belief that a living oral tradition was housed in the church, attesting to the true apostolic interpretation of Scripture.

The Nature of Tradition
In contrast to Gnosticism, Irenaeus held this tradition to be public. It emanated from the apostles, and them alone, who were the sole authority on the matter.[27] He contended also, that regardless of differences in language and expression "the force of the tradition" communicated by the apostles was one and the same.[28]

The Locus of the Tradition
Unlike Papias, who could refer to personal reminiscences of the apostles,[29] Irenaeus believed in "the tradition from the apostles" which he said was available in the church for all who care to look for it,[30] having been faithfully "preserved by means of the succession of Presbyters in the Churches."[31] He also pointed to Barbarian tribes whom he believed had it in unwritten form.[32] For all practical purposes this tradition could be found in what he called "the canon of truth," which Kelly calls a "condensed summary, fluid in its wording but fixed in content, setting out the key points of the Christian revelation in the form of a rule."[33] Irenaeus makes numerous allusions to this body of truth.[34]

The Relation of Scripture and Tradition
While some infer that Irenaeus exalted tradition alongside of, or even over, Scripture, this is to be rejected for the reasons given by Kelly. First, this only *appears* to be the case, since in his controversy with the Gnostics Irenaeus appealed to apostolic tradition as the proper way to interpret the Bible. Second, "the Gnostics' appeal to their supposedly secret traditions forced him to stress the superiority of the Church's public tradition, [yet] *his real defense of orthodoxy was founded on Scripture.*"[35] Third, "*tradition itself, on his view, was confirmed by Scripture,*

---

27. Ibid., 3.1.1.
28. Ibid., 1.10.2; 5.20.1.
29. Kelly, *Early Christian Doctrines*, 37.
30. *Haer.*, 3.4.2–5.
31. Ibid., 3.2.2.
32. Ibid., 3.4.1.
33. Kelly, *Early Christian Doctrines*, 37.
34. *Haer.*, 1.10.1; 22.1; 5.20.1, etc.
35. Kelly, *Early Christian Doctrines*, 38–39.

which was 'the foundation and pillar of our faith.'"[36] Fourth, even the "canon of truth" which converts supposedly received at baptism was used to help preserve orthodoxy was itself based on Scripture. Finally, Kelly said that Irenaeus believed that *"Scripture and the Church's unwritten tradition are identical in content."* Kelly adds, "If tradition as conveyed in the "canon" is a more trustworthy guide, this is not because it comprises truths other than those revealed in Scripture, but because the true tenor of the apostolic message is there unambiguously set out."[37]

Further, considering the overall context of Irenaus's polemic against the Gnostics, who were misinterpreting Scripture, it is understandable that Irenaeus would stress the value of valid tradition supporting the orthodoxy of his anti-Gnostic views.

On the Apostolicity of the Church

It is evident from repeated statements that the final authority for the church rests in the apostles, not in any one apostle. Even the founding of the church at Rome was said to be by two apostles, Paul and Peter.[38] Irenaeus repeatedly speaks of "the apostolic tradition"[39] and "the blessed apostles" who "founded and built up the Church,"[40] "the doctrine of the apostles,"[41] and "the tradition from the apostles."[42] He wrote: *"these* [apostles] *are the voices of the Church from which every Church had its origin;* these are the voices of the apostles; these are the voices of the disciples of the Lord, the truly perfect, who after the assumption of the Lord, were perfected by the Spirit."[43] For "He [God] sent forth His own apostles in the spirit of truth, and not in that of error, He did the very same also in the case of the prophets."[44]

Summary

The traditional Roman Catholic view emanating from the infallible pronouncements of the Council of Trent (AD 1545–1563) is there are two sources of divine revelation: Scripture and tradition. Trent proclaimed that "this truth and instruction are contained in (1) the written books *and*

36. *Haer.*, 3.1.1, emphasis added.
37. Kelly, *Early Christian Doctrines*, 39, emphasis added.
38. *Haer.*, 3.1.1.
39. Ibid., 3.3.2.
40. Ibid., 3.3.3.
41. Ibid., 3.12.4.
42. Ibid., 3.5.1.
43. Ibid., 3.12.4, emphasis added.
44. Ibid., 4.35.2.

(2) in the unwritten traditions, which have been received by the apostles
... at the dictation of the Holy Spirit." Thus Trent "receives and holds in
veneration with equal affection or piety and reverence [1] all the books
of the Old and the New Testament, since God is the author of both, *and*
also [2] the traditions themselves ... as having been dictated either by
Christ's own word of mouth, or by the Holy Spirit."[45] Denzinger speaks
of "the Sources [plural] of Revelation" which include [1] "the written
source of revelation [which] is the canonical books of both Testaments.
... [2] *Another* source of revelation is ecclesiastical tradition."[46] Thus
attempts by post-Vatican II scholars to claim only one source of revelation are contrary to the infallible pronouncements of Trent.

Clearly, there is no evidence to support elevating tradition alongside
of infallible Scripture in the earliest fathers of the church. Irenaeus is
the key figure in this early period, and he held no such view. While
there was a growing episcopal view in this period, there is no evidence
of either the primacy of Peter (see chap. 3) or the divine authority of
tradition. At most, tradition was used instrumentally and supplementally
to support Scripture.

First, it was employed historically to show that the interpretation later
Fathers had of the Scripture was the same as that of the apostles, since
an unbroken chain of teachers exists all the way back to the apostles.
In this sense it was no different from a historical verification through
witnesses of witnesses that the later church held the same teaching as
that of Christ and the apostles.

Second, it was used, along with a proper method of interpreting the
biblical text, as a supplementary and confirming testimony to the plain
commonsense interpretation of Scripture, which in itself was sufficient to
convey the meaning of Scripture. For, as shown above, Irenaeus believed
in both the exclusivity of Scripture as the divine revelation (*sola Scriptura*) and the perspicuity of Scripture, namely, that the main teachings
of the Bible are sufficiently clear in and of themselves. Thus, tradition
was not necessary to understand the essential truths of Scripture. The
normal historical-grammatical method of interpreting the Bible, and the
Bible alone, was sufficient. Tradition (historical testimony) was merely
instrumental and supplemental. It had no divine authority in itself and
certainly no infallible authority as Rome subsequently claimed.

---

45. Henry Denzinger, *The Sources of Catholic Dogma* (St. Louis, MO: Herder, 1957), 244 (from
Session 4 of Trent, 1546).
46. Ibid., 11–12.

Indeed, as late as the thirteenth century the greatest Roman Catholic theologian of all time declared: "We believe the prophets and apostles because the Lord has been their witness by performing miracles.... And *we believe the successors of the apostles and prophets only in so far as they tell us those things which the apostles and prophets have left in their writings.*"[47] In short, tradition can be helpful, but it is not infallible. Scripture is not subject to interpretation by tradition. All tradition is subject to the authority of the Scriptures.

---

47. Thomas Aquinas, *On Truth*, 14.10.11, emphasis added.

SOLA SCRIPTURA

ola Scriptura can be understood in two senses. In the *material* sense it simply means that all the content of salvific revelation exists in Scripture. In this sense, progressive Catholics and Protestants agree. *Sola Scriptura* in the formal sense means that the Bible *alone* is sufficiently clear so that no infallible magisterium of the church is necessary to interpret it. In this sense Protestants affirm and Catholics deny it.[1] The chart below provides clarity on these two crucial concepts.[2]

Sola Scriptura: Two Views	
Material Sufficiency	*Formal Sufficiency*
Content	Form
Revelation	Interpretation
Protestantism Affirms	Protestantism Affirms
Catholicism Allows	Catholicism Denies
Traditional Catholicism Denies	
Progressive Catholicism Affirms	

In principle, the Catholic Church denies both the formal and material sufficiency of Scripture (except for "progressive" Catholics), while Protestants affirm both concepts. While the Bible contains all the truths that are necessary for salvation, Catholicism holds that the church is

1. Norman L. Geisler and Ralph E. MacKenzie, *Roman Catholics and Evangelicals: Agreements and Differences* (Grand Rapids, MI: Baker, 1995), 180–81.
2. Chart borrowed and adapted from ibid.

the vehicle by which Scripture is interpreted and understood (and by which one is ultimately saved). Congar writes that in "the establishment of the canon three elements unite: Scripture, tradition, the Church."[3] Concerning the distinction between formal versus material sufficiency, Congar, in mentioning the Church Fathers in his exposition of tradition, writes, "[Protestants] admitted a material sufficiency of Scripture, the Fathers and medieval theologians affirmed its formal *insufficiency*." Scripture, they held, does not itself suffice to yield its true meaning; it must be read within the church, within tradition. Further, "Scripture itself is sovereign and is not subject to any rule which could judge it. But it does not itself fulfill all the functions that are necessary for fixing the faith of Christians. Moreover, Scripture itself does not claim to be an exclusive rule: it witnesses, on the contrary, to the fact that Jesus, who wrote nothing himself, gave to men the gift of the Church together with his Spirit and the apostolic ministry . . ."[4]

---

3. Yves Congar, O. P., *Tradition and Traditions* (New York: MacMillan, 1967), 419. Congar's assessment of the relationship between Scripture and the church is to the point here, especially as it relates to canon. For he says, "This intervention by authority [with respect to the canon] . . . does not imply that the Church could create the normative value of Scripture; it can only recognize it. One cannot say, therefore, that Scripture takes its authority from the Church, or even its canonicity, fundamentally. There is, however, in the establishment of the canon, that is to say in the giving of a character of normativity to certain definite writings to the exclusion of others, *an act of the Church* which is posited in virtue of a charism, although in continuity with it, with a view to completing its work for mankind's benefit. It is *from the Church* that the faithful learn which are the books of the Old and New Testaments. Without the Church, the Bible could be known as a remarkable book but we could exclude from it neither the *Odes of Solomon*, nor more than sixty Jewish writings and fifty gospel narratives, which we regard in fact as apocryphal. The question of the canon is linked in such a way with that of the Church that certain sects have often wanted to make up their own."
4. Ibid.

IRENAEUS ON SCRIPTURE AND TRADITION

Irenaeus (ca. 130–200) is an important figure in the early church. He was the bishop of Lyons, France who heard Polycarp (the disciple of the apostle John) when he was a boy, and was thought to be a native of Smyrna who studied at Rome. He was the first great father in the West. His major work was titled *Against Heresies* (hereafter, *Haer.*).

His View of Scripture

Irenaeus stood soundly on the doctrine of the verbal inspiration of Scripture. He also held to its inerrancy. Further, he is an important testimony to the authorship and dates of the Gospels.

On the Authority of Scripture

Irenaeus attests to the Scriptures' divine authority by referring to them as "divine Scriptures."[1] He calls the Bible "the ground and pillar of our faith."[2] It is "the Scripture of truth" as opposed to the "spurious writings" of heretics.[3] For "all Scripture, which has been given to us by God, shall be found by us perfectly consistent."[4] He affirms that "even the

---

1. *Haer.*, 2.35.4; 3.19.2.
2. Ibid., 3.1.1.
3. Ibid., 1.20.1.
4. Ibid., 2.28.3.

Gentiles present perceived that the Scriptures had been interpreted by the inspiration of God."[5] Indeed, the apostle Paul's words came from "the impetus of the Spirit within him."[6]

On the Inerrancy of Scripture

Irenaeus declares that "the Scriptures are indeed perfect, since they were spoken by the Word of God and His Spirit."[7] He also said they are "divine" (from God), and God cannot err (Rom. 3:4; Titus 1:2; Heb. 6:18). They are called "the Scripture of truth" as opposed to the "spurious writings" of heretics.[8] The fact that "all Scripture . . . has been given to us by God" is further evidence of the Bible's inerrancy.[9] Likewise, the fact that they are "found by us perfectly consistent" bespeaks of their flawless character. Indeed, Irenaeus speaks of the authors of Scripture as being beyond error, saying, "The apostles, likewise, being disciples of the truth, are above all falsehood" in what they taught.[10] The Gospels, written by the apostles, are based on the words of our Lord. And "our Lord, therefore, being the truth, did not speak lies."[11]

On the Authenticity of the Gospels

Irenaeus held that the traditional authorship of the Gospels was by the contemporary eyewitness apostles and disciples whose names they bear. He speaks of "the Gospel of truth,"[12] in that the Gospels were written by the true apostles. He wrote: "Matthew also issued a written Gospel among the Hebrews in their own dialect, while Peter and Paul were preaching at Rome and laying the foundation of the Church. After their departure, Mark, the disciple and interpreter of Peter, did also hand down to us in writing what had been preached by Peter." Further, "Luke also, the companion of Paul, recorded in a book the Gospel preached by him. Afterwards, John the disciple of the Lord . . . did himself publish a Gospel during his residence at Ephesus in Asia."[13] Irenaeus exhorts, "let us revert to the Scriptural proof furnished by those apostles who did also write the Gospel."[14] He speaks also of the certainty we have of the

5. Ibid., 3.21.2.
6. Ibid., 3.6.7.
7. Ibid., 2.28.2.
8. Ibid., 1.20.1.
9. Ibid., 2.28.3.
10. Ibid., 3.5.1.
11. Ibid.
12. Ibid., 3.11.9.
13. Ibid., 3.1.1.
14. Ibid.

Gospel, which we would not have were it not for the apostles. "For how should it be if the apostles themselves had not left us writings?"[15] Hence, "these [four] Gospels alone are true and reliable, and admit neither an increase nor diminution of the aforesaid number, I have proved by so many and such arguments."[16]

The Transmission of the Truth of Scriptures
Irenaeus offers two main arguments for the accuracy of the transmission of biblical truth. First, the translations are accurate. Second, the interpretation is the same as that of the apostles and associates who produced them and with whom we have an unbroken historical connection.

The Accuracy of the Copies
Irenaeus said little on this point because little needed to be said. After all, the available copies were only about a hundred years old after the New Testament was completed. Nonetheless, Irenaeus does make some comments about both Testaments.

As for the Old Testament, he bases his belief in the reliability of the translation on the widely believed story of the alleged miraculous origin of the Septuagint (LXX). It was supposedly produced by some seventy different translators, each working independently and yet producing identical translations from Hebrew to Greek. He wrote, "For all of them read out of the common translation which they had prepared in the very same words and the very same names from beginning to end, so that even the Gentiles present perceived that the Scriptures had been interpreted by the inspiration of God."[17] As unlikely as this story is, it contains a core of truth: abundant available manuscripts verify that the Old Testament has been accurately reproduced down through the centuries.[18]

Irenaeus adds to this the argument that the content has not been corrupted because "the Scriptures have been interpreted with such fidelity, and the grace of God has prepared and formed again our faith towards His Son, and has preserved to us the unadulterated Scriptures in Egypt, where the house of Jacob flourished; . . . This interpretation[19] of these

15. Ibid., 3.4.1.
16. Ibid., 3.11.9.
17. Ibid., 3.21.2. Justin Matyr had this same view (*To the Greeks*, 13), as did St. Augustine after this time.
18. See Norman L. Geisler and William Nix, *A General Introduction to the Bible*, rev. ed. (Chicago: Moody, 1986), chap. 21.
19. The word *interpreted* includes the idea of translated, since one must interpret a text correctly in order to properly translate it.

Scriptures was made prior to the Lord's descent to earth, and came into being before the Christians appeared ... but Ptolemy was much earlier, under whom the Scriptures were interpreted."[20] Irenaeus's argument is similar to that of current Christian apologists who point out that Isaiah 53 is a messianic prediction about Christ, since even the rabbis before the time of Christ understood it to be about the Messiah, not about a suffering nation.[21]

As for the New Testament manuscripts available in the second century, Irenaeus bases their authenticity on several factors. He wrote: "But our faith is steadfast, unfeigned, and the only true one, having clear proof from the Scriptures, which were interpreted [transmitted] in the way I have related; and the preaching of the Church is without interpolation." This is evident because "the apostles, since they are of more ancient date than all these heretics, agree with this aforesaid translation; and the translation harmonizes with the tradition of the apostles. For Peter, and John, and Matthew, and Paul, and the rest successively, as well as their followers, did set forth all prophetical announcements, just as the interpretations of the elders contain them."[22] He adds, "For the one and the same Spirit of God, who proclaimed by the prophets what and of what sort the advent of the Lord should be, did by the elders give a just [right] interpretation of what had been truly prophesied."[23] In short, the Holy Spirit who inspired the Scriptures also guided the early Fathers in interpreting them.

On the Unbroken Chain of Transmission

Irenaeus refers to the links in this unbroken chain transmitting the apostolic understanding of the gospel, namely, it came from John the apostle to Polycarp to Irenaeus, who knew him. Indeed, he spoke of Polycarp as one "not only instructed by apostles, and conversed with many who had seen Christ, but also, by the apostles in Asia appointed bishop of the Church in Smyrna, whom I also saw in my early youth."[24]

Irenaeus wrote: "But, again ... we refer them [heretics] to that tradition which originates from the apostles, and which is preserved by means of the successions of presbyters in the Churches."[25] Indeed, Irenaeus

20. *Haer.*, 3.21.3.
21. See *The Fifty-Third Chapter of Isaiah According to the Jewish Interpreters*, trans. S. R. Driver and A. D. Neubaur (Oxford: James Parker, 1877).
22. *Haer.*, 3.21.3.
23. Ibid., 3.21.4.
24. Ibid., 3.3.4.
25. Ibid., 3.2.2.

refers to the "presbyters" as "the disciples of the apostles."[26] For, "It is within the power of all, therefore, in every Church, who may wish to see the truth, to contemplate clearly the tradition of the apostles manifested throughout the whole world; and we are in a position to reckon up those who were by the apostles instituted bishops in the Churches, and to demonstrate the succession of these men to our own times."[27] Irenaeus added, "These things are borne witness to in writing by Papias, the hearer of John, and a companion of Polycarp [who was a disciple of the apostle John], in his fourth book."[28]

On the Primacy of Scripture

No one reading the apostolic and other early Fathers can help but be struck by their extensive and authoritative use of Scripture. Seven major Fathers from Justin Martyr to Eusebius cite 36,289 verses from the New Testament—all but eleven verses (most of which are from 3 John). Irenaeus alone cites 1,819 verses.

Further, the manner in which they are cited reveals their great respect for the Scriptures as the very written Word of God. As we have already seen, Irenaeus believed that the very words of Scripture were God-given, perfect, and without error. It is the very ground and pillar of truth.

Other than a few scant references in early Fathers to the oral words of apostles confirming what is in their written word, which alone is God-breathed (2 Tim. 3:16; cf. 2 Pet. 1:20–21; 3:15–16), the Bible is not only the primary source of divine authority cited; it is the only source. Hence, it is not simply a matter of the primacy of Scripture but the exclusivity of Scripture as the sole written, God-breathed authority from God. Indeed, Irenaeus criticizes heretics because "they gather their views from other sources than the Scriptures."[29] Likewise, he condemns them because they "adduce an unspeakable number of apocryphal and spurious writings."[30] In this sense, Irenaeus held to *sola Scriptura* (the Bible alone)—one of the great principles of the later Reformation.

On the Perspicuity of Scripture

As J. N. D. Kelly notes, "Provided the Bible was taken as a whole, its teaching was self-evident."[31] Only when heretics wrenched texts out of

26. Ibid., 5.35.2.
27. Ibid., 3.3.1.
28. Ibid., 5.333.4.
29. Ibid., 1.8.1
30. Ibid., 1.22.1.
31. J. N. D. Kelly, *Early Christian Doctrines* (New York, Harper, 1960), 38.

their proper context did the basic message seem confused. Of course, because the Bible is "spiritual in its entirety" it is not surprising that there are some obscurities.[32] Nonetheless, with proper exegesis and aid of the Holy Spirit, the main message of the Bible is clear.

Irenaeus criticized those who "accuse these Scriptures, as if they were not correct, nor of authority, and assert that they are ambiguous, and that the truth cannot be extracted from them by those who are ignorant of tradition."[33] This shows clearly that he not only believed in the perspicuity (clarity) of Scripture but also the sufficiency of the literal hermeneutic, apart from tradition, to understand what the Scriptures are teaching.

Irenaeus recognized, of course, that as clear as the Scriptures are there are depraved minds that will not accept them. He said, "I shall for the benefit of those at least who do not bring a depraved mind to bear upon them, devote a special book to the Scriptures referred to . . . and I shall plainly set forth from these divine Scriptures proofs to satisfy all the lovers of truth."[34]

On the Interpretation of Scripture

Following on the clarity of Scripture is the belief in a literal historical-grammatical hermeneutic, which alone can yield this clear message. Irenaeus believed that proper interpretation yields a harmonious and unambiguous understanding of Scripture. He wrote: "A sound mind . . . will eagerly meditate upon those things which God has placed with the power of mankind . . . and will make advancement in them, rendering the knowledge of them easy to him by means of daily study."[35] He added, "These things are such as fall plainly under our observation, and are clearly and unambiguously in express terms set forth in the Sacred Scriptures."[36]

Irenaeus concludes: "Since, therefore, the entire Scriptures, the prophets, and the Gospels, can be clearly, unambiguously, and harmoniously understood by all, although all do not believe them . . . those persons will seem truly foolish who blind their eyes to such clear demonstrations."[37]

32. Ibid., 61.
33. *Haer.*, 3.2.1.
34. Ibid., 2.35.4.
35. Ibid., 2.27.10.
36. Kelly, *Early Christian Doctrines*, 38.
37. Ibid.

As for difficult passages, "the parables shall be harmonized with those passages which are perfectly clear."[38] Hence, there is a proper and improper way to read a text. And "if, then, one does not attend to the proper reading of the passage . . . there shall be not only incongruities, but also, when reading, he will utter blasphemy."[39] While Irenaeus did not hesitate to offer "proofs [of] the truths of Scripture" he was quick to point out that "proofs of the things which are contained in the Scriptures cannot be shown except from the Scriptures themselves."[40] That is, the Bible speaks best and most clearly for itself.

Referring to the New Jerusalem, Irenaeus speaks against the allegorical method of interpreting prophecy, saying, "Nothing is capable of being allegorized, but all things are steadfast, and true, and substantial, having been made by God for righteous men's enjoyment. For as it is God truly who raises up man, so also does man truly rise from the dead, and not allegorically, as I have shown repeatedly. . . . Then, when all things are made new, he shall truly dwell in the city of God."[41]

As for Irenaeus's affirmation that the true exposition of the Scriptures is to be found in the church alone, the context indicates he simply means that, as the repository of the true teaching that has come down from the apostles, the church alone, as opposed to heretics outside it, contains the true meaning of Scripture. This is clear from what he says in elaborating on this very point. For he wrote: "It behooves us to . . . adhere to those who, as I have already observed, do hold the doctrine of the apostles."[42] And, "it is also incumbent to hold in suspicion others who depart from the primitive succession."[43]

Likewise, Irenaeus attributes the correctness of his teaching to this close link to the apostles, saying, "I have heard from a certain presbyter, who had heard it from those who had seen the apostles, and from their disciples, the punishment declared in Scripture was sufficient for the ancients in regard to what they did without the Spirit's guidance."[44] Hence, "True knowledge is that which consists in *the doctrine of the apostles,* and the ancient constitution of the Church throughout all the world, and the distinctive manifestation of the body of Christ according to the succession of the bishops, *by which they have handed down* that

38. Ibid.
39. *Haer.,* 3.7.2.
40. Ibid., 3.12.9.
41. Ibid., 5.35.2.
42. Ibid., 4.26.4.
43. Ibid., 4.26.2.
44. Ibid., 4.27.1.

Church which exists in every place, and *has come even unto us, being guarded and preserved, without a forging of Scripture,* by a *very complete system of doctrine, and neither receiving addition nor suffering curtailment* in the truths which she believes; and *it consists in reading the word of God without falsification, and a lawful and diligent exposition in harmony with the Scriptures;* and above all it consists in the preeminent gift of love."[45]

It is evident from the emphasized words in the foregoing quote that the correct interpretation of Scripture is found by: reading a text (1) in its proper context; (2) in harmony with other Scripture; (3) as the apostles meant it; (4) as it is expressed in the apostolic doctrines; and (5) which is known to us by historical links with the apostles.

Thus, the succession of elders in the church was to be followed not because of any special divine revelatory authority that rests in them, but because their known historical link to the apostles gives validity to their claim to be offering a correct interpretation of what the apostles taught.

On the Canonicity of Scripture

Irenaeus cites freely from every major section of the Old Testament and from most of the books. He also cites from more New Testament books than any other early writer (all but Philemon, James, 2 Peter, and 3 John). And he gives no reason to believe he rejected any of these; he simply had no occasion to quote from them, two of them being one-chapter books.[46] Further, he chides heretics because they "adduce an unspeakable number of apocryphal and spurious writings"[47] as opposed to the authentic Scriptures.

Because the basis of the New Testament revelation is the authority of the apostles—both what they had originally proclaimed orally and later committed to writing[48]—"it was not simply church custom but apostolicity, i.e., the fact that they had been composed by apostles and followers of the apostles" that was the basis for discovering their canonicity.

Not only does Irenaeus cite every New Testament writer as an apostle or accredited mouthpiece for God (like an associate of an apostle), but he also cites from the vast majority of the twenty-seven New Testament

45. Ibid., 4.33.8, emphasis added.
46. Geisler and Nix, *A General Introduction to the Bible,* 193.
47. *Haer.,* 1.22.1.
48. Ibid., 3.1.1.

books. The same is true of him regarding the Old Testament. So, there is no reason to believe he rejects any one of the sixty-six canonical books of Scripture. As for the so-called apocryphal books of the Old Testament later accepted by the Roman Catholic Church, there is no definitive evidence that Irenaeus believed they were inspired. Of the fourteen apocryphal books (eleven of which are accepted as inspired by the Roman Catholic Church), only two are alluded to by Irenaeus: (1) *History of Susanna*[49] is quoted but not used as a divine authority to establish any doctrine. (2) The other book, *Wisdom*[50] is only a possible allusion, not a quotation or an authoritative citation at all. This contrasts with 1,819 citations from a vast array of Old Testament books and twenty-three of the twenty-seven books of the New Testament.

On the alleged citations of the Old Testament Apocrypha by Irenaeus and other early Fathers, the canonical authority Roger Beckwith notes:

> When one examines the passages in the early Fathers which are supposed to establish the canonicity of the Apocrypha, one finds that some of them are taken from the alternative Greek text of Ezra (*1 Esdras*) or from additions or appendices to Daniel, Jeremiah or some other canonical book, which . . . are not really relevant; that others of them are not quotations from the Apocrypha at all; and that, of those which are, many do not give any indication that the book is regarded as Scripture.[51]

His View on Tradition

In defense of his orthodox interpretation of Scripture, Irenaeus appealed to several arguments:

First, he used the correct means of interpretation of Scripture. This entails several factors: taking words in their literal sense and in the context of the overall theme of Scripture.

Second, he believed the presence of the Holy Spirit in the church guides it to correct interpretation.[52] Indeed, he viewed the church as the home of the Holy Spirit, who through its Spirit-endowed men vouchsafed the truth of the gospel.[53]

49. Ibid., 4.26.2.
50. Ibid., 2.18.9.
51. Roger Beckwith, *The Old Testament Canon of the New Testament Church and Its Background in Early Judaism* (Grand Rapids, MI: Eerdmans, 1986), 382–83.
52. *Haer.*, 3.21.4.
53. Ibid., 4.26.2, 5.

Third, he referred to an unbroken chain of bishops going back to the apostles to verify it was the correct interpretation.[54]

Finally, in connection with this later argument Irenaeus believed that a living oral tradition was housed in the church, which attests to the true apostolic interpretation of Scripture.

The Nature of Tradition

According to J. N. D. Kelly, noted authority on the early Fathers, "Scripture and the Church's living tradition [are viewed] as coordinate channels of this apostolic testimony."[55] In contrast to Gnosticism, Irenaeus held this tradition to be public. It emanated from the apostles, and them alone, who were the sole authority on the matter.[56] He contended also, that regardless of differences in language and expression "the force of the tradition" communicated by the apostles was one and the same.[57]

The Locus of the Tradition

Unlike Papias, who could refer to personal reminiscences of the apostles,[58] Irenaeus believed in "the tradition from the apostles" which he said was available in the church for all who care to look for it,[59] having been faithfully "preserved by means of the succession of Presbyters in the Churches."[60] He also pointed to barbarian tribes whom he believed had it in unwritten form.[61] For all practical purposes this tradition could be found in what he called "the canon of truth," which Kelly calls a "condensed summary, fluid in its wording but fixed in content, setting out the key points of the Christian revelation in the form of a rule."[62] Irenaeus makes numerous allusions to this body of truth.[63]

The Relation of Scripture and Tradition

While some infer that Irenaeus exalted tradition alongside, or over, Scripture, this is to be rejected for the reasons Kelly has given.

First, this inference only *appears* to be the case, since in his controversy with the Gnostics, Irenaeus appealed to apostolic tradition to inter-

54. Ibid., 3.2.2.
55. Kelly, *Early Christian Doctrine*, 35–36.
56. *Haer.*, 3.1.1.
57. Ibid., 1.10.2; 5.20.1.
58. Kelly, *Early Christian Doctrine*, 37.
59. *Haer.*, 3.4.2–5.
60. Ibid., 3.2.2.
61. Ibid., 3.4.1.
62. Kelly, *Early Christian Doctrine*, 37.
63. *Haer.*, 1.10.1, 22.1; 5.20.1; etc.

pret the Bible. Second, "the Gnostics' appeal to their supposedly secret traditions forced him to stress the superiority of the Church's public tradition, [yet] *his real defense of orthodoxy was founded on Scripture.*"[64] Third, *"tradition itself, on his view, was confirmed by Scripture,* which was 'the foundation and pillar of our faith.'"[65] Fourth, even the "canon of truth," which converts supposedly received at baptism and was used to help preserve orthodoxy, was itself based on Scripture.

Finally, Kelly said that Irenaeus believed that *"Scripture and the Church's unwritten tradition are identical in content."*[66] Kelly added, "If tradition as conveyed in the "canon" is a more trustworthy guide, this is not because it comprises truths other than those revealed in Scripture, but because the true tenor of the apostolic message is there unambiguously set out."[67]

Considering the overall context of Irenaeus's polemic against the Gnostics, who were misinterpreting Scripture, it is understandable that Irenaeus would stress the value of valid tradition for supporting the orthodoxy of his anti-Gnostic views.

On the Apostolicity of the Church

It is evident from repeated statements that Irenaeus believed the final authority for the church rests in the apostles, not in any one apostle. Even the founding of the church at Rome was said to be by two apostles, Paul and Peter.[68] Irenaeus repeatedly spoke of "the apostolic tradition"[69] and "the blessed apostles" who "founded and built up the church,"[70] "the doctrine of the apostles,"[71] and "the tradition from the apostles."[72]

He wrote: *"These [apostles] are the voices of the Church from which every Church had its origin;* these are the voices of the apostles; these are the voices of the disciples of the Lord, the truly perfect, who after the assumption of the Lord, were perfected by the Spirit."[73] For "He [God] sent forth His own apostles in the spirit of truth, and not in that of error, He did the very same also in the case of the prophets."[74]

64. Kelly, *Early Christian Doctrine,* 38–39, emphasis added.
65. Ibid., 39, emphasis added. Cf. *Haer.,* 3.1.1.
66. Kelly, *Early Christian Doctrine,* 39, emphasis added.
67. Ibid.
68. *Haer.,* 3.1.1.
69. Ibid., 3.3.2.
70. Ibid., 3.3.3.
71. Ibid., 3.12.4.
72. Ibid., 3.5.1.
73. Ibid., 3.12.4, emphasis added.
74. Ibid., 4.35.2.

Conclusion

Taken in the total context of his writing, Irenaeus favored the non-Catholic position on almost all the major areas of concern. First, he held to the Protestant canon, rejecting the Apocrypha canonized by the Catholic Council of Trent (1546). Second, he believed in *sola Scriptura* (see Appendix 4), the Protestant sense of both material and formal sufficiency. Third, this means Irenaeus held to the perspicuity of Scripture. Fourth, Irenaeus did not hold the Roman Catholic views of tradition as a second source of revelation. Nor did he believe tradition was divinely authoritative. Fifth, he has written nothing that supports the primacy of Peter, let alone any alleged infallibility.

Even with a more Catholic interpretation, at the very most Irenaeus would be no more than an incipient Anglican. There is nothing in his writing to support either the primacy of Peter or the infallibility of the pope. At best, one can see only a developing episcopal form of government, along with a belief in the reliability of the chain of interpretation leading back to the apostles. But this is a long way from post-Trent or post-Vatican I Rome.

That this more Catholic interpretation of Irenaeus could be used as steps in the Roman Catholic justification of its hierarchy of bishops position is not surprising. John the apostle spoke of it in his third epistle when he warned: "I wrote to the church, but Diotrephes, who loves to have the preeminence among them, does not receive us" (3 John 9 NKJV).

Further, Irenaeus was writing more than a century after most apostles had died—the very time that even apocryphal gospels were emerging. Indeed, he was writing some time after the apocryphal *Gospel of Thomas* (c. 140). So there was plenty of time for false views to emerge, even among those who were otherwise orthodox. What is more, considering the attacks on Christianity at the time, there was strong motivation to develop an ecclesiology that would provide a united front against the divergent heretical groups emerging then, which is reflected in Irenaeus's emerging episcopal view of church government.

In any event, Irenaeus did not support the later Roman Catholic pronouncements on the infallibility of the pope. His constant appeal was to the original "apostles" (plural) as the God-established authority. Peter was not singled out by him as superior to others. He, at best, was only a cofounder of the church at Rome along with Paul. He was in fact on the same level as Paul and the other "apostles" to whom Irenaeus repeatedly refers. Furthermore, his stress on the primacy of Scripture as the final written authority of the Christian faith demonstrates that all ecclesiastical authority is based on Scripture, not the reverse.

Finally, his stress on the sufficiency of the Holy Spirit and the proper mode of interpretation as sufficient to understand the Scripture denies the later Roman Catholic view that the church, in an organizational authoritative sense, is necessary to interpret Scripture.

Sources

Beckwith, Roger. *The Old Testament Canon of the New Testament Church and Its Background in Early Judaism*. Grand Rapids, MI: Eerdmans, 1986.

Behr, John. "Irenaeus and the Word of God." In *Studia Patristica* 36, 2001.

Driver, S. R., and A. D. Neubauer. *The Fifty-Third Chapter of Isaiah According to Jewish Interpreters*. Vol. 2. Oxford: James Parker, 1877.

Geisler, Norman, and William Nix. *A General Introduction to the Bible*, rev. Chicago: Moody, 1986.

Jacobsen, Anders-Christian. "The Philosophical Argument in the Teaching on the Resurrection of the Flesh." In *Studia Patristica* 36, 2001.

Leach, Charles. *Our Bible: How We Got It*. Chicago: Moody, 1897.

Morris, Richard. "Irenaeus." In *Historical Handbook of Major Interpreters*. Downers Grove, IL: InterVarsity, 1998.

Osborn, Eric F. "Reason and the Rule of Faith in the Second Century." In *Making of Orthodoxy*, edited by Rowan Williams. Cambridge: Cambridge University Press, 1989.

Peters, George. *The Theocratic Kingdom*. Grand Rapids, MI: Kregel, 1952; originally published in 1884.

Tiessen, Terrance. "Gnosticism and Heresy: The Response of Irenaeus." In *Hellenization Revisited*. Lanham, MD: University Press of America, 1994.

SCRIPTURE INDEX